ALSO BY CLAUDIA RODEN

The New Book of Middle Eastern Food

The Book of Jewish Food: An Odyssey from Samarkand to New York

Coffee: A Connoisseur's Companion

Mediterranean Cookery

The Good Food of Italy—Region by Region

Everything Tastes Better Outdoors

A Book of Middle Eastern Food

Arabesque

Arabesque

A Taste of Morocco, Turkey,
and Lebanon

Claudia Roden

ALFRED A. KNOPF   NEW YORK   2006

THIS IS A BORZOI BOOK
PUBLISHED BY ALFRED A. KNOPF

www.aaknopf.com

Originally published in Great Britain by Michael Joseph, Penguin Books, Ltd.,
London, in 2005.

Library of Congress Cataloging-in-Publication Data
Roden, Claudia.
Arabesque : a taste of Morocco, Turkey, and Lebanon / by Claudia Roden.
p.   cm.
ISBN 0-307-26498-X
1. Cookery, Arab.   2. Cookery, Moroccan.   3. Cookery, Turkish
4. Cookery, Lebanese.   I. Title.
TX725.A7R63   2006
641.59′2927—dc22   2006045258

Manufactured in China
First American Edition

For my children, Simon, Nadia, and Anna;
my grandchildren, Cesar, Peter, Sarah, Ruby, and Nell;
and also for Clive and Ros

Contents

Arabesque

Introduction

Three great cuisines—of Morocco, Turkey, and Lebanon—developed around the Mediterranean where the Occident meets the Orient and where, long ago, medieval *jihadis* and crusaders clashed. The three are part of the Mediterranean culinary culture that the West has come to love and also share legacies from the Islamic world, with echoes of ancient Persia and medieval Baghdad, Moorish Spain and the Ottoman Empire.

The three countries have been centers of empire (Lebanon as part of historic Syria) with imperial capitals where high culinary styles developed. Damascus was the first capital of the Islamic Arab Empire during the Umayyad dynasty from the seventh to the eighth century when the empire spread all the way to Spain. Morocco was the center of the Almoravide and Almohad dynasties that ruled over Spain and North Africa from the eleventh to the thirteenth century. And Istanbul was, for more than 400 years, the glittering capital city of the huge Ottoman Empire. Empires have a way of drawing in culinary riches from distant lands, and court kitchens are places of creativity and refinement. Something of the old grandeur and sophistication of their golden ages has passed down into the kitchens of today.

The cuisines, especially Moroccan cooking, are known for their aromatic flavorings, for the subtlety of combinations and the harmonious equilibrium. Since early times, the countries were transit areas on the spice routes between the Far East, Central Africa, the Spice Islands, and Europe. (My ancestors were involved in the camel-caravan trade through Aleppo.) Today, practically every main town has its spice shops in the *souk* or bazaar and each country has its own characteristic spices and aromatics. If you traveled with your eyes closed, you could know where you were by the taste of the food.

Lately there has been a renaissance of interest in the culinary past. Restaurants in Istanbul are re-creating Ottoman cuisine, Fez recently had a festival dedicated to medieval dishes from a thirteenth-century manuscript, and Lebanese gastronomes regularly quote medieval Arab recipes. And at the same time, in each of these countries, the rural regional cuisines have become immensely popular.

There have been great social and technological changes that have affected the way people cook and eat. Until not very long ago, most cooked on braziers and Primus stoves and in outside clay ovens, or they sent dishes to the public oven to be cooked. The modern generation has less time to spend in the kitchen and is part of the global world with the same interests in new trends and concerns about healthy eating as we have. They feel they can do things in a different way without losing their age-old traditions, and that the new approaches do not have to kill the old. I love tradition and respect cuisines that have a past and are part of an old civilization—that is what this book is about. But cooking does not stand still, it evolves, and I want to celebrate tradition while reflecting the changes. For me, what matters is what makes the food more delicious and appealing and also easier and more accessible.

In the 1960s, when I began researching the cooking of the Middle East and North Africa, the dishes were entirely strange in Britain and America. Now they are fashionable and some have been adopted as our own. The aim of this book is to offer new, recently discovered recipes, and variations to those already known, with some of the more famous classics that I have featured in previous books.

Using the Book

Trust your taste and allow yourself a certain freedom in the preparation of the dishes. This is in the spirit of these cuisines that, although faithful to tradition, have no absolute rules and are rich in variations and poor in precision. You are told to "weigh with the eye" and to taste as you go along. And that is what cooking is about. We are dealing with products of nature and these vary. You can have a small lemon that has more juice and is sharper than a larger one. Garlic cloves vary in size and flavor; there are many varieties and they can be young or old and more or less strong. Much of the vegetables available to us come from different countries and are grown in different soils, under a different sun. They have a different taste and respond differently to cooking. Rice, even of the same variety and the same provenance, varies from one year to another and, depending on whether it is new or old, in the amount of water it absorbs. Once upon a time the recommendation for many recipes (also those using flour) was to add "as much water as it takes" and there was much sense in that.

The flavors of fresh herbs vary as do those of spices, depending on where they come from and the particular harvest. There are different grades and qualities. If spices or dry herbs are old they lose their strength, which is why you may have to use more or less and why you should buy small quantities at a time. Even rose and orange blossom waters, which come in bottles, can be more or less diluted according to the producer and depending on whether they were the first or last batch in the distillation process. I do not generally give precise quantities of salt in my recipes, because I believe salting is so much a matter of personal taste and it is the one seasoning that people know how to use and have an "eye" for, even before tasting. It is best to start with less and add more later. It is quite possible to substitute oil for butter in dishes without spoiling them, and onions and garlic may be used abundantly or omitted entirely if you don't like them.

The book is divided by country, so that you can choose to have dishes of the same country in one meal. But you can also have a mixed menu, which is what I often do. Each country is divided into first, main, and dessert courses to make it easier to plan a menu. Ours is a different society from the ones whose dishes we are adopting, so we can be flexible and we can plan around our own ways of eating and entertaining. For instance, you can feel free to serve appetizers—*mezze* or *kemia*—with drinks, as starters, or as side dishes. You can make a casual meal out of two or three, accompanied by bread and perhaps cheese or yogurt and olives, while a large assortment can be produced for a buffet party. You can make a meal out of a soup accompanied by bread. A pie or an omelette—both of which can be quite substantial—can also serve as a one-course snack. For most of the fish dishes you may use alternative kinds of fish. Lamb is the traditional meat of the three countries, but beef or veal can be used instead; in many recipes, such as stews, meat and poultry are interchangeable. Rice, couscous, and bulgur are staples that make good accompaniments to many dishes.

It is important to use good ingredients—free-range, corn-fed, or organic chickens; plain whole milk yogurt; whole milk cheese; good extra virgin olive oil. A mild-tasting olive oil is best with all the dishes. You will find the ingredients you need in Middle Eastern (Turkish, Lebanese, Persian), North African, Greek, and Asian food stores, and many of the best food stores now also stock most of what you require.

About Aromatics

A certain magic surrounds the use of spices and aromatics, which are not only used for their flavor but also for their medicinal, therapeutic, and even sometimes aphrodisiac value. They are variously believed to increase the appetite, help digestion, or calm the nerves; to be good for the heart and circulation; to be antitoxic or sexually stimulating; and even to kill microbes. Attributes may be well founded or romantic; ginger is said to make people loving, rose water to give a rosy outlook, dill and aniseed to have digestive qualities, and garlic to be both health-giving and antiseptic. Herbs are so popular in the three countries that they are sometimes placed in a bunch on the table for people to pick at. The most commonly used are flat-leaf parsley, coriander, and mint.

Gum mastic has nothing at all to do with the waterproof filler called mastic, nor with the glue called "gum Arabic" sold in the building trades. It is an aromatic resin from the lentisc tree or bush, a small evergreen tree that grows on the Greek island of Chios. When tiny incisions are made in the branches in the summer, sticky oval tears of resin appear. It is pronounced *miskeh* in Lebanon and some London restaurants misleadingly spell it "musk."

It is sold in tiny, hard, dry, translucent lumps. To use them, you must first pound them and grind them to a fine powder with a pestle and mortar, together with a pinch of sugar, or use a spice grinder. Use very little as otherwise the taste can be quite unpleasant.

Olive oil is native to all three countries. Although other oils such as sunflower and peanut oil are also used in cooking, olive oil has come to be seen as the oil of choice for gourmets. Use mild-tasting, extra virgin oil for all the recipes and refined non-virgin for deep-frying.

Orange blossom water, produced by boiling the blossom of the sour orange tree and condensing the steam in an alembic or still, lends a delicate perfume to syrups, pastries, and puddings. As the flavor is rather powerful, and because the distilled water comes in varying degrees of strength, it is worth adding a little less than the amount stated to begin with, and adding more to taste.

Pomegranate molasses, also called concentrate and syrup, is made from the juice of sour (not sweet) pomegranates boiled down to a thick syrup. Some varieties are a bit too sweet for my liking. A little added lemon juice or wine vinegar can improve on the sweet-and-sour flavor.

Preserved (or pickled) lemons lend a unique and distinctive flavor to Moroccan dishes. (Some British importers call them "pickled," claiming that "preserved" here denotes a "sweet" preserve.) Pickled in salt, they lose their sharpness. To make them yourself, see pages 36–37.

Rose Water, produced by boiling rose petals and condensing the steam in an alembic or still, is used to perfume syrups, pastries, and puddings. It is weaker than orange blossom water and can be used less sparingly. The two are often used together.

Saffron, highly prized red threads—the pistils of the purple *Crocus sativus*—are much used in Moroccan cooking. There are various grades. The highest have an incomparable flavor. It is better to buy the threads than the powders, but in certain dishes a powder is more useful for giving color. Some commercial powdered saffron is very good and worth buying (it is cheaper than the threads), but some is adulterated or not the real thing.

Sumac, a dark wine-colored spice with an astringent sour flavor, is made from the coarsely ground dried berries of the sumac shrub. Turks and Lebanese use it frequently to sprinkle on grills and salads, or on fish. It can be used instead of lemon.

Tahini is a paste made of ground sesame seeds. It is used very much in Lebanon, where it is spelled *tahina* or *tehineh*. (We call it *tahini* because it was first imported from Cyprus.) Because it separates, with the oil coming to the top and the thick paste remaining at the bottom, it needs to be stirred with a spoon before use.

Preparing Vegetables

To Prepare Artichoke Bottoms: Choose large globe artichokes and cut off the stems at the base. With a pointed knife and cutting around it spirally, trim off all the leaves and any hard bits around the base. Putting the artichoke on its side, cut away the top leaves, then remove the chokes. Rub each prepared artichoke bottom with a squeezed lemon half, and drop it into a bowl of water acidulated with 2 to 3 tablespoons vinegar or lemon juice to keep it from discoloring.

Salting Eggplants: It is the custom to salt eggplants to make them sweat and rid them of their bitter juices and to make them absorb less oil when they are fried. These days, eggplants are not bitter, and even if they have been salted, they absorb a lot of oil when they are fried. I now prefer to broil or roast eggplants, in which case salting is not necessary. But if you are frying, it is worth salting them. There are two traditional ways: One is to soak them in salted water for 30 minutes to 1 hour—this also stops them from discoloring if you have to wait for some time before you use them. Another is to sprinkle them with plenty of salt, leave them in a colander to disgorge their juices, then rinse them and pat them dry with absorbent paper towels.

To Roast and Mash Whole Eggplants: Prick the eggplants in a few places with a pointed knife to prevent them from exploding. Turn them over the flame of a gas burner or barbecue, or under a preheated broiler on a sheet of foil on an oven tray, until the skin is charred all over and they feel very soft. Alternatively, place them on a sheet of foil on an oven tray and roast them in the *hottest* oven for 45 to 55 minutes, until they are very soft. When cool enough to handle, peel the eggplants (you can do this under cold running water), drop the flesh into a colander or strainer, and chop it with a knife, then mash it with a fork, letting their juices escape. Adding a squeeze of lemon juice helps to keep the purée looking pale and appetizing.

Garlic: Garlic cloves must be firm, not soft or hollow. If it has begun to sprout inside a clove, cut into the middle of the clove and remove the pale green sprout, which has a bitter taste. To crush the garlic clove, bash it on a board under the flat blade of a large knife, then chop it or scrape it to a mush on the board. Or use a garlic press—I have nothing against them but so many are useless. My own works very well and dates from my school days in Paris.

To Roast and Peel Bell Peppers: Grill them over the flame of a gas burner or barbecue, or put them on a sheet of foil on an oven tray under a preheated broiler. Turn them until their skins are black and blistered. Alternatively, roast them in the hottest oven for

30 minutes, turning them once, until they are soft and their skins blistered and blackened. To loosen the skins further, put them in a strong plastic bag, twist it shut, and leave for 10 to 15 minutes. When cool enough to handle, peel them and remove and discard the stems and seeds. Strain the juice that comes out since it can be added to the dressing.

To Peel Tomatoes: Prick the skins with a pointed knife, pour boiling water over them, and leave for 1 minute before draining and pulling off the skin.

About Fillo Pastry

Fillo is used in Turkey and Lebanon. In Lebanon, another pastry called *rakakat*, like a very thin, soft, large round pancake, softer and more malleable and also tougher than fillo, is used to make savory pies. I have used fillo instead of *rakakat* and instead of the Moroccan paper-thin pancake called *warka* or *brick* with perfect results.

Fillo is widely available both fresh and frozen. Commercial brands generally weigh 14 ounces (packages used to be 1 pound) but vary in the size of sheets and their fineness. I have come across the following sizes: 20 inches × 12 inches, 19 inches × 12 inches, 18 inches × 13³/4 inches, 18 inches × 12 inches, 12 inches × 7 inches, and 11¹/2 inches × 5 inches, and they will often vary by a fraction of an inch even within the same brand. Sizes are not given on the packaging. Supermarket brands usually contain fresh sheets in the smaller size, while packages containing large-size sheets are usually sold, frozen, in specialty stores. If you are using a frozen brand, it is important to find a reliable one, as some are totally unsatisfactory, with damp sheets sticking together when defrosted and tearing when you try to use them.

Frozen fillo must be allowed to defrost slowly for 2 to 3 hours. Packages should then be opened just before using, and the sheets should be used as quickly as possible since they become dry and brittle when exposed to the air. Keep them in a pile as you work, always brushing the top one with melted butter so the air has no opportunity to dry them out. If you have to leave them for a few minutes, cover them with plastic wrap. Any leftover pieces can be wrapped in plastic wrap and kept in the refrigerator for later use.

Fillo pies with any filling, except one that is too moist, can be frozen uncooked and put straight from the freezer into the oven without thawing. They will need a little more cooking time.

Morocco

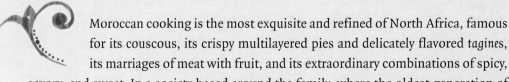Moroccan cooking is the most exquisite and refined of North Africa, famous for its couscous, its crispy multilayered pies and delicately flavored *tagines*, its marriages of meat with fruit, and its extraordinary combinations of spicy, savory, and sweet. In a society based around the family, where the oldest generation of women is still mostly illiterate, cooking is a woman's art and still an oral tradition with its secrets passed down from mother to daughter. It is the lore learned in the kitchen, a precious heritage, which a bride brings to her husband's home. It is an all-important activity, central to every aspect of life. In Morocco, any reason, any event, happy or sad, is an occasion for meeting around the table.

Styles of cooking go back hundreds of years. Some are rooted in the rural traditions of the indigenous Berber populations of Morocco, while an important grand style is a legacy from the royal kitchens of the great Moroccan dynasties—the Almoravides, Almohads, Merinids, Saadians, and Alaouites—that has echoes from medieval Baghdad and Muslim Spain. Morocco was invaded by the Arabs in several waves from the seventh until the fourteenth century. More than any other country that adopted Islam, it inherited most directly the high culinary culture of Baghdad in the time of the Abbasid caliphs when that city was the capital of the Islamic Empire, and its court cuisine was influenced by Persian styles. In 711, the Arabs invaded Spain with North African Berber foot soldiers. They conquered the peninsula and remained in the south, which became known as Al Andalus, for almost 800 years. From the eleventh to the thirteenth centuries, the ruling dynasties in Muslim Spain—the Almoravides and the Almohads—were Berber. The capital cities of their vast empire that spread through Spain, Tunisia, Algeria, and into Senegal, were in Morocco, this country becoming a center of excellence and sophistication.

Until the final expulsion of the Moors from Spain in 1492, there was constant cultural exchange between Spain and Morocco. A new eclectic style of cooking developed in the part of Spain that was under Muslim occupation. It was a multicultural civilization with people from various parts of the Muslim and Mediterranean world, including Jews and the indigenous Christians. A Kurdish lute player known as Ziryab, a freed slave from the court of Harun al Rashid in Baghdad who joined the court of Cordoba, is credited in particular for transforming the art of living and cooking in Andalusia. He introduced new music and taught people how to dress and wear makeup. He established rules of etiquette—table manners and table setting, and the order of serving three different courses—and encouraged refinements in the kitchen.

When the Moors were finally thrown out, many found refuge in Morocco, where they settled mostly in Tangier, Tetouan, and Fez. These "Andalusians," as they were called, brought with them the exuberant and convivial lifestyle that had blossomed in Spain. They also started a culinary renaissance. You can see their influence in the country's architecture, you can hear it in the music, and you can taste it in the food.

Other influences on Moroccan cuisine are through the influx of thousands of black slaves from central Africa in the seventeenth century, and also Ottoman influences via refugees from Algeria and Tunisia who migrated while those countries were under Ottoman rule.

Regional Cooking

Some years ago I was invited to a festival celebrating the regional cooking of Morocco, held in Fez. Each night, we were offered a taste of at least twenty-five dishes coming from two or three cities, while musicians, singers, and dancers entertained us. It was an enthralling experience. In Moroccan cooking, there are traditions that come from the countryside, the mountains, and the sea—both the Atlantic and the Mediterranean—and there is urban cooking that varies from one city to another. Some dishes are common throughout Morocco, varying only by the spicing and by one or two ingredients, but every city also has its own special dishes and distinctive style, which reflects its geographic position and climate as well as its past. In Tangier and Tetouan in the north, the influences are Andalusian and Mediterranean and there is also, unusually for Morocco, an Ottoman influence, especially in the pastries such as *ktaief* (see page 230) and *baklava*. In the south, in Marrakesh, Safi, and Essaouira, the influences come from Africa and the Atlantic. The cooking of Fez reflects the mix of its past inhabitants, Arab, Andalusian, Berber, and Jewish (the old Jewish quarter, the *Mellah*, situated in the *medina*, backs on to the Royal Palace), as well as the city's position on the camel-caravan spice route. A particularly refined and sophisticated bourgeois cuisine emanates from cities such as Fez, Meknès, and Marrakesh that were once imperial capitals and are now gastronomic rivals with very distinctive styles of cooking.

A Festive Meal in a Traditional Moroccan Home—a Riad

You arrive at the traditional Moroccan house from a narrow street in the *medina*. There is a blank wall, with a tiny window. You enter by a heavily studded wooden door through a dark, narrow corridor carpeted with fragrant rose petals and arrive in a glorious inner *patio* filled with little fruit trees and scented flowers. The floor and arched walls around it are lined with cobalt blue, turquoise, and yellow mosaics called *zeligs*. Water trickles from a fountain. Alcoves around the courtyard are ornately decorated. Brilliantly colored hangings line the walls of the living area. Placed against them are low sofas with embroidered cushions. The meal is served in the *patio*. The scent of jasmine hangs in the air. A band plays Andalusian music. The tables are large brass trays on low, folding legs. You sit on cushions around them. The crockery is classic Chinese. Long ago, Moroccans fell in love with Chinese porcelain with blue designs; now they make it themselves.

You wash your hands in water poured from a jug and then in rose water sprinkled from a silver flagon. Dishes follow one another. A multitude of appetizers (*kemia*): pickles; spiced vegetable purées; fried fish in a sauce flavored with cumin, chili, and green cilantro; pastry "cigars" filled with chopped meat and with shrimp. Then pigeon pie—baby pigeons stuffed with nutty couscous in a saffron and ginger honey sauce, followed by a *tagine* of lamb with wild artichokes, broad beans, and preserved lemon, and another with quinces. And next, couscous—mountains of it—crowned with meat cooked to melting tenderness, and with vegetables pressed into the sides of the mountains of grain. Then platters of fruit, followed by mint tea and almondy pastries. You might be worried by how much food is left uneaten. But the next day, family, friends, and neighbors have their feast, and what is left—every bit of it—is eaten by the cooks, staff, and helpers. That, too, is part of the ritual.

The Dadas and their Secrets

Men are excluded from all kitchens. The great cooks—family cooks, professional cooks, those who cook for weddings and parties, the guardians of the great culinary traditions—are the *dadas*. They are all women and most of them are black. Who they are is a taboo subject; the hidden face of Morocco. The women are descended from African slaves who were brought from the Sudan, which was once part of the Moroccan empire.

In the seventeenth century, the sultan Moulay Ismail recruited 150,000 slaves from the Sudan and the states of the African Sahel. The men became the origin of the Sherifan black guard. The women became domestics in people's homes. Some became concubines, some wives, some were freed and became midwives. In imperial Fez, it was not uncommon for men of great families to choose young *dadas* as their fourth wives so that they would look after their children and cook. Their children were often formally recognized and took on the father's name. A form of bondage went on until not so long ago, and the women remained illiterate. That is why it is still a taboo subject. I heard this from Fatema Hal, anthropologist, food writer, and owner of the restaurant La Mansouria in Paris.

In more recent times *dadas* have joined cooks' corporations, catering for great occasions such as weddings, circumcisions, and receptions. A man is in overall charge on such occasions, an *amine*, or chief. It is he who discusses the menu with the host, works out quantities, and hires the giant saucepans and piles of crockery, silver teapots, ornate tea glasses, and trays.

The women arrive, heads tied in fringed and floral scarves, with their helpers and their pots and pans, and stay several days with the families. They shop, slaughter sheep and pigeons, prepare the *warka* for *bstilla*, set up the big, copper pans on braziers, and prepare all the dishes while the ladies of the house and their relatives busy themselves with the sweet pastries. These *dadas* pass on the oral traditions of grand cooking to each other. They also pass, from one kitchen to another, the inside stories and scandals of the top families. Their stories of sorcerers and devils frighten the children who gather to watch the activities around the giant pans and to see the *dadas* throw a grain of incense in the fire to drive away the *jnoun* (devil). They are paid little but they are fed and they can take home the offals and leftovers.

Some *dadas* have become famous itinerant specialists of one dish only or a culinary style. A few lead the battalions of women in the kitchens of the best hotels. Most of the great ones who lived all their lives with families are old now. They are disappearing, and people have had to learn to do without them. Some of their specialties, such as the paper-thin pancakes called *warka* (or *brick*) (see page 29), can now be bought loose at the *souk* and vacuum-packed in supermarkets.

Street Food

Donkeys carry produce from the country—great bundles of fresh green mint and cilantro, baskets of fat tomatoes, little wild purple artichokes, long fleshy cardoon stalks—into the heart of the *medina* through the narrow, meandering streets and into the *souk*. Powerful aromas emanate from the mounds of red, gold, and brown powders, curious looking roots, bits of bark, shriveled pods, seeds, berries, bulbs, rose buds, and orange blossoms, which are on display in the spice shops. Vendors pack the spices into tightly rolled cones of newspaper and offer them as though they were magic potions. Some of the spice merchants are also magic men. I got to know one who said he was a white magic man who defeated the evil eye and black magic spells. Mostly it meant he dealt with any mischief from co-wives and restored potency to men.

In every town, in the *souks*, in the old *medinas*—the squares where weekly markets set up—at bus stops on inter-city roads, there are street vendors. From tiny cafés and boutiques as small as a cupboard, from carts or stands, or sometimes from an upturned box with a chair for customers, they offer their specialties: boiled carrot salad with cumin, *harira* (soup with meat or chicken, chickpeas, lentils, or other beans), tiny spicy snails, grilled minced meat on skewers, spongy pancakes, fritters in sugar syrup.

Place Djemaa-el-Fna in Marrakesh is the most enthralling gastro-theater. One of my friends has a medical clinic there. I stayed in the family home and hung around the square day and night. During the day, musicians and dancers from the mountains, snake charmers, fire-eaters, letter writers, storytellers, fortune-tellers, have possession of the huge square. As the sun begins to fall, the entire area is taken over by hundreds of cooks. They set up stands and trestle tables, and start charcoal fires. Clients sit on benches around each stand. All night long the vendors serve soups from huge pots, often accompanied by dates. The smoke of fish frying and meat grilling on braziers and the mingled aromas of mint and cilantro, cumin and turmeric, fill the air.

Restaurants

There have always been small modest establishments where travelers and country folk who bring their products to market can find something to eat—soups simmering in large copper pans, fried fish, mountains of couscous, pancakes oozing with honey and melting butter. But it is only in the last decade or two that grand restaurants that serve traditional local foods have opened. Moroccans are not used to eating out. They are used to entertaining at home. The local hospitality is legendary. Even strangers, poor travelers knocking at a door of a home in the *medina*, will be offered at least soup and a piece of bread.

Tourist hotels used to serve French cuisine, but now they mostly serve international food. Recently, grand restaurants that employ family cooks or *dadas* who can make exquisite refined dishes have opened in old *riads*—palaces that were family homes. It is an extraordinary experience to eat in one of those restaurants with their fabulous decor. The best meal I had on a recent visit to Fez was in one such *riad* built in the eighteenth century, the *maison d'hôte* Dar El Ghalia. It has been converted by descendants of the original owners into a restaurant with hotel rooms, but otherwise it has kept the reception area as it was, with inner *patio* and fountain, mosaics, alcoves with low sofas, and seating around huge brass trays. For me, it is a bit of heaven. In Morocco hospitality is an art, and this restaurant emulates the traditions of the home. The owners receive you with effusive warmth, offer you mint tea poured from a silver teapot held high into little glasses, and serve you the local dishes cooked in the traditional way.

Of Tagines, Qdras, and Other Long-Cooked Dishes

During a round-table discussion at a festival of culinary arts in 2001 entitled "*Saveurs d'hier et d'aujourd'hui*" ("Flavors of Yesterday and Today"), there were heated arguments between those who did not accept any changes to tradition and those who wanted to be free to invent and to do dishes their way. The latter were Moroccan restaurateurs abroad. Local restaurateurs were concerned with the loss of their beloved traditions and were prickly about every little detail. The "modernizers" in between advocated making dishes lighter and healthier by using less fat.

One man regretted the passing of the time, not long ago, when people would walk down the street and know, by the smells, exactly what their neighbors were cooking, and what stage of readiness the stews had reached. I am not sure if this is because they have cars

now and have moved out of the *medina*, or because many cooks now use the *cocotte minute* or *mijotte* (pressure cooker). Years ago when I was traveling through Morocco, I was told that I had to go to see a woman who had developed a new style of "fast" Moroccan cuisine. I contacted her and she invited me to lunch. On the table was a pressure cooker in which she made her *tagine*s. It was the start of a trend that, a long time later, has taken the country by storm.

The word *tagine* derives from the shallow, round clay cooking pot with the pointed cone-shaped lid in which stews are traditionally cooked. The word has become so glamorous and prestigious in our western world, and so misused in restaurants in Morocco, that it has come to mean any kind of stew or braise. Cooking in a clay *tagine*, very gently over a brazier (*kanoun*) of constantly replenished embers, diffuses the heat all around the pot and produces, at the end, a reduced sauce sizzling in its fat. *Tagine*s are distinguished by their cooking fats and spicing, although the distinctions have become blurred these days. *M'qualli* denotes those cooked in oil where there is saffron and ginger and the sauce is yellow. *M'hammer* refers to those cooked with olive oil or butter, and spiced with cumin and paprika, where the sauce is red.

For parties and great occasions it has never been possible to cook in *tagine*s because they don't contain enough. The cooking, then, is done in giant pots. You see them in copper, aluminum, or stainless steel in the *souk*s, for sale or to rent. The word *qdra*, the name of the big pots used for the grand parties in the royal cities, has come to mean the kind of grand dishes with noble ingredients that are cooked in them on such occasions. The cooking fat is butter (although nowadays many substitute olive oil), the flavor is that of saffron, sometimes combined with ginger and cinnamon, and they nearly always include chickpeas or almonds. Huge quantities of chopped onions are reduced to melting softness to produce a rich, creamy sauce. There is often also a touch of honey. The varieties of stews cooked and sold in the streets and in the *souk*s, and those cooked in the countryside in ordinary saucepans with oil and turmeric instead of saffron, are called *marqa*. They are the poor man's *qdra*.

Until recently, people did not have ovens. Nowadays, most city families have every modern appliance and utensil. They can make life easier for themselves without betraying the memory of the old gastronomy. It is more convenient to cook in saucepans and casseroles over gas than in a *tagine* over a dying fire. The result can be as good if you cook slowly with very little water, adding more as it evaporates, and if you reduce the sauce until it is rich and unctuous. In restaurants, stews are cooked in large pans and finished off and brought to the table in beautiful, individual *tagine*s decorated with blue, green, turquoise, and yellow arabesques. People also do more roasting and baking in their ovens.

Moroccan dishes change little even when they are "modernized." As with legends that vary in small details as they travel from place to place and are passed from one person to another, the differences in cooking lie in the use of spices, fats, and local seasonal produce, as well as in method. While in many places they brown the meat and soften the onions in oil or butter before adding water, in Fez they never fry first but put all the ingredients in together with the water. *Smen*, the "matured" clarified butter that was once very common, is now little used. (To outsiders, including myself, and also to many local people these days, it appears to give the food an unpleasant rancid taste.) Some braise their chickens whole, others joint them. Although lamb and mutton are the traditional meats, beef and veal are now also used. There are also differences as to when to put in olives and preserved lemon—ten minutes before the end of cooking, or as a garnish just before serving.

About Couscous

Couscous is the national dish of Morocco. The name refers to the grain as well as to the combined dish of broth with meat, chicken, or fish with vegetables over which the grain is traditionally steamed and which is served with the grain. The processed grain is semolina made from durum hard wheat that has been ground then moistened and coated or "rolled" in flour. The resulting granules are cooked by steaming. Other grains—maize, millet, and especially barley—are also used in the same way.

In Morocco, where all foods based on grain are considered sacred, couscous has a quasi-mystical character. It is served on all great occasions, both happy and sad—at weddings and at funerals. It is a celebratory dish served at the end of great feasts to make sure that no one is left hungry. It is usually the musicians and the *tolbas*—people who come to pray and recite the Koran at weddings, funerals, or during Ramadan, in expectation of a good meal—who get to eat it. It is the family's Friday meal, where any vegetables left over from the week's provisions go in, and also famously the food sent to the mosque by the pious to be distributed to the poor.

Couscous is associated with the indigenous Berbers, who call it *kesksou*, a name said to be derived from the sound steam makes as it passes through the grain. No written reference was made of it until the thirteenth century—a time when the Berber Almohad dynasty ruled Andalusia and all of North Africa—when it featured prominently in Arabic culinary manuscripts of the Maghreb (North Africa) and Andalusia. The special type of durum wheat that is used originated in Ethiopia and was supposedly introduced in the region by the Arabs by the tenth century. But it is in the Berber lands, where steaming in a clay colander placed over a boiling pot was an age-old practice, that the special way of rolling the grain and then cooking it over a broth was developed.

Until not very long ago, every family bought its wheat at the market and took it to the local mill to be ground to the degree of fineness they preferred, then brought it home to be processed or "rolled" by hand. This is traditionally done by the following method: A few handfuls of semolina (medium-ground durum wheat) are spread in a wide shallow wooden or clay dish. The semolina is sprinkled with a little cold salted water to moisten it and rolled with the open hand with a circular clockwise movement as it is gradually sprinkled with flour, until the granules are evenly coated with a fine film of flour to form very tiny balls. These are shaken through two or three sieves with different size holes (the first with larger holes) to sort them by size, and lastly through a very fine sieve to eliminate any excess flour. Larger granules are enlarged with more moistening and rolling in flour and are used as a type of pasta called *berkoukes* or *mhammas*. Without this coating of flour, the couscous would cook into a stodgy porridge.

Large amounts of couscous were prepared in advance, either to be stored or for special occasions such as a wedding or circumcision or a return from a pilgrimage to Mecca. Women from the family and neighbors assembled to work together. It took hours but it was a day of fun and rejoicing as they gossiped and laughed and sang. Before the rolled grain was stored, it was first steamed for about 20 minutes then dried for two days on sheets laid out on rooftops. This ensured it would keep for a long time.

Nowadays, very few women roll their own grain, even in the country areas. The process has been industrialized and the vast majority now buy it ready-processed or in an instant precooked variety, which can be bought in three different grades: fine, medium, and large. Those who insist on having the time-honored homemade couscous for a special event call in professional artisans—Berber women or *dadas* (see page 16)—to the house to make it. Traditional purists find the precooked instant variety unacceptable, even offensive. It does not have the special quality of the real thing made by hand, but I suspect they are also mourning the loss of an old culture and the rituals that accompanied it. Nevertheless, the precooked instant couscous is used in many North African restaurants abroad and by busy North African families in France as well as in Morocco. It can be perfectly good if handled properly.

I visited a couscous processing factory in Sfax during an international conference in 1993, which took us on a fabulous gastronomic tour of Tunisia. We were received with welcoming banners and offered a tasting of dozens of couscous dishes, both savory and sweet. Women in Berber dress gave demonstrations of the old ancestral ways of rolling

US
GROß
متوسط •
F.A.G
ZAKIA
كسكسي
MOYEN - MEDIUM - MITTELGROB
MIDDELGROTE - MEDIO - متوسط
1kge

couscous by hand and steaming it. When the owner of the factory showed us around the plant, I asked him what he advised was the best way to use his product since packages sold abroad gave different instructions. He said that, although steaming is a ritual and part of the culture of North Africa that the people are used to and hold on to, you can just as well add water and heat it through in the oven—even, he added very quietly, in a microwave, which many of the women now do.

The couscous we get in the United States is the precooked, instant variety. Supermarkets sell the medium-size granules that are best for ordinary couscous dishes, while the "fine" variety called "couscous *seffa*," used for stuffings and sweet couscous (see the dessert section), can be found in specialty Moroccan and a few Middle Eastern stores. With care, it is possible, even with precooked couscous, to prepare it so that it swells and becomes light, fluffy, and airy, each grain soft and separate from its neighbor. Moroccans describe it as "velvety."

There are many regional and seasonal versions of couscous dishes. It can be very simple, with the couscous plus just one vegetable such as fresh green peas, or it can be quite grandiose with stuffed pigeons sitting on a mountain of couscous mixed with almonds and raisins. Every family makes it in their own special way, and it is always different every time they make it. It can, with experience, be the easiest thing to prepare in advance and to serve at a large dinner party. It can be spectacular and there is something about the dish that inspires conviviality. By tradition, couscous is a communal dish. The old traditional way was to eat it with one hand straight from the serving dish. Nowadays, couscous is eaten with a spoon—the meat is supposed to be so tender that you can pull it apart with your fingers and you don't need to cut it with a knife.

The traditional method of cooking couscous is by steaming it over a broth or over water in a *couscoussier*—a large round pot with a colander on top that holds the couscous. The couscous needs to be steamed three times, and between each steaming it is taken out and moistened with cold water and rubbed so any lumps are removed. In all, the process takes about three-quarters of an hour.

Since almost all the couscous available in America is of the precooked variety, it requires a different treatment. I use a very simple method (see page 112), which cannot fail. However, even with this method of preparing precooked couscous, there is an art in achieving light, airy, separate grains.

Warka *or* Brick *for* Bstilla *and* Briwat

Large, ever-so-thin pancakes called *warka* are used to make large round pies called *bstilla* (or *pastilla*) and small ones called *briwat*. These are made in the shape of cigars, triangles, cornets, and square parcels with a variety of fillings and are deep-fried.

Making *warka* is a highly skilled operation and these days it is left to specialists. A dough is made with hard-wheat (or bread) flour, a pinch of salt, and warm water, and then kneaded for a long time as more water is worked in to obtain a soft, very moist, spongy elasticity. Then the dough is left to rest for an hour, covered with a film of warm water. Lumps the size of an egg are picked up with one hand and dabbed onto the oiled surface of a round tray placed bottom side up over a fire. As the dough touches the tray with repeated dabs, a thin, almost transparent, film of pastry is built up and gradually expanded into a round about 12 inches in diameter.

Nowadays, you can buy the vacuum-packed, round pastry sheets in Moroccan stores as *"feuilles de brick."* Brick is the Tunisian name of the little fried pies. I buy these sheets from North African stores in Golborne Road, London W10, and they are in all French supermarkets. They freeze very well. Quality varies, and they are never as good as homemade ones. I personally prefer to use fillo instead, because I like baking rather than frying the pies, and the round sheets of *brick* are wonderful and crisp when they are deep-fried, but come out unpleasantly tough when baked.

I started using fillo for Moroccan pies long ago but I always felt a little guilty about not using the real thing until a young Moroccan cook who had been sent to Disneyland in the United States to demonstrate Moroccan cooking at an international festival of tourism told me about her team's experience. They had not anticipated the extent of the demand for *briwat* and quickly ran out of pastry. A Lebanese contingent nearby loaned the Moroccan cooks fillo and they continued to make the pies with this pastry, which turned out perfectly satisfactory.

About Spices and Aromatics

What is most surprising and fascinating to us is the way Moroccans mix savory with sweet, and the way they mix a number of spices to achieve a very delicate, subtle flavor. There are no sweet-and-sour dishes, but sugar or honey can be part of savory dishes such as meat stews and vegetable dishes. Dozens of aromatics are used and some are ubiquitous. Cumin, which is believed to stimulate the appetite, ginger, paprika, and chili are common in appetizers as well as in fish dishes. Saffron, ginger, and cinnamon are the constant aromatics of sweet *tagines*. There are spice mixtures for ground meat, *kefta* (cilantro seed, cumin, mace, allspice, paprika, or chili pepper), and mixtures for soup (cinnamon, caraway, cumin, ginger, pepper). *Ras el hanout* (meaning "the head of the shop") is a legendary mixture of twenty-seven spices including the golden beetle that is the aphrodisiac Spanish fly. Spice merchants have their own secret blends and now there are brands made by small local producers that you can buy in Europe.

The most prestigious and also ubiquitous spice used extensively in soups and *tagines* is saffron. In Morocco, it is cultivated in the region of Taliouine between Taroudannt and Ouarzazate. Because it is expensive, many Moroccans use a low-grade adulterated powder that gives a yellow color and has hardly any taste or aroma, but using the "threads" or stigmas of the *Crocus sativus*, or a very good quality powder, makes the difference to a dish. Turmeric is the poor man's saffron. You can smell it in the aroma of stews and soups sold by street vendors. It is yellow but the flavor is nothing like that of saffron.

When you cook a Moroccan dish, it is most important to achieve a delicate marriage of flavors and, with the sweet *tagines* especially, a balance between sweet and salty. Dishes with sugar and honey must have enough salt and also plenty of black pepper to mitigate the sweetness. They say you must "weigh with your eye," but of course you must also taste and you must learn to trust your taste. Preserved lemon peel is used as an aromatic, and oils also contribute their flavor. Sophisticated cooks now commonly replace the traditional peanut oil with extra virgin olive oil for cooking as well as for dressings. Argan oil (see page 31), which has a distinctive nutty flavor, is also used as a dressing. Flower waters, made from the blossoms of bitter oranges and roses (see pages 6 and 7), are used to perfume puddings and pastries. People make them at home. In the spring, mountains of the flowers are to be seen for sale in huge, floppy baskets in all the markets.

About Argan Oil

Argan oil is obtained from the nut in the yellow fruit of the argan tree, which grows exclusively in southwest Morocco. It has a distinctive nutty flavor and is used as a dressing. It does not keep very well.

Goats famously climb in the trees and jump from one branch to another, munching the argan fruit. The pulp is digested and the stone is expelled. The stones are then collected and cracked to release the nut from which the oil is made. Nowadays the pulp is removed by an industrial process at a women's cooperative, but the nuts are still cracked by the women. The oil is believed locally to have aphrodisiac properties. It is also valued for its medicinal and cosmetic qualities. Women rub it on their faces and necks as a night lotion, and in their hair.

About Bread

In Moroccan society bread is considered almost sacred. It is a symbol of generosity and conviviality, of giving and taking. If a piece falls on the ground, someone is sure to pick it up, kiss it, and place it somewhere high. When you see the extraordinary bread bins with cone-shaped hats made of wicker and brightly colored leather or, more grandly, of copper or silver, you realize how favorably bread is held.

Hardly any dish is eaten without bread. It is used to mop up sauces and also to pick up morsels of food. Loaves are round and dense, made from wheat flour and semolina, and also from maize, barley, and rye flours; sometimes they are embellished with seeds such as sesame and aniseed. Families used to take their wheat to be ground at the mill. They would make bread at home every morning with leaven they kept in a clay pot, and then send the loaves to the public oven with errand boys who carried them on trays balanced on their heads, a sight that can still sometimes be seen today. Every family makes a distinctive mark on their uncooked loaves so that when the baker puts them in the oven with his wooden oar, he knows whose they are, and can bake them as each family likes them—soft and white or crisp and brown. In the last twenty years, since people have had home ovens, the old public ovens have mostly closed down. They are now seen mainly in poorer neighborhoods near the public baths, as the wood they burn also heats the water for the baths.

In courtyards of large town houses and in the countryside, rustic breads are baked in small outdoor conical clay ovens with a hole on top, called *tannours*. The dough is slapped on to the inside walls of the *tannour*. When it is cooked, it falls and continues to cook in the ashes. Flat breads, leavened or unleavened, are cooked on domed griddles and in clay *tagines*. In city *souks* you see vendors making small, thick, spongy pancakes called *baghrir* and a kind of soft, greasy puff pastry called *trid* and *rghaif*.

About Beverages

Alcoholic drinks are forbidden by Islam, but Morocco is nevertheless a wine-producing country. Established since Roman times, wine-making was developed extensively by French colonizers, but production has shrunk since they left in 1956. Now it is still made for export, and tourists can find it locally. Their *rosés* and *gris* (light reds) go well with the spicy flavors of Moroccan food, as does the light beer. A spirit called *mahya*, made by Jews from figs or dates, is drunk as an aperitif or digestive on festive occasions. *Samet* is a drink made from a mix of fruits such as grapes, apples, pears, and plums that are left to ferment together in an earthenware pot.

Nonalcoholic beverages are fresh fruit juices—orange, date, grape, apple, and pomegranate—sometimes with a drop of orange blossom water, and also almond milk. Water (often from a well in the courtyard) is perfumed with orange blossom water or with the aroma of burning gum mastic (see page 6). Infusions are made from orange blossom petals, verbena, marjoram, thyme, and sage. The rural drink of welcome is milk served with dates. Milk with a touch of orange blossom and the slightly acid buttermilk called *lben* are drunk with certain couscous dishes.

The famous, very sweet, mint tea is a symbol of hospitality: it is served as soon as guests arrive at a house, and at all times of the day. English traders introduced tea in the nineteenth century, and the drink, with added fresh mint, acquired a ceremonial ritual with its own rules. On grand occasions, a specialist is hired to prepare and pour the tea in front of the guests. It is served in ornate Victorian-style silver teapots (once upon a time they came from Manchester) on silver trays with tiny legs and poured from a great height into small ornamented colored glasses.

The old-style Turkish coffee, scented with orange blossom water or gum mastic or spiced with cardamom, cinnamon, cloves, or *ras el hanout*, has been generally replaced by espresso and is only rarely to be found.

About Olives

A recurring feature in many *tagines* is the use of olives in partnership with preserved lemon peel. Moroccan olives are among the best in the world. There are basically three varieties—green, violet, and black—that reflect the stage of their ripeness (all olives start green and gradually turn violet and then black as they ripen). After they are picked, they are soaked in changes of water for days or weeks to get rid of their bitterness and mellow their flavor. The violet ones are cured in the juice of bitter oranges. Green olives cured in salt are also variously flavored with herbs, garlic, and chili pepper. Black olives are salted and allowed to lose their juices and are then dried in the sun.

Use green or violet olives for your *tagines*. If you find them too salty, soak them in water for up to an hour.

About Preserved Lemons

Lemons pickled in salt lose their sharpness and acquire a distinct flavor. They are one of the most common ingredients in Moroccan cooking. They are sold loose in Moroccan markets where you see them, soft and oozing with juice, piled high on stalls beside mountains of different colored olives. The two are often used together in dishes.

Although preserved lemons can now be bought in some supermarkets, it is worth making your own. They are not difficult to make, and they will taste better. They take about four weeks to mature to be ready to use and will keep for a year. Normally the peel alone is used and the pulp is thrown away, but some people like to use the pulp too. You can use small lemons with thin skins or ordinary lemons with thick ones, and they must be unwaxed. There are three common ways of making them.

LEMONS PRESERVED *in* SALT *and* LEMON JUICE

In this method, which is considered the most prestigious and gives the best results, no water is used. The lemon juice, which is the pickling liquor, can be reused for further batches.

> 4 lemons
> 4 tablespoons sea salt
> juice of 4 additional lemons, or more to taste

Wash and scrub the lemons. The classic Moroccan way is to cut each lemon in quarters but not right through, so that the pieces are still attached at the stem end, and to stuff each with a tablespoon of salt and squeeze it closed. Put them in a sterilized preserving jar, pressing them down so that they are squashed together, and close the jar.

Leave for 3 to 4 days, by which time the lemons will have disgorged some of their juices and the skins will have softened a little. Open the jar and press the lemons down as much as you can, then add fresh lemon juice to cover them entirely.

Close the jar and leave in a cool place for at least a month. The longer they are left, the better the flavor. (If a piece of lemon is not covered, it develops a white mold that is harmless and just needs to be washed off.)

Before using, scoop out and discard the pulp and rinse the lemon peel under the tap to get rid of the salt.

LEMONS PRESERVED in BRINE

This is the same procedure as on the preceding page, but instead of adding lemon juice, cover the lemons with brine made by adding 2 tablespoons of salt to warm (boiled) water. Lemons prepared this way take longer to mature. Some people pour a little oil on top as a protective film.

LEMONS BOILED in BRINE and PRESERVED IN OIL

I am especially fond of this quick unorthodox method, which gives delicious results in four days.

With a sharp knife, make 8 superficial, not deep, incisions into the skin from one end of the lemon to the other. Put the lemons in a large pan with salted water (4 tablespoons salt for 4 lemons) to cover. Put a smaller lid on top of them to weigh them down since they float, and boil for about 25 minutes, or until the peel is very soft, then drain.

When cool enough to handle, scoop out the flesh, pack the skins in a glass jar and cover with sunflower or light vegetable oil.

Starters and Kemia

A Moroccan meal begins with an assortment of cold appetizers called *kemia* served with bread. These are mostly vegetable salads, either raw or cooked, in which cumin, ginger, and paprika—which are believed to whet the appetite—are ubiquitous aromatics and preserved lemon peel and olives are characteristic ingredients. The salads are usually left on the table to act as side dishes with the main course.

Among the hot dishes that you can serve as a first course are soups, grilled meats on skewers (see page 99 in main courses), and pies.

SWEET TOMATO PURÉE
Matesha Masla

The honey sweetness of this specialty from Marrakesh is surprising and enchanting. Serve it cold as an appetizer with bread, or hot to pour over meat or chicken, and sprinkle, if you like, with chopped, toasted almonds or sesame seeds.

SERVES 6

2 tablespoons extra virgin olive oil
2 pounds ripe tomatoes, peeled and chopped
salt
1 tablespoon sugar
1/2 teaspoon ground cinnamon
1/4 to 1/2 teaspoon black pepper
1 tablespoon clear honey

Heat the oil in a pan and add the tomatoes, a little salt, and the sugar.

Cook for 45 minutes, or until the liquid has gone and the purée is thick and jammy and almost caramelized. It is vital to stir often so that it doesn't stick to the pan and burn.

Add the cinnamon, pepper, and honey and a little salt to taste, and stir well. Cook for a minute or so more.

BELL PEPPER PURÉE
Slada Felfla

This bright red, creamy purée has an alluring mix of flavors. Serve it as a dip or to accompany fish.

SERVES 6 TO 8

6 red bell peppers
2 garlic cloves, crushed
4 to 5 tablespoons vinegar or the juice of 11/2 lemons
pinch of ground chili pepper
1 teaspoon ground cumin
4 tablespoons extra virgin olive oil
salt
2 tablespoons chopped flat-leaf parsley
2 tablespoons chopped cilantro
peel of 1/2 preserved lemon, chopped (see page 7)

Place the peppers on a sheet of foil on an oven tray under a preheated broiler, 2 1/2 to 3 1/2 inches from the broiler. Turn them until their skins are black and blistered all over. Alternatively—and more easily—roast them in the hottest oven for about 30 minutes, or until they are soft and their skins blistered and blackened, turning them once after 15 minutes.

To loosen the skins further, put them in a strong plastic bag, twist it shut, and leave for 10 to 15 minutes. Another old way that has the same effect is to put them in a pan with a tight-fitting lid for the same length of time. When the peppers are cool enough to handle, peel them, and remove and discard the stems and seeds.

Blend the peppers to a purée in the food processor with the garlic, vinegar or lemon juice, chili, cumin, olive oil, and a little salt to taste.

Put the purée into a serving bowl and mix in the chopped parsley, cilantro, and preserved lemon peel.

ZUCCHINI PURÉE and BABY PLUM TOMATOES
Slada Bil Gharaa Wal Tamatem

I like the contrasts of color and texture in this little dish that can be served hot or cold.

SERVES 6
- 1 pound zucchini, cut into thick slices
- 4 tablespoons extra virgin olive oil
- 1 pound baby plum tomatoes, cut lengthwise in half
- 6 garlic cloves, sliced
- salt and black pepper
- 2 to 3 tablespoons chopped flat-leaf parsley or cilantro

Boil the zucchini in salted water until very tender. Drain and chop them with a sharp knife in the colander or strainer, then mash them with a fork, letting their excess water escape.

In a large skillet, heat 2 tablespoons olive oil, then take it off the heat. Put in the tomatoes, cut side down, and the garlic. Cook over a medium-high heat until the tomatoes have softened and the garlic begins to color. Turn over the tomatoes once, and season with salt and pepper.

Add the zucchini purée to the pan with the tomatoes, and stir in 2 more tablespoons olive oil, a little salt, and the chopped parsley or cilantro.

Serve hot or cold.

MASHED EGGPLANT and TOMATO SALAD
Zaalouk

I love this popular Moroccan salad. It is best made several hours in advance so that the flavors have time to penetrate.

SERVES 6

1 1/2 pounds eggplants
juice of 1/2 to 1 lemon
1 pound tomatoes, peeled and chopped
5 garlic cloves, chopped coarsely
salt
4 tablespoons argan (see page 31) or extra virgin olive oil
1/2 teaspoon paprika
good pinch of ground chili pepper, to taste
1 teaspoon ground cumin
2 tablespoons chopped flat-leaf parsley
2 tablespoons chopped cilantro
To garnish: a handful of black olives

Prick the eggplants with a pointed knife to prevent them from bursting in the oven. Place them on a large piece of foil on a baking sheet and roast them in a hot oven preheated to 475°F for about 45 to 55 minutes, or until they feel very soft when you press them and the skins are wrinkled. When cool enough to handle, peel and drop them in a bowl of water with a little lemon juice to keep their flesh pale.

Drain the eggplants in a strainer or colander with small holes and press out as much of the water and juices as possible. Still in the colander, chop the flesh with a pointed knife, then mash it with a fork or wooden spoon, letting the juices escape through the holes.

Cook the tomatoes with the garlic and a little salt over a low heat for about 20 minutes, or until reduced to a thick sauce, stirring occasionally. Mix with the mashed eggplants and the rest of the ingredients and add salt to taste.

To serve, spread flat on a plate and garnish with olives.

GRATED CUCUMBER and MINT SALAD
Khiar Bil Na'na

This is a wonderfully refreshing salad. The tiny bit of orange blossom water gives it a mysterious flavor. Try to get small cucumbers from Middle Eastern or Asian stores. They have a better taste and texture than the large ones found in our supermarkets.

SERVES 4

1 large or 3 small cucumbers
3 tablespoons extra virgin olive oil
2 tablespoons lemon juice
1 teaspoon orange blossom water, or to taste
salt
leaves of 2 sprigs of mint, finely chopped

Peel and grate the cucumber or cucumbers. You can do this in the food processor.

Drain off the juices in a colander, and then mix the cucumbers with the rest of the ingredients.

POTATO and OLIVE SALAD
Slada Batata Bil Zaytoun

Moroccan olives are among the best in the Mediterranean and find their way into many salads. Look for good ones for this salad, which is best made in advance so that the dressing and flavors are absorbed. The potatoes will attract the dressing and flavors better if they are peeled.

SERVES 4

1 pound new potatoes

3 tablespoons extra virgin olive oil

juice of 1/2 lemon

1/2 teaspoon paprika

1/2 teaspoon ground cumin

pinch of chili pepper

salt

2 tablespoons chopped flat-leaf parsley

1/2 large mild red or white onion, chopped finely

12 black olives

Peel the potatoes and boil them in salted water until tender. Drain them and cut them in half, or quarters if large, but leave them whole if small.

Prepare the dressing in the serving bowl. Mix the oil with the lemon juice, paprika, cumin, chili pepper, and salt.

While still warm, turn the potatoes in the dressing, add the parsley, onion, and olives and mix gently.

PEAR and LEAF SALAD
Slada Bouawid

Use pears that are ripe but still firm (Comice is a good variety) and salad leaves such as curly endive, chicory, cress, arugula, and lamb's lettuce (mâche). You can stick to one type only or use a mix.

SERVES 4

juice of 1/2 lemon

3 tablespoons extra virgin olive oil or a 50/50 mix with argan oil (see page 31)

salt and black pepper

2 ripe but firm pears

about 4 ounces salad leaves

Prepare the dressing in a flat serving dish, mixing lemon juice, oil, salt, and pepper.

Peel the pears and cut them lengthwise into eight slices each, removing the cores. Turn the slices in the dressing, ensuring that the pear pieces are all well coated in order to avoid discoloration.

Just before serving, toss the pear pieces with the salad leaves.

VARIATION

You can make this salad with figs, washed or peeled and cut into quarters.

CARROT SALAD with CUMIN and GARLIC
Jazar Bil Kamoun Wal Toum

Carrot salads are very common in Morocco. This one is sold by street vendors and is particularly delicious. Use older carrots, which have a better taste than young ones.

SERVES 4 TO 6
5 large carrots (about 1 1/4 pounds)
4 tablespoons extra virgin olive oil
4 garlic cloves, crushed
1 teaspoon ground cumin
salt and black pepper
juice of 1/2 lemon

Peel or wash and scrape the carrots and trim off the tops and tails. Cut them in quarters lengthwise and then cut each quarter in half to produce sticks. Boil in salted water for 10 to 15 minutes, until tender but not too soft, then drain.

In a large skillet, heat the oil and put in the carrots, garlic, cumin, and some salt and pepper. Sauté on a medium-high heat, stirring and turning the carrots over, until the garlic just begins to color.

Sprinkle with lemon juice and serve cold.

CARROTS with GARLIC and MINT
Jazar Bil Na'na

These minty carrots are tasty and aromatic. Serve them hot or warm as an appetizer or to accompany grilled or roast meat or chicken.

SERVES 4
1 pound carrots
salt
2 garlic cloves, crushed
1 tablespoon dried mint
2 tablespoons extra virgin olive oil

Peel or wash and scrape the carrots and trim off the tops and tails, then cut them crosswise into slices about 1/3 inch thick. Put the carrots in a pan and barely cover with water. Add salt and simmer, covered, for 10 minutes, or until almost tender. Uncover to let the liquid reduce, and cook for about 10 minutes more.

Add the garlic, mint, olive oil, and more salt to taste, if necessary, and cook for a few minutes more.

ORANGE, OLIVE, and ONION SALAD
Slata Bortokal Bil Zaytoun

Bitter oranges—Seville oranges—are commonly used in Morocco, but this salad is also good with sweet ones. Argan oil (see page 31) gives it a nutty flavor.

SERVES 6

4 oranges
16 black olives
1 large mild red onion, finely chopped
juice of 1/2 to 1 lemon
3 tablespoons argan or extra virgin olive oil
salt
1/2 teaspoon ground cumin
1/2 teaspoon paprika
pinch of ground chili pepper
2 tablespoons chopped flat-leaf parsley

Peel the oranges, removing the pith. Cut them into thick slices and then into quarters with a fine serrated knife. Put them on a flat serving plate with the olives and chopped onion on top.

Make a dressing with a mixture of lemon juice, argan or olive oil, salt, cumin, paprika, and chili pepper and pour over the salad. Sprinkle with the chopped parsley.

VARIATION

Instead of lemon juice, add a whole lemon, peeled, pith removed, cut into slices, and then into small pieces.

ROASTED TOMATOES
Tamatem Halwa

These sweet tomatoes confites have a deliciously intense flavor. Serve them hot or cold as an appetizer or with grilled meat or fish. Considering their versatility and their great use in Moroccan cuisine, it is extraordinary that tomatoes were adopted by Morocco as late as 1910. It is best to use plum tomatoes. Although they take a long time to cook, you can cook them in advance, even days in advance, as they keep well in the refrigerator.

SERVES 6 TO 8
12 ripe but firm plum tomatoes
olive oil
3 tablespoons sugar
salt and black pepper

Cut the tomatoes in half lengthwise. Brush an oven dish or baking sheet (or a piece of foil) with olive oil and place the tomatoes on it, cut side up. Sprinkle each with sugar, salt, and pepper and cook in an oven preheated to 275°F for 3 1/2 to 4 hours, until shriveled and shrunken. Serve them, cut side up, on a flat serving plate.

ROAST PEPPER, TOMATO, and APPLE SALAD
Slada Felfla Bil Tamatem Wal Tofah

Peppers and tomatoes are often partnered around the Mediterranean, but the surprise of finding sweet apples and chili peppers makes this a very special first course to serve with bread. The peppers can also be fried with the onion, but I like to roast them.

SERVES 6
3 fleshy red bell peppers
1 large onion, sliced
3 to 4 tablespoons extra virgin olive oil
4 garlic cloves, chopped
1 pound tomatoes, peeled and chopped
1 or 2 chili peppers, left whole
salt and black pepper
2 sweet apples (such as Golden Delicious)

Place the peppers on a sheet of foil on an oven tray under a preheated broiler, 2 1/2 to 3 1/2 inches from the broiler. Turn them until their skins are black and blistered all over. Alternatively—and more easily—roast them in the hottest oven for about 30 minutes, or until they are soft and their skins blistered and blackened, turning them once after 15 minutes.

To loosen the skins further, put them in a strong plastic bag, twist it shut, and leave for 10 to 15 minutes. Another old way that has the same effect is to put them in a pan with a tight-fitting lid for the same length of time. When the peppers are cool enough to handle, peel them and remove and discard the stems and seeds. Now cut the peppers lengthwise into ribbons.

In a wide pan, fry the onion in 2 tablespoons of olive oil over a medium heat, stirring often until they are lightly colored. Add the garlic and stir until it just begins to color, then add the tomatoes and chili peppers. Season with salt and pepper and cook gently for about 15 to 20 minutes.

Leaving the peel on, quarter and core the apples. Stir the red pepper ribbons into the onion mixture then put in the apple quarters, cut side down. Cook gently until the apples are tender, adding a little water if the pan becomes too dry. Turn the apples skin side down toward the end.

Serve cold, drizzled with the remaining olive oil.

ROAST PEPPERS and CHICKPEAS with FRESH GOAT CHEESE
Felfla Wal Hummas Wa Jban

A mild and soft fresh goat cheese, jban, is one of the rare cheeses produced in Morocco. If you are not keen on raw garlic, you can leave it out.

SERVES 4 TO 6 4 fleshy red bell peppers
one 14-ounce can of chickpeas
4 tablespoons extra virgin olive oil
juice of 1 lemon
salt and black pepper
3 garlic cloves, crushed
3 sprigs of oregano, chopped, or 1 tablespoon dried
10 ounces fresh goat cheese

Place the peppers on a sheet of foil on an oven tray under a preheated broiler, 2 1/2 to 3 1/2 inches from the broiler. Turn them until their skins are blackened and blistered all over. Alternatively—and more easily—roast them in the hottest oven for about 30 minutes, or until they are soft and their skins blistered and blackened, turning them once after 15 minutes.

To loosen the skins further, put them in a strong plastic bag, twist it shut, and leave for 10 to 15 minutes. Another old way that has the same effect is to put them in a pan with a tight-fitting lid for the same length of time. When the peppers are cool enough to handle, peel them and remove and discard the stems and seeds. Now cut them lengthwise into thin ribbons.

Drain the chickpeas. Dress them with a mixture of 3 tablespoons of olive oil, the lemon juice, salt, and pepper, 2 crushed garlic cloves, and about one-third of the oregano; mix well, then gently mix with the peppers.

Mash the goat cheese with the remaining crushed garlic clove, the last tablespoon of olive oil, and the remaining oregano, and shape it into a mound on a serving plate. Arrange the peppers and chickpeas in a ring around it.

SWEET POTATO SALAD
Slada Batata Halwa

Sweet potatoes are very popular in Morocco. In this recipe, their sweet, delicate flavor marries well with the mixture of aromatics.

SERVES 4

1 large onion, chopped coarsely
5 tablespoons extra virgin olive oil
1 pound orange-fleshed sweet potatoes, peeled
1/2 teaspoon ground ginger
1/2 teaspoon ground cumin
1/2 teaspoon paprika
salt
6 or 7 green olives
peel of 1/2 preserved lemon, chopped (optional) (see page 7)
juice of 1/2 lemon
2 tablespoons chopped flat-leaf parsley

Fry the onion in 2 tablespoons of oil until golden. Cut the sweet potatoes into pieces (about 1-inch cubes), add to the pan, and barely cover with water. Add the ginger, cumin, paprika, a little salt, and two more tablespoons of oil. Cook until the potato pieces are tender, and the liquid has reduced to a sauce, turning the potatoes over once, and keeping watch so that they do not suddenly fall apart.

Serve at room temperature, mixed with the olives and preserved lemon peel, if using, and sprinkled with lemon juice, the remaining olive oil, and the chopped parsley.

SWEET POTATOES with ONIONS and TOMATOES
Batata Halwa Bil Tamatem

This lovely combination of vegetables makes a great accompaniment to roast or grilled meat or chicken.

SERVES 6

2 onions, chopped
2 tablespoons extra virgin olive oil
2 garlic cloves, crushed
3 tomatoes, peeled and chopped
1/2 teaspoon ground ginger
2 pounds sweet potatoes, peeled
2 to 3 tablespoons chopped cilantro
salt and black pepper

In a large pan, fry the onions in the oil until soft. Add the garlic, and when the aroma rises, add the tomatoes and ginger.

Cut the sweet potatoes into 1-inch cubes, and put them in the pan with the cilantro. Add about 1 1/2 cups water, or enough to half-cover the potatoes, and season with salt and pepper. Cook, uncovered, for 15 minutes, until the potatoes are tender and the liquid has almost evaporated, turning the potatoes over once.

Serve hot or cold.

POTATOES with CELERY and FENNEL
Batata Bil Bisbas

This herby vegetable dish is as good hot as it is cold. The potatoes can be peeled or not, as you wish.

SERVES 4

4 to 5 tablespoons extra virgin olive oil
14 ounces new potatoes, peeled or not
3 stalks celery
2 fennel bulbs
2 garlic cloves, crushed
salt and black pepper

4 sprigs mint, chopped coarsely

4 sprigs basil, chopped coarsely

juice of 1/2 to 1 lemon

In a large pan, put 2 tablespoons olive oil and the potatoes. If large, cut the potatoes in half or in quarters. Cut the celery into 3/4-inch pieces, and quarter the fennel bulbs and cut each quarter in half. Place the celery and fennel on top of the potatoes. Add the garlic, salt and pepper, and enough water to almost cover the green vegetables. Bring to a boil and simmer, covered, for about 15 minutes.

Stir in the chopped mint and basil and cook, uncovered to reduce the liquid, for about 10 minutes, or until the vegetables are very tender.

Serve sprinkled with lemon juice and the remaining olive oil.

VARIATION

Add the peel of 1/2 a preserved lemon (see page 7) and about 12 green olives at the same time as the herbs.

ARTICHOKE and FAVA BEAN SALAD with PRESERVED LEMON
Slada L'Korni Wal Ful

I use the frozen artichoke bottoms obtainable from Middle Eastern and Asian grocers, who also sometimes sell frozen skinned fava beans. Some supermarkets sell freshly shelled fava beans. You do not need to remove the skins if they are young. If you wish to use fresh artichokes, see page 8.

SERVES 4

2 tablespoons extra virgin olive oil

1 teaspoon ground cumin

1/2 teaspoon ground ginger (optional)

3 to 4 garlic cloves, crushed

7 ounces artichoke bottoms, defrosted, quartered or halved

7 ounces fresh fava beans (shelled weight)

salt

peel of 1/2 preserved lemon (see page 7)

To garnish: 8 green olives (optional)

In a pan, stir the oil with the cumin, ginger, if using, and garlic, then put in the artichoke bottoms and the fava beans. Cook over low heat for a moment, stirring, until the aroma of the garlic rises.

Almost cover with about 1 cup water and add salt. Simmer, covered, for the first 5 minutes, then uncovered for 10 to 15 minutes, until the beans are very tender and the sauce is reduced. Add the preserved lemon, cut into thin slices, toward the end.

Serve warm, garnished, if you like, with a few olives and a little more thinly sliced preserved lemon peel.

SPINACH SALAD with PRESERVED LEMON and OLIVES
Salkh Bil Hamid Wal Zaytoun

Preserved lemons bring one of the defining flavors to Moroccan salads and are often used together with olives. Cook the spinach in two batches if your saucepan is not large enough for all the bulky spinach leaves. Keep back 4 or 5 whole olives as a garnish.

SERVES 6 TO 8

2 pounds fresh spinach

3 garlic cloves, chopped

3 to 4 tablespoons extra virgin olive oil or argan oil (see page 31)

peel of 1/2 preserved lemon, chopped (see page 7)

1/2 cup violet olives, pitted and chopped

salt and black pepper

Wash the spinach and remove the stems only if they are thick and hard. Put the leaves in a large pan, cover with a lid, and set over low heat until the leaves crumple into a soft mass. They will steam in the water that clings to them in 1 to 2 minutes. Drain well.

Heat the garlic in 1 tablespoon of oil in a large pan until the aroma rises. Add the chopped preserved lemon peel, the chopped olives, and the cooked spinach. Season with salt and pepper, mix well, and cook over high heat for a moment or two.

Stir in the remaining oil, garnish with the reserved olives, and serve cold.

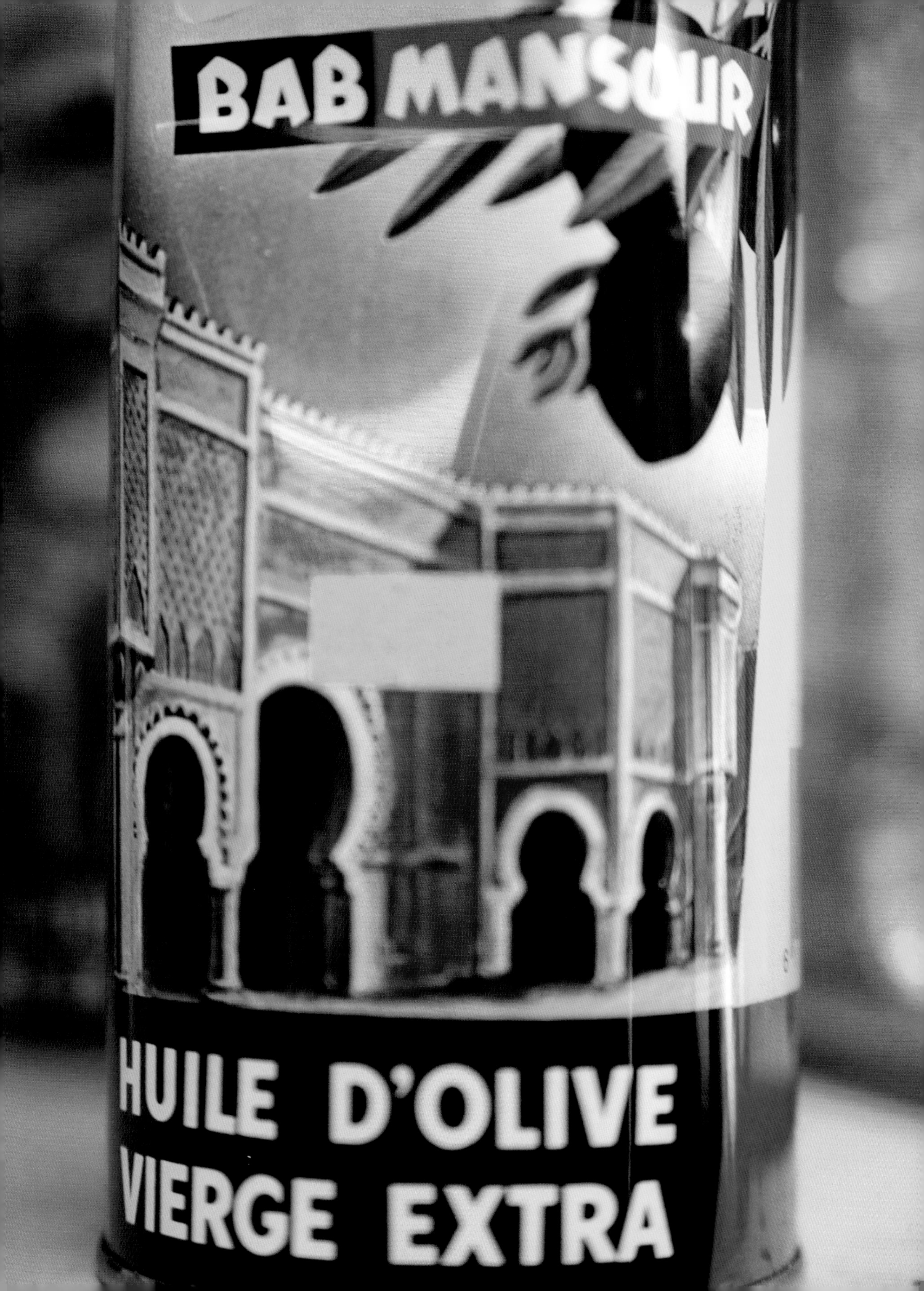
BAB MANSOUR
HUILE D'OLIVE
VIERGE EXTRA

TOMATOES STUFFED *with* ROAST PEPPERS, TUNA, CAPERS, *and* OLIVES
Tamatem Ma'Amrine

The tomatoes can be served hot or cold. I prefer them cold. For vegetarians, they make an elegant main dish accompanied by a potato or carrot salad. Use large or beefsteak tomatoes.

SERVES 6

4 red bell peppers
salt
3 tablespoons extra virgin olive oil
one 7-ounce can of tuna, flaked
2 tablespoons capers
4 tablespoons chopped black olives
peel of 1/2 preserved lemon, chopped (optional) (see page 7)
2 tablespoons chopped flat-leaf parsley
6 large tomatoes

Place the peppers on a sheet of foil on an oven tray under a preheated broiler, 2 1/2 to 3 1/2 inches from the broiler. Turn them until their skins are black and blistered all over. Alternatively—and more easily—roast them in the hottest oven for about 30 minutes, or until they are soft and their skins blistered and blackened, turning them once after 15 minutes.

To loosen the skins further, put them in a strong plastic bag, twist it shut, and leave for 10 to 15 minutes. Another old way that has the same effect is to put them in a pan with a tight-fitting lid for the same length of time. When the peppers are cool enough to handle, peel them and remove and discard the stems and seeds. Now cut the peppers into strips about 3/4 inch wide. Mix with the rest of the ingredients except the tomatoes.

Cut a small circle around the stalk of each tomato and cut out a cap. Remove the center and seeds with a pointed teaspoon. Fill the cavities with the roast pepper mixture and replace the caps. Arrange in a shallow baking dish and bake in a preheated oven at 350°F for 20 to 30 minutes, or until the tomatoes are a little soft. Keep a watch, however, that they do not fall apart.

CHICKPEAS with TURMERIC
Hummas

In Morocco, this is considered "poor food." It is eaten hot with bread to soak up the juices. You could make it with canned chickpeas, in which case it would take only a few minutes to cook, but for a large quantity like this, it is worth using dried chickpeas, as their taste and texture is better and they will have time to absorb the flavors. You need to soak them in water for a few hours or overnight.

SERVES 6

3 tablespoons extra virgin olive oil

1 large onion, chopped

4 garlic cloves, crushed

1/2 teaspoon ground turmeric

1 1/2 cups dried chickpeas, soaked in plenty of water overnight

salt and black pepper

3 tablespoons chopped cilantro

3 tablespoons chopped flat-leaf parsley

Heat the oil in a large pan and fry the onion until lightly colored. Add the garlic and stir for a moment or two. Stir in the turmeric, then add the drained chickpeas.

Cover with about 2 1/4 cups water and simmer for 1 1/2 hours, or until the chickpeas are very tender, adding salt and pepper when they have softened, and extra water if it becomes too dry. The liquid should be reduced to a thick sauce at the end of the cooking.

Stir in the chopped cilantro and parsley and cook for 5 minutes more.

VARIATIONS

◆ A grander version served as a first course is made with 1/2 teaspoon saffron threads or powder instead of the turmeric.

◇ Add the juice of 1 lemon at the end.

◆ Dried cannellini beans, soaked overnight, or the canned variety, drained, can be used in the same way as chickpeas.

PEAS and FAVA BEANS with MINT and GARLIC
Jekban Wal Ful Bil Na'na

I am lucky enough to find freshly shelled fava beans and peas at my local supermarket. If you grow your own, or have a source of really young vegetables, use them, but it is better to use frozen petits pois and fava beans rather than old fresh ones.

SERVES 4

2 garlic cloves, finely chopped

3 tablespoons extra virgin olive oil

7 ounces young fava beans (shelled weight)

salt

7 ounces young peas (shelled weight)

1 teaspoon sugar

black pepper

handful of chopped mint

juice of 1/2 lemon

Heat the garlic in 1 tablespoon oil for a few seconds only, stirring. Before it begins to color, add the fava beans and a little salt, and barely cover with water. Simmer, covered, for 10 minutes, until the beans are tender.

Add the peas, sugar, pepper, a little more salt, the mint, and lemon juice and simmer, covered, until the peas are tender. If they are very young, this takes only a minute. (If you are using older peas, put them in at the same time as the beans.) They do not need to be covered with water as they cook in the steam, but do not let the vegetables dry out. Add a little water, if necessary, and reduce excess liquid by cooking uncovered.

Stir in the remaining olive oil and serve hot or cold.

FISH CAKES
Kefta Bil Hout

These Moroccan fish cakes can be served as a first course with green salad leaves. They also make good finger food for a party. Use cod, haddock, or another firm white fish.

MAKES 15 FISH CAKES

1 pound firm, white fish fillets, skinned
1 1/2 teaspoons ground cumin
good pinch of chili pepper
1/2 to 1 teaspoon salt
3 garlic cloves, crushed
1 egg, beaten lightly
peel of 1/2 to 1 preserved lemon, finely chopped (see page 7) (optional)
handful of chopped flat-leafed parsley or cilantro, or a mix of both
about 5 tablespoons all-purpose flour
olive oil for deep-frying
To garnish: 1 lemon, cut into wedges

Cut the fish fillets into pieces and put them in the food processor with the rest of the ingredients except the flour and oil. Process for about 5 seconds only, until it is finely chopped and the ingredients are well mixed. It is important not to let it turn into a paste.

Sprinkle the flour onto a plate. Wet your hands, take a lump of the fish mixture the size of a small egg, roll it into a ball, and flatten it. Do the same with the rest of the mixture, then turn the fish cakes in the flour to cover them all over.

Shallow-fry the cakes in hot oil until browned, turning them over once. Lift them out and drain on paper towels. Serve hot or cold, accompanied by lemon wedges.

VARIATION

You can use the same fish mixture as above to make balls rather than cakes. These are very good poached in a tomato sauce. For the sauce, fry 4 to 5 finely chopped garlic cloves in 2 tablespoons olive oil for a moment or two, add 2 pounds peeled and chopped tomatoes, 1 to 2 teaspoons sugar, salt, a pinch of chili pepper, and cook for 10 minutes. Roll the fish mixture into balls, drop them into the sauce, and simmer for 5 minutes.

LITTLE PIES *with* FRESH GOAT CHEESE *and* OLIVES
Briwat Bil Jban

Use a soft, fresh-tasting, mild goat cheese for these little pies. Use the fillo in sheets that measure 12 inches × 7 inches, which you can find fresh in some supermarkets, or use the large sheets measuring 19 inches × 12 inches and cut them in half. See the note on fillo on page 9.

You can freeze these pies and you can put them straight from the freezer into the oven without thawing, but they will need a little more cooking time. They make elegant and tasty party fare.

MAKES 20
TRIANGLES

10 ounces fresh goat cheese
1 egg, beaten lightly
14 black olives, pitted and chopped
10 large or 20 small sheets of fillo (see above)
3/4 stick (6 tablespoons) butter, melted

First, prepare the filling by mixing the goat cheese with the beaten egg and olives.

Take out the sheets of fillo from their wrapper only when you are ready to use them since they dry out quickly, and cover them with plastic wrap when you are not using them.

Keeping the first sheet of fillo on the pile, brush it lightly with melted butter. Fold it lengthwise to produce a strip about 3 1/4 inches wide. Brush the top of the strip lightly with melted butter. Take a heaping teaspoon of filling. Place it at one end of the strip, about 1 1/4 inches from the edge, and fold the end over the filling. Now pick up a corner and fold diagonally, making a triangle. Continue to fold, trapping the filling, until the whole strip has been folded into a triangular parcel. Make sure that you close any holes as you fold so that the filling does not ooze out.

Place the little parcels close to each other on a greased baking sheet. Brush the tops with melted butter, and bake in a preheated oven at 350°F for 30 minutes, or until crisp and golden.

Serve them hot or warm. You can make them in advance and warm them up.

MEAT CIGARS
Briwat Bil Kefta

In Morocco, these briwat bil kefta are made with warka (see page 29) and deep-fried, but it is not only much easier to use fillo and to bake them, but the result is very good. See the note on fillo on page 9. I used sheets measuring about 6 inches × 12 inches. It is very good finger food to serve at a party.

MAKES ABOUT
60 CIGARS

1/4 cup vegetable oil

1 medium onion, chopped finely

1 1/2 pounds ground beef or lamb

2 teaspoons ground cinnamon

1/2 teaspoon ground ginger

salt

black pepper or good pinch of ground chili pepper

3 tablespoons chopped flat-leaf parsley

3 tablespoons chopped cilantro

5 eggs, lightly beaten

1 pound large fillo sheets

2/3 cup melted butter or vegetable oil

First prepare the filling. Heat the oil in a large skillet, and sauté the onion in the oil until softened. Add the meat, spices, salt, and pepper or chili pepper, and cook, crushing the meat with a fork and turning it over, for 5 to 10 minutes, until it changes color. Then stir in the chopped parsley, cilantro, and the beaten eggs, and cook gently for a moment or two, stirring all the time, until the eggs set to a creamy consistency. Let the filling cool. Taste and add more spices and pepper, if you like.

With large scissors, cut all the sheets of fillo together, without separating them, into 3 strips of about 6 inches × 12 inches, and put the three piles together in one pile so that they do not dry out. Brush the top sheet very lightly with melted butter or oil.

Put a tablespoon of filling in a line along one of the short ends, about 3/4 inch from the three edges. Roll up like a cigar, folding in the long sides at the halfway point so that the filling does not fall out, then continue to roll, letting the sides unfold so that the cigars appear open.

Place the rolls side by side on a greased baking tray, brush the tops with melted butter, and bake in a preheated oven at 350°F for 30 minutes, or until golden.

Serve them hot. You can make them in advance and warm them up.

VARIATIONS

◇ Before serving, dust the rolls first with confectioners' sugar and then with cinnamon.

◆ These rolls are *very* nice deep-fried, so if you want to fry a few for an instant snack, do so in medium-hot vegetable oil, turning them over once, until browned, and drain on paper towels.

CHICKEN *and* ONION CIGARS
Briwat Bil Djaj

The rolls are delicious if made with the chicken and onion filling on page 66. Prepare in the same way as the meat cigars above and bake for 30 minutes in an oven preheated to 350°F. Dust with confectioners' sugar and then with cinnamon.

CHICKEN and ONION PIE
Bstilla Bil Djaj

This is a "poor man's" version of the famous pigeon pie called bstilla (or pastilla), which is such a favorite at weddings and festive occasions, and which Moroccans say was brought back by the Moors from Andalusia. I have to admit that this pie, which comes from Fez, is very much more to my taste than the grander version. Don't be put off by what might seem like a difficult recipe; it is truly scrumptious and you must try it.

In Morocco, the pie is made with trid, an oily puff pastry made by pulling an elastic dough until it is paper-thin and layering it. Since trid is not available in this country, use fillo, which is a perfect substitute. It comes in various commercial sizes. It is best to use the large-size sheets, which are available frozen in packages from Middle Eastern and other specialty stores. The sheets I use for this pie (from a popular brand) measure about 19 inches × 12 inches. If you can find only smaller sheets, you can have more of them overlapping. Wrap any sheets that are left over in plastic wrap and keep in the refrigerator for future use.

SERVES 4 TO 6
2 large onions, sliced (about 1 pound)
3 tablespoons sunflower oil
1/3 cup blanched almonds
1/2 teaspoon ground ginger
1 1/2 teaspoons ground cinnamon
10 ounces boneless, skinless chicken thighs
salt and black pepper
1/2 cup chopped cilantro
7 large sheets of fillo (about 7 ounces)
about 3/4 stick (6 tablespoons) butter, melted
1 egg yolk
To decorate: confectioners' sugar and cinnamon

Put the onion in a wide saucepan with 2 1/2 tablespoons oil and cook, over a low heat, with the lid on, stirring occasionally, for up to 30 minutes, until it is very soft and only just beginning to color.

Fry the almonds in the remaining drop of oil, stirring and turning them over, until lightly golden. Drain on paper towels and chop them coarsely.

When the onions are cooked, stir in the ginger and cinnamon, then put in the chicken, cut in bite-size pieces, and season with salt and pepper. Cook, uncovered, stirring occasionally, for about 15 to 20 minutes, until the onions are pale gold. If by this time there is still some liquid left (which would make the pastry soggy), remove

the chicken pieces from the pan and continue to cook the onion until the liquid has evaporated and you can see the oil sizzling. Now return the chicken to the pan, add the cilantro, and mix very well.

Open out the sheets of fillo when you are ready to use them and leave them in a pile so they don't dry out. Fit the first sheet in a greased round baking pan or dish about 9 1/2 inches in diameter and brush it entirely with melted butter, pressing the fillo into the corners with the brush and letting the longer edges hang over the sides. Repeat with 4 sheets, brushing each with melted butter, including the ends that overhang the sides at different points (again, to prevent them from drying out).

Spread the chicken and onion mixture evenly in the hollow, then bring the overlapping fillo up over the filling to cover it. Sprinkle all over with the chopped almonds.

Lay another sheet of fillo over the top, brush it with melted butter, then lay the final sheet on top of that. Do not brush the last sheet with melted butter. Cut the longer overhanging ends of the sheets in a curve, leaving a wide margin round the pan. Now tuck these edges into the sides of the pan around the pie.

Brush the top with egg yolk mixed with a drop of water. Bake the pie in an oven preheated to 350°F, for 30 to 40 minutes, until it is puffed up, crisp, and golden. Now put the pie on the bottom surface of the oven for about 15 minutes, which will help to brown the bottom. Turn out the pie or serve it in the baking dish.

Serve the pie hot, dusting the top with confectioners' sugar and then making a geometric pattern on the white confectioners' sugar with the golden-brown cinnamon.

VARIATION

For a version that comes from Tetouan, add the juice of 1/2 lemon and the chopped peel of 1/2 preserved lemon (see page 7) to the filling. In this case, do not sprinkle the top of the pie with sugar or cinnamon.

POTATO and TOMATO CAKE
Almokhtalitat Bil Tamatem Wal Batata

This thick omelette can be made in advance. Served hot or cold, and cut into big or small wedges, it makes a substantial first course or vegetarian main dish.

SERVES 4 TO 6

1 pound baking potatoes, peeled

1 large onion, chopped

2 tablespoons extra virgin olive oil

2 garlic cloves, chopped finely

10 ounces tomatoes, peeled and chopped

salt and black pepper

1 teaspoon sugar

1/2 chili pepper, finely chopped (optional)

4 eggs

3 to 4 tablespoons chopped flat-leaf parsley

1 tablespoon butter

Boil the potatoes in salted water until tender, then drain and mash them. In a wide skillet, fry the onion in the oil until golden, stirring occasionally. Stir in the garlic and fry briefly without letting it color. Add the tomatoes, season with salt, pepper, and sugar, add the chili pepper, if using, and cook the mixture over a high heat, stirring every so often, until it is reduced to a thick, jammy sauce.

Beat the eggs lightly, then beat them into the mashed potatoes. Add this to the tomato sauce and mix vigorously. Stir in the chopped parsley and adjust the seasoning.

Heat the butter in a large skillet, preferably nonstick. When it sizzles, pour in the omelette mixture. Cook over low heat until the bottom sets (about 10 minutes), then cook the top under a preheated broiler until it is firm and lightly browned.

Serve hot or cold, turned out, and cut into wedges.

CHICKPEA and LENTIL SOUP
Harira

Harira is the generic term for a soup full of pulses—chickpeas, lentils, or beans—with little meat, few vegetables, and plenty of herbs and spices. Every day during the holy month of Ramadan, when Muslims fast between sunrise and sunset, the smell of this soup permeates the streets as every household prepares its own version to be eaten when the sound of the cannon signals the breaking of the fast.

While ingredients and spices vary, a particular feature is the way it is given what is described in Morocco as a "velvety" touch by stirring in a sourdough batter or simply flour mixed with water. In the cities in Morocco, it serves as a one-dish evening meal, and in rural areas it is also eaten as breakfast before peasants go out to work in the fields. During Ramadan, it is served with lemon quarters and accompanied by dates and honeyed pastries.

The soup can be made a long time in advance, but if you are adding the tiny bird's-tongue pasta—douida in Morocco (you find it in Middle Eastern stores), orzo in Italian stores (or you can use broken vermicelli)—these should be added only about 10 to 15 minutes before you are ready to serve, otherwise they will get bloated and mushy. I have given measurements for a large quantity because it is a rich, substantial soup that you might like to serve as a one-dish meal at a party. The best cuts of meat to use are shoulder or neck fillet.

SERVES 10

2 marrowbones, washed (optional)
1 pound lamb or beef
2 large onions, chopped coarsely
1 cup chickpeas, soaked overnight
3/4 cup large brown lentils, rinsed
1 pound ripe tomatoes, peeled and chopped
4 celery stalks, diced
1 tablespoon tomato paste
1 teaspoon black pepper
1 teaspoon ground ginger
2 sticks cinnamon
1/2 teaspoon saffron threads or powder or 1 teaspoon turmeric
salt
5 tablespoons all-purpose flour
5 ounces orzo (bird's-tongue) pasta or broken vermicelli (optional)
juice of 1 lemon
3/4 cup chopped cilantro
1/3 cup chopped flat-leaf parsley
To serve: 3 lemons, cut into quarters; dates (optional)

If using marrowbones, blanch them in boiling water for a few minutes, then throw out the water. Put the bones in a large pan with the meat, cut into 1/2-inch pieces, the onions, and the drained chickpeas. Cover with about 13 cups water and bring to the boil. Remove the scum and simmer, covered, for 1 hour.

Remove the bones (if using), scoop out the soft marrow with a knife, and drop it back into the soup.

Add the lentils, tomatoes, celery (include some leaves), tomato paste, pepper, ginger, cinnamon, and saffron or turmeric. Simmer 15 minutes more, adding more water, if necessary, as the level drops, and salt when the lentils begin to soften.

In the meantime, put the flour in a small pan and gradually add 2 1/4 cups cold water, a little at a time, beating vigorously with a wooden spoon to blend well and to avoid lumps. Put over a medium heat and stir constantly until the mixture thickens, then simmer for 10 minutes. Pour this batter into the soup, stirring vigorously, and cook for a few minutes, until the soup acquires a light, creamy texture.

If you are using the tiny pasta or vermicelli (crush the vermicelli with your hand into small pieces), add this to the soup 10 minutes or so from the end, adding the lemon juice, chopped cilantro, and parsley at the same time.

Serve with lemon wedges and, if you like, dates.

VARIATION

Instead of meat, you can use 1 pound boneless, skinless chicken, preferably thighs, and crumble in 3 chicken bouillon cubes.

CREAM *of* DRIED
FAVA BEAN SOUP
Bessara

Bessara is the name of the soup as well as a creamy paste, made in the same way but with less water (see Variation). You can buy the split and skinless dried fava beans in Asian and Middle Eastern stores. They look creamy white without their dried brown skins.

SERVES 4

1 1/4 cups split skinless dried fava beans, soaked overnight
3 whole garlic cloves
2 chicken bouillon cubes
1 teaspoon ground cumin
1 teaspoon paprika
good pinch of ground chili pepper
salt
To serve: extra virgin olive oil; 2 lemons, cut into quarters

Rinse and drain the soaked beans and put them in a pan with the garlic and 6 cups water. Simmer, covered, for about 1 hour. Crumble in the bouillon cubes and simmer another 30 minutes, or until the beans fall apart.

Still in the pot, mash the beans with a potato masher and add the cumin, paprika, and chili pepper and, if necessary, a little salt, bearing in mind the saltiness of the bouillon cubes. Stir thoroughly and cook a few minutes more. Add a little water if you would like to thin the soup. For a thicker soup, cook, uncovered, for a while longer.

When serving, pass around the olive oil for people to dribble onto their soup and the lemon quarters for them to squeeze over.

VARIATION

Make a fava bean purée, using half the quantity of water. Serve it with little bowls of ground cumin, paprika, ground chili pepper, lemon juice, and extra virgin olive oil for people to sprinkle on their purée as they wish. Serve it as a dip with bread.

COUSCOUS

ZAKIA

FIN - FINE - FIJN

هدا الكسكسي مصنوع هنا سب
القمح القمح كما في العادة
القديمة

PRODUCT OF FRANCE

INGREDIENTS : Semoule de blé dur
Durum wheat semolina

INGREDIENTEN : Harde tarwe griesmeel

Main Courses

The most common and most typical of the Moroccan main dishes, apart from couscous, is a braise or stew of chicken or meat called a *tagine*, which takes its name from the clay pot in which it is cooked. In Morocco, these *tagines* are served with bread, never with couscous. In the West, however, with the increasing popularity of Moroccan dishes, the grain is sometimes served as an accompaniment. In North African restaurants in Paris, it is not uncommon to accompany *tagines* with a separate dish of the fine ground couscous called *seffa* (see page 28), which comes decorated with lines of cinnamon and a few almonds or raisins. Many *tagines* differ only by one or two main ingredients, such as the vegetable or the fruit, and often chicken and meat are interchangeable in the same recipe. Do try the different versions, because each is special and unique.

Tagines that marry meat or chicken with fruit, and are delicately flavored with saffron, ginger, and cinnamon and sometimes also honey, are celebratory dishes cooked on festive and special occasions. Many of these sweet *tagines* originate in Fez, the oldest imperial city in Morocco, which was founded by Idriss I, who came from Baghdad with his Arab entourage in the eighth century. Fez kept its ties with Baghdad over many centuries and, in later times, the city became the refuge of Jews and Muslims chased from Andalusia. Its cooking is a fusion of culinary memories of the court of Harun al Rashid and those of Muslim Spain. Fez is now a city of artisans—dyers, tanners, weavers, potters, silversmiths—crowded in a labyrinth of narrow streets in the *medina*. Most of the grand old families have left for Rabat and Casablanca, but the city is still the intellectual, artistic, and religious capital of Morocco, and it boasts the most refined and exquisite cuisine.

The long, slow cooking in a clay *tagine* produces meat so tender that you can pull it off the bone with your fingers. A good alternative to a *tagine* is a lidded, heavy-bottomed casserole or stainless steel pan. The meat most commonly used for *tagines* is boned shoulder of lamb. You may use other cuts of lamb such as the neck fillet, shank, or the leg. Veal or beef, which now sometimes replace lamb in Morocco, may also be used. The liquid in a *tagine* must be almost completely reduced at the end, producing a rich, thick, and unctuous sauce. It is best to start with only a little water and to add more, if necessary, as you go along. If you have too much liquid at the end, you should lift out the meat and reduce the sauce over high heat.

ROAST COD with POTATOES and TOMATOES
Hout Bi Batata Wa Tamatem

The marinade and sauce called chermoula that gives the distinctive flavor to this dish is used in most Moroccan fish dishes, whether fried, steamed, or cooked in a tagine. Every town, every family, has its own special combination of ingredients. Bream, haddock, and turbot can also be used.

SERVES 6

6 cod fillets (each weighing 7 to 8 ounces), skin left on
salt

FOR THE CHERMOULA MARINADE AND SAUCE
2/3 cup chopped coriander
4 garlic cloves, crushed
1 teaspoon ground cumin
1 teaspoon ground paprika
1/2 teaspoon ground chili pepper
6 tablespoons extra virgin olive oil
juice of 1 lemon or 3 tablespoons white wine vinegar

2 pounds new potatoes
1 pound tomatoes, peeled
extra virgin olive oil

Slash the skin of the fish in a few places across the thickest part. This ensures that the fish does not curl, and cooks evenly. Sprinkle with salt.

Mix all the *chermoula* ingredients in a dish, and marinate the fish in half the quantity for about 30 minutes.

Peel the potatoes, if you wish, and cut them into slices about 1/4 inch thick, and the tomatoes into slices 1/3 inch thick. Brush the bottom of a baking dish with olive oil, put in the potatoes and tomatoes, and drizzle a little oil on top. Sprinkle with salt, then turn the vegetables so they are well seasoned and lightly coated all over with oil. Put the dish in a very hot oven preheated to 475°F for 50 minutes, or until the potatoes are tender. During the cooking, turn them over once so that the top ones bathe in the juice released by the tomatoes.

Take the potatoes and tomatoes out of the oven, place the fish fillets on top, skin side up, and return the dish to the oven. Bake for 10 to 12 minutes, or until the fish is cooked through; it is cooked when the flesh flakes when you cut into the thickest part.

Just before serving, pour the remaining *chermoula* over the fish, letting it dribble onto the vegetables.

DEEP-FRIED BREAM *with* CHERMOULA SAUCE
Hout Maqli Bil Chermoula

This is good hot or cold and can be made well in advance. The best fish to use is bream, cod, haddock, or turbot.

SERVES 4

4 fillets bream (each weighing 7 to 8 ounces), skin left on
1 teaspoon ground cumin
salt
juice of 1 lemon
1/3 cup chopped coriander
1 to 4 garlic cloves, crushed
1/2 chili pepper, seeded and finely chopped (optional)
4 tablespoons extra virgin olive oil
flour
olive oil for frying

Rub the fish with a mixture of cumin and salt.

Prepare a sauce by mixing the lemon juice with the chopped coriander, crushed garlic (I like the larger amount but you may prefer to use only one clove), the chili pepper, if using, a little salt, and the oil.

Dredge the fish fillets in flour, turning to cover them lightly all over. Deep-fry very briefly in sizzling oil until golden, turning the pieces over once. Test the fish by cutting into one piece with a pointed knife. When the flesh begins to flake, lift out and drain on paper towels.

Serve hot with the sauce poured over. If serving cold, turn the fish in the sauce and leave to marinate, covered, in the refrigerator for an hour or longer.

TUNA *with* RED BELL PEPPER SAUCE
Hout Bil Felfla

Tuna steaks are best seared quickly, leaving the flesh still pink and almost raw inside. The sauce is also good with other grilled or pan-fried fish.

SERVES 4

FOR THE SAUCE

4 fleshy red bell peppers
2 garlic cloves, unpeeled
3 tablespoons red or white wine vinegar
3 tablespoons extra virgin olive oil

3 tablespoons olive oil
4 thick tuna steaks
salt
1 to 2 tablespoons chopped flat-leaf parsley

Prepare the sauce first. Place the peppers and garlic on a sheet of foil on an oven tray and place under a preheated broiler, 2 1/2 to 6 1/2 inches from the broiler. Turn the peppers until their skins are black and blistered all over. Remove the garlic when it feels soft. Alternatively—and more easily—roast both the peppers and garlic in the hottest oven for about 30 minutes (take out the garlic much sooner, when it feels soft), or until the peppers are soft and their skins blistered and blackened, turning them once after 15 minutes.

To loosen their skins further, put the peppers in a strong plastic bag, twist it shut, and leave for 10 to 15 minutes. Another old way that has the same effect is to put them in a pan with a tight-fitting lid for the same length of time. When the peppers are cool enough to handle, peel them and remove and discard the stems and seeds. Peel the roasted garlic cloves.

Blend the roasted peppers and garlic in a food processor with the rest of the sauce ingredients.

Heat the oil in a large, preferably nonstick, skillet. Put in the tuna steaks and cook over high heat for less than 1 minute on each side, sprinkling lightly with salt. The time depends on the thickness of the piece. Cut into a steak with a pointed knife to test it; it should be soft and still pink inside.

Serve the tuna steaks on top of the sauce, sprinkled with the chopped parsley.

ROAST SEA BASS with HERBS and ONION CONFIT
Hout Bil Bassal M'Zgueldi

Other large white fish such as sea bream and turbot can be cooked in this way. When you buy the fish, ask the fishmonger to scale and clean the fish but to keep the head on.

SERVES 4

1 pound onions, sliced
4 tablespoons extra virgin olive oil
pinch of saffron threads
1 tablespoon clear honey
salt and plenty of black pepper
1 large sea bass (about 3 to 4 1/2 pounds)
2 to 3 tablespoons chopped flat-leaf parsley
2 to 3 tablespoons chopped coriander
4 garlic cloves, crushed
juice of 1 lemon
To serve: 1 lemon, cut into quarters

In a covered pan, cook the onions in 2 tablespoons oil over a very low heat, for about 30 minutes, stirring occasionally, until they are very soft and lightly colored. Stir in the saffron and honey, and season with salt and pepper. Cook, uncovered, for another 10 minutes, or until most of the liquid has evaporated, then spread over the bottom of an overproof dish.

Slash the fish in a few places across the thickest part to ensure that it cooks evenly. Rub the fish with salt and the remaining olive oil, then stuff with a mixture of the parsley, coriander, garlic, lemon juice, and a little salt and pepper.

Place the stuffed fish on the bed of onions and roast in an oven preheated to 375°F for about 25 minutes, or until the flesh flakes away from the bone when you cut into the thickest part with the point of a knife. Serve with the lemon quarters.

COD STEAKS *in* TOMATO SAUCE *with* GINGER *and* BLACK OLIVES
Hout Bil Tamatem Wal Zaytoun

I like to make this dish with cod, but other fish such as bream, turbot, monkfish, and grouper may also be used.

SERVES 4

4 thick cod steaks (each weighing 1/2 pound) or fillets (each weighing 7 to 8 ounces)

salt

4 tablespoons extra virgin olive oil

5 to 6 garlic cloves, chopped

1 small chili pepper, seeded and finely chopped (optional)

1 1/2 to 2 pounds ripe tomatoes, peeled and chopped

2 teaspoons sugar

1/2 teaspoon ground ginger

peel of 1 preserved lemon, chopped (see page 7)

12 or more black olives, pitted

Sprinkle the fish lightly with salt.

In a large skillet, heat the oil with the garlic and chili, if using, for moments only, stirring, until the aroma rises. Add the tomatoes, a little salt, sugar, and ginger and simmer for 20 minutes.

Add the lemon peel and olives and put in the fish. Simmer for about 3 to 8 minutes (depending on the type of fish and thickness of the steak or fillet), or until the flesh begins to flake when you cut into it with a pointed knife. Turn the fish over once during the cooking.

Serve hot with the sauce poured over.

SKATE with PRESERVED LEMON and GREEN OLIVES
Hout Bil Laymoun M'Rakade Wal Zaytoun

All kinds of white fish fillets can be cooked in this way, but I am particularly fond of skate wings with these flavors. The flesh is fine and delicate and easily parts from the layer of soft cartilaginous ribs. Small skate wings can be sautéed but the thicker, more prized wings of the larger fish must be poached (see Variations).

SERVES 4

4 tablespoons extra virgin olive oil
4 small skate wings, skinned (about 2 pounds)
salt
juice of 1 lemon
peel of 1 preserved lemon, chopped (see page 7)
8 to 12 large green olives, pitted and chopped
2 tablespoons chopped flat-leaf parsley or coriander
To serve: 1 lemon, cut into quarters

Heat the oil in a nonstick skillet and put in the skate wings. Sprinkle lightly with salt and cook over a low heat for 4 minutes, then turn over, add the lemon juice, and cook for another 4 minutes, or until the flesh begins to come away from the long soft bones. The time depends on the thickness of the wings.

Add the preserved lemon peel, green olives, and chopped parsley or coriander and let them heat through in the oil and juices. Serve with the lemon wedges.

VARIATIONS

◆ For a spicy version using small wings, stir into the oil, just before you put in the fish, 2 crushed garlic cloves, a pinch of ground ginger, a pinch of ground cumin, and a pinch of ground chili pepper.

◈ Instead of olives, you can add 1 to 2 tablespoons capers.

◆ If using larger wings, buy 4 thick middle strips weighing about 1/2 pound each (they are sold skinned) rather than side wedge pieces. Poach them in salted water, just below simmering point, for 15 to 20 minutes, then drain thoroughly. Heat the oil and lemon juice with the preserved lemon peel, olives, and herbs and pour over the fish.

PRAWNS *in* SPICY TOMATO SAUCE
Kimroun Bil Tamatem

These prawns are deliciously rich in flavor and are good hot or cold. Serve them with mashed potatoes (see page 168) or with a little couscous (page 112) moistened with olive oil.

Use raw king prawns: they are gray and turn pink when they are cooked. Some supermarkets sell them fresh and ready-peeled. You can also buy them frozen with their heads off from some fishmongers. The weight of these packs is inclusive of a thick ice glaze, which means that you need to double the weight—that is, for 1 pound of peeled prawns (about 25), you need a 2-pound package.

SERVES 6

1 pound raw king prawns, peeled, or a 2-pound package frozen prawns
1 medium onion, chopped
2 tablespoons extra virgin olive oil
3 garlic cloves, chopped finely
14 ounces tomatoes, peeled and chopped
1/2 teaspoon ground ginger
pinch of saffron threads (optional)
pinch of chili pepper
salt
1 to 2 tablespoons chopped flat-leaf parsley
1 to 2 tablespoons chopped coriander

If using frozen prawns, defrost them thoroughly. Pull the legs off the prawns, then peel off the shells and pull off the tails (they are usually sold headless). If you see a dark vein along the back, make a fine slit with a pointed knife and pull it out.

In a large skillet, fry the onion in the oil, stirring, until it begins to color. Add the garlic and cook until the aroma rises. Then add the tomatoes, ginger, saffron, if using, chili pepper, and some salt and cook for about 20 minutes, until the sauce is reduced.

Now put in the prawns and cook them for 3 to 5 minutes, until they turn pink, turning them over once. Stir in the chopped parsley and coriander at the end.

CHICKEN with CARAMELIZED BABY ONIONS and HONEY
Djaj Bil Assal

This is one of the classics of Moroccan cooking and this version, with shallots or baby onions, is sensational. The art is to reduce the sauce at the end until it is rich and caramelized. It is important to taste it in order to get the right balance between sweet and savory.

SERVES 4

1 pound shallots or baby onions

1 onion, chopped

4 tablespoons sunflower oil

good pinch of saffron threads

1 teaspoon ground ginger

1 teaspoon ground cinnamon

1 chicken, cut up in 6 or 8 pieces

salt and black pepper

1 to 1 1/2 tablespoons clear honey

To garnish: 1/2 cup blanched almonds or a handful of
sesame seeds (optional)

To peel the shallots or baby onions, blanch them in boiling water for 5 minutes, drain, and when cool enough to handle, peel off the skins and trim the root ends.

Sauté the chopped onion until softened in the oil over a medium heat in a pan or casserole large enough to hold the chicken pieces in one layer. Stir in the saffron, ginger, and cinnamon, then put in the chicken pieces. Season with salt and pepper, and turn to brown them lightly all over.

Add about 1 cup water and cook, covered, over a low heat, turning the pieces over, for 15 minutes, or until the chicken breasts are done. Lift out the breasts and put them to one side. Add the shallots or baby onions and continue to cook, covered, for about 25 minutes, or until the remaining chicken pieces are very tender. During the cooking, turn the chicken pieces and stir the onions occasionally; add a little water, if necessary.

Lift out the chicken pieces and set to one side. Stir the honey into the pan. Check the seasoning. You need quite a bit of pepper to mitigate the sweetness. Cook, uncovered, until all the water has evaporated, and the onions are brown, caramelized, and so soft that you could crush them, as they say in Morocco, "with your tongue."

Return the chicken pieces to the pan, spoon the onions on top of them, and heat through. A few minutes should be enough. Serve, if you wish, sprinkled either with blanched almonds fried in a drop of oil until they are lightly golden, or with toasted sesame seeds.

CHICKEN with CARAMELIZED BABY ONIONS and PEARS
Djaj Bil Bouawid

This is one of my favorites. You will be surprised by just how good it is. Follow the recipe on the preceding page for Chicken with Caramelized Baby Onions and Honey. Choose firm pears; if the fruit is too soft, they tend to collapse during the cooking. Comice and Bosc are good varieties.

Cook the chicken as on the preceding page. Peel, quarter, and core 4 small or 2 large pears. Over medium heat, sauté the pieces in a large skillet in about 1/3 to 1/2 stick (3 to 4 tablespoons) unsalted butter and 1 tablespoon sunflower oil until they are soft and lightly colored.

When serving, present them on top of the chicken pieces or beside them.

CHICKEN with CARAMELIZED BABY ONIONS and QUINCES
Djaj Bil Sfargal

I love quinces and love this dish. Quinces are now available for a good part of the year since they are imported from several countries where their seasons vary. Follow the recipe for Chicken with Caramelized Baby Onions and Honey (page 85).

Start with the quinces, as they take a long time to cook. Wash and scrub 2 quinces, then boil them whole for about 1 hour, or until they feel soft. The time varies greatly depending on their size and degree of ripeness, so watch them and don't let them fall apart. Drain them, and when the chicken is nearly ready, cut them into quarters and cut away the cores, but do not peel them. Then cut each quarter in half so you end up with fat slices.

Fry the slices in shallow sunflower or vegetable oil until they are brown on the cut sides. This gives them a delicious caramelized taste. Lift them out and drain on paper towels. Serve the chicken surrounded by the quince slices.

CHICKEN *with* CHESTNUTS
Djaj Bil Kastal

There are some excellent varieties of vacuum-packed or frozen chestnuts now available, making this dish very easy.

SERVES 4

1/4 stick (2 tablespoons) butter
1 tablespoon sunflower oil
2 large onions, sliced
1 teaspoon ground ginger
good pinch of saffron threads
1 teaspoon ground cinnamon
1 chicken, cut up in 4 to 6 pieces
salt and black pepper
1 to 2 tablespoons clear honey
1 pound chestnuts, vacuum-packed, or frozen and defrosted

Heat the butter and oil in a large pan. Put in the onions, cover, and let them soften slowly over medium heat, stirring from time to time. When they begin to color, stir in the ginger, saffron, and cinnamon. Put in the chicken pieces, season with salt and pepper, and turn to brown them lightly all over.

Add 1 cup water and cook, covered, turning the chicken pieces over at least once. Lift out the breasts when they are done, after about 15 to 20 minutes, and put them to one side. Lift out the remaining chicken pieces about 25 minutes later, when they are very tender.

Let the onions reduce to a rich, brown sauce. Stir in the honey (I use only 1 tablespoon) and taste to make sure you have enough salt to balance the sweetness and enough pepper to mitigate it.

Put in the chestnuts and simmer for 5 to 10 minutes, or until they are tender, adding a little water, if necessary. Return the chicken pieces to the pan and simmer for a few minutes until the chestnuts are soft, and the chicken has absorbed the honeyed flavors.

CHICKEN with DATES
Djaj Bil Tmar

Morocco is a country of dates and there are several varieties. Use 3/4 cup dates of a soft, moist variety such as the Tunisian Deglet Nour or Californian ones that you can find in supermarkets. Remove the stones, replacing each one with a blanched almond.

Follow the recipe on the preceding page for Chicken with Chestnuts until the sauce has reduced but omit the honey. At this point, add the dates instead of the chestnuts. Cook 2 to 5 minutes, turning them over once; take care that the dates do not fall apart. Put the chicken pieces back into the sauce under the dates and heat through.

CHICKEN with FRESH FIGS and WALNUTS
Djaj Bil Karmous Wal Joz

Follow the recipe on page 88 for Chicken with Chestnuts until the sauce has reduced and become caramelized. At this point, add 1/2 cup walnut halves and 4 to 8 fresh figs (4 black ones or 8 little green ones), peeled or simply washed, and cut in half. Cook them for 2 to 5 minutes, turning them over once. Take care that the figs do not fall apart. Put the chicken pieces back into the sauce under the figs, and cook a few minutes more to heat through and to absorb the honey flavors.

Another appealing way with the figs is to slash their stalk ends, making a cross. Sprinkle inside with a little lemon juice and a little superfine sugar, and put them under the broiler for a few minutes to barely caramelize. Then serve them as a garnish on top of the chicken pieces.

ROAST CHICKEN with COUSCOUS, RAISIN, and ALMOND STUFFING
Djaj M'Ammar Bil Kesksou

The couscous stuffing is the traditional one used for all birds, especially Mediteranean pigeons (the French pigeonneaux or squabs) and chickens. A generous amount of stuffing is made, enough to fill the chicken and to have some on the side, but it makes more sense not actually to bother stuffing the chicken. It is best to use the fine-ground couscous called seffa (see page 28) but you can use the ordinary medium one.

SERVES 4

1 chicken (about 3 to 3 1/2 pounds)
1 1/2 tablespoons extra virgin olive oil
juice of 1/2 lemon
1/2 teaspoon ground ginger
1/2 teaspoon ground cinnamon
salt and black pepper
2 tablespoons clear honey

FOR THE STUFFING
1 1/4 cups fine couscous
1 1/4 cups warm water
salt
2 tablespoons sunflower oil
1 tablespoon superfine sugar
1 teaspoon ground cinnamon
1 tablespoon orange blossom water
2 tablespoons raisins, soaked in water for 10 minutes
1/2 cup blanched almonds
1/2 stick (4 tablespoons) butter

Rub the chicken with a mixture of olive oil, lemon juice, ginger, cinnamon, salt, and pepper. Put it breast side down in a roasting dish so that the fat runs down and prevents the breasts from drying out. Pour about 4 to 5 tablespoons water into the dish.

Cook in an oven preheated to 400°F for about 1 1/2 hours. Turn the chicken breast side up after about 50 minutes, brush it with the honey, and continue to cook until it is well done and brown. Test that it is ready by cutting into a thigh with a pointed knife. The juices should run clear, not pink. You will find that most of the honey will have slid down the chicken to mix with the juices and make a delicious honey sauce.

For the stuffing, put the couscous in a baking dish and moisten with 1 1/4 cups warm water mixed with 1/2 teaspoon salt. Stir vigorously so that it is evenly absorbed. After about 10 minutes, add the oil and rub the couscous between your hands to air it and break up any lumps. Stir in the sugar, cinnamon, orange blossom water, and drained raisins. Fry the almonds in the remaining oil until lightly colored, coarsely chop them, and mix them into the stuffing. The butter will be stirred in later, just before serving.

Put the couscous stuffing in the oven with the chicken 20 to 30 minutes before you are ready to serve. Stir in the butter, cut into small pieces, and fluff up the couscous with a fork. Taste, since you might like to add a little salt.

Carve the chicken and serve with the sauce poured over, accompanied by the stuffing.

TAGINE *of* CHICKEN *with* PRESERVED LEMON *and* OLIVES
Tagine Djaj Bi Zaytoun Wal Hamid

This is the best-known Moroccan chicken dish. It was the only one, apart from appetizers, served during an evening of Arab poetry and storytelling, accompanied by musicians, that I attended in a Paris restaurant. The olives do not have to be pitted. If you find them too salty, soak them in 2 changes of water for up to an hour.

SERVES 4

3 tablespoons extra virgin olive oil

2 onions, grated or very finely chopped

2 to 3 garlic cloves, crushed

1/2 teaspoon crushed saffron threads or saffron powder

1/4 to 1/2 teaspoon ground ginger

1 chicken, cut up in 6 or 8 pieces

salt and black pepper

juice of 1/2 lemon

2 tablespoons chopped coriander

2 tablespoons chopped flat-leaf parsley

peel of 1 large or 2 small preserved lemons (see page 7)

12 to 16 green or violet olives (see above)

In a wide casserole or heavy-bottomed pan that can hold all the chicken pieces in one layer, heat the oil and put in the onions. Sauté, stirring over low heat, until they soften, then stir in the garlic, saffron, and ginger.

Put in the chicken pieces, season with salt and pepper, and pour in about 1 1/4 cups water. Simmer, covered, turning the pieces over a few times and adding a little more water if it becomes too dry. Lift out the breasts after about 15 minutes and put them to one side. Continue to cook the remaining pieces for another 25 minutes or so, after which time return the breasts to the pan.

Stir into the sauce the lemon juice, the chopped coriander and parsley, the preserved lemon peel cut into quarters or strips, and the olives. Simmer uncovered for 5 to 10 minutes, until the reduced sauce is thick and unctuous. If there is too much liquid, lift out the chicken pieces and set aside while you reduce the sauce further, then return the chicken to the pan and heat through.

Present the chicken on a serving dish with the olives and lemon peel on top of the meat.

VARIATION

Add 1/2 chili pepper, seeded and chopped, with the onions at the start, and the juice of 1/4 lemon (instead of 1/2) toward the end of cooking.

TAGINE *of* CHICKEN *with* ARTICHOKE BOTTOMS, PRESERVED LEMON, *and* OLIVES
Djaj Bil Korni

This is marvelous! I use frozen artichoke bottoms that come from Egypt and are available here in Middle Eastern and Asian stores. You get about 9 in a 14-ounce package and that is enough for 4 servings.

Follow the recipe above for *Tagine of Chicken with Preserved Lemon and Olives*. Ten minutes before the end, when you put in the coriander and parsley, lemon peel, and olives, lift the chicken pieces and put the artichoke bottoms in the sauce beneath them. Add a little water, if necessary, and cook about 10 minutes, or until the artichokes are tender.

MEDITERRANEAN PIGEONS, SQUABS, *or* POUSSINS *with* COUSCOUS STUFFING
L'Hamam M'Ammar Bil Kesksou

Because they are small birds, with one per person, it is worth stuffing them. A few butchers sell the special baby Mediterranean pigeons or pigeonneaux or squabs. Otherwise, buy the smallest poussins possible.

Make the same couscous stuffing as in the recipe for Roast Chicken with Couscous, Raisin, and Almond Stuffing (page 92). Fill each pigeon or poussin with about 3 table-spoons of stuffing—they should not be too tightly filled, or the stuffing may burst out— and use toothpicks to secure the openings.

Rub the birds with double the quantities of olive oil, lemon juice, ground ginger, ground cinnamon, salt and pepper as given above. Roast them in an oven preheated to 400°F, breast side down for the first half hour, then turn them breast side up, and brush them with 3 to 4 tablespoons honey. Return the birds to the oven for another 1/2 hour (it takes longer to cook them than usual because they are stuffed).

Heat through the remaining stuffing for 20 to 30 minutes in the same oven and serve alongside the pigeons.

MEDITERRANEAN PIGEONS or SQUABS STUFFED with DATE and ALMOND PASTE
L'Hmam Bel Tamr Wal Loz

This is great and also easy to make. Use a moist variety of dates such as the Deglet Nour of Tunisia or Californian ones. If you cannot get the special pigeons or squabs use small poussins.

SERVES 4

FOR THE STUFFING

1/2 cup blanched almonds

5 ounces dates (a little more than 3/4 cup), pitted

2 tablespoons butter

4 small Mediterranean pigeons, squabs, or small poussins

1/4 cup extra virgin olive oil

juice of 1 lemon

salt

1/2 teaspoon ground ginger

1 tablespoon clear honey

For the stuffing, grind the almonds in the food processor. Add the dates and the butter and blend to a paste. Stuff the birds with this, and close the openings with toothpicks.

Rub the birds with a mixture of oil, lemon juice, and salt, and place them breast side down in a baking dish. Roast them in an oven preheated to 400°F. The time depends on their size. I used 12-ounce poussins (not very small), and it took as long as 1 1/2 hours. The reason they take so long is because they are stuffed. Small Mediterranean pigeons or squabs take less time. Turn them over after 1 1/4 hours, when their backs are brown, and brush their breasts with a mix of ginger and honey. Put them back into the oven until the juices run clear when the inside leg is cut with a pointed knife.

Serve hot.

ROAST DUCK with APRICOTS
Bata Bil Mashmash

I have used the ingredients of a chicken tagine as a relish to accompany duck (which is not a Moroccan bird) because the combination of fatty duck with sharp apricots is great.

SERVES 4

1 duck (about 5 pounds)
salt and black pepper
1 teaspoon ground ginger
3 tablespoons sunflower oil
1 pound baby onions or shallots
1/2 teaspoon ground cinnamon
1/4 stick (2 tablespoons) butter
1 1/4 pounds fresh apricots
juice of 1/2 lemon
3 tablespoons clear honey

Sprinkle the duck with salt, pepper, and 1/2 teaspoon ginger, then rub with 1 tablespoon oil. Prick the skin with a fork or pointed knife in several places so that the melting fat can ooze out. Put the duck, breast side down, on a rack in a baking dish or roasting pan and into an oven preheated to 400°F.

Cook for 1 hour, then pour off the fat and turn over the duck. Return the duck to the oven and cook for another hour, or until the juices run clear, not pink, when you cut into the inside leg with a pointed knife. The skin should be crisp and brown and the flesh still soft and juicy.

Blanch the onions or shallots in boiling water for 5 minutes, and when cool enough to handle, peel off the skins and trim the roots. Sauté them in the remaining 2 tablespoons oil for about 15 minutes, covered, over a low heat until softened; shake the pan occasionally so the onions brown all over. Stir the remaining ginger and the cinnamon into the oil, add the butter and put in the apricots. Cook, covered, over low heat until the apricots begin to collapse. Add the lemon juice and honey and cook, stirring, for about 15 minutes, until jammy.

Serve the duck accompanied by the apricots and onion relish.

GROUND MEAT KEBAB
Kefta Kebab

In Morocco, men are masters of the fire, in charge of the brochettes, the small kebabs threaded on little wood or metal skewers, which are traditional street food.

The ground meat kebabs are deliciously aromatic—full of fresh herbs and spices. The meat is usually pressed around skewers and cooked over dying embers, but it is easier simply to pat the meat into sausage or burger shapes and cook them under the broiler or on a griddle. There should be a good amount of fat (it melts away under the fierce heat), enough to keep the meat moist and soft. Otherwise, work 3 tablespoons extra virgin olive oil into the paste.

Bite-size keftas can be served as appetizers at a party, but en famille burger-size ones, accompanied by a salad, represent a main dish.

SERVES 4 TO 6
2 pounds fatty ground lamb or beef
1 small onion, finely chopped or grated
large handful of chopped flat-leaf parsley
large handful of chopped coriander
handful of chopped mint
1/2 teaspoon ground cumin
1/2 teaspoon ground cinnamon
1/2 teaspoon ground ginger
good pinch of ground chili pepper
salt

Put all the ingredients together in a bowl. Mix well and work with your hands into a soft paste. Wash your hands and rub them with oil. Take lumps of paste the size of a tangerine and roll them into sausage shapes about 3/4 inch thick, then press them around flat wooden skewers. Alternatively, shape the meat into burgers.

Place the *keftas* on a heat-proof serving dish or on a piece of foil on a baking tray and cook under the preheated broiler for about 10 minutes, turning them over once, until browned on the outside but still pink inside.

Serve hot with good bread and a salad of cucumber, tomato, and red onion, dressed with lemon juice and olive oil.

ROAST SHOULDER of LAMB with COUSCOUS and DATE STUFFING
Dala M'Aamra Bi Kesksou Wa Tmar

This is sumptuous and extremely easy. The meat is cooked very slowly for a long time until it is meltingly tender and you can pull the meat off the bones with your fingers. The stuffing—it is the traditional stuffing for a whole lamb—is sweet with dates and raisins and crunchy with almonds. (In Morocco, they add sugar or honey but that makes it too sweet for me.) The couscous needs plenty of butter as there is no sauce, but you can substitute oil if you prefer. Try to get the fine-ground variety of couscous called seffa (see page 28), otherwise use the ordinary medium-ground one. For the dates, use the Tunisian Deglet Nour or Californian varieties that you can find in supermarkets.

A shoulder of spring lamb is always fatty but most of the fat melts away during the long cooking. If it appears too fatty, as might be the case with an older lamb, carefully remove some of the fat before cooking.

SERVES 4 TO 5 1 shoulder of lamb (about 3 to 4 1/2 pounds)
salt and black pepper
1 1/4 cups couscous
1 tablespoon orange blossom water
1 teaspoon ground cinnamon
2 tablespoons sunflower or vegetable oil
5 ounces (not quite 1 cup) dates, pitted and cut into small pieces
1/3 cup raisins
1/2 cup blanched almonds, chopped coarsely
2/3 stick (5 1/2 tablespoons) butter, cut into small pieces
To garnish: 8 dates and 8 blanched almonds

Put the lamb skin side up in a baking dish or roasting pan, sprinkle with salt and pepper, and roast in an oven preheated to 475°F for 15 minutes. Then lower the heat to 350°F and cook for 3 hours, until the skin is crisp and brown and the meat is juicy and meltingly tender. Pour off the fat after about 2 hours.

For the stuffing, put the couscous in another baking dish, and add the same volume of warm water, about 1 1/4 cups, mixed with a little salt, the orange blossom water, and cinnamon. Stir well so that the water is absorbed evenly. After about 10 minutes, add the oil, and rub the couscous between your hands to air it and break up any lumps. Mix in the remaining ingredients, apart from the butter, cover with foil, and put in the oven with the lamb for the last 20 minutes, or until it is steaming hot.

Before serving, stir in the butter so that it melts in and is absorbed evenly. With a fork, fluff up the couscous stuffing, breaking up any lumps. Add a little salt to taste, if necessary.

For the garnish, remove the pits from each date and replace them with the blanched almonds. Serve the meat with the couscous stuffing decorated with these dates.

ROAST SHOULDER *of* LAMB *with* CARAMELIZED BABY ONIONS *and* HONEY
Dala Bil Basal Wal Asal

A favorite joint for a family roast in Morocco is a shoulder of lamb, and honeyed onions are a specially delicious accompaniment. The lamb is cooked very slowly for a long time, until it is so tender that the meat can be pulled away from the bone with the fingers. In the past, the lamb was cooked on the spit in the family courtyard or taken to the public oven.

A shoulder roast of young spring lamb is always fatty, but most of the fat melts away during the long cooking, keeping the meat moist and succulent. If an older lamb is too fatty, carefully remove some of the fat with a sharp knife before cooking. Use the smaller amount of honey to begin with, and add more, to taste.

SERVES 4 TO 5

1 shoulder of lamb (about 3 to 4 1/2 pounds)
salt and black pepper
2 pounds (about 4 cups) baby onions or shallots
4 tablespoons extra virgin olive oil
2 to 4 tablespoons clear honey

Put the lamb skin side up in a baking dish or roasting pan. Sprinkle with salt and pepper and roast in an oven preheated to 475°F for 15 minutes. Then lower the heat to 350°F and cook for 3 hours, until the skin is crisp and brown and the meat is juicy and meltingly tender. Pour off the fat after about 2 hours.

Blanch the baby onions or shallots in boiling water for 5 minutes, drain, and when they are cool enough to handle, peel off the skins and trim the roots.

Heat the olive oil in a wide pan, and put in the onions. Half-cover with about 1 cup water and add a little salt and pepper. Braise for about 35 minutes, covering the pan at first, then removing the lid to reduce the liquid. Cook, stirring occasionally, until all the liquid has disappeared and the onions are soft and brown in the sizzling oil. They will be ready when the point of a sharp knife goes in easily. Add the honey and cook, stirring often, for 15 minutes, until the onions are caramelized and soft enough to, as they say in Morocco, "crush with the tongue."

Serve very hot. Accompany the lamb with the onions, and pass around salt and pepper for the meat, which is needed to mitigate the sweetness of the onions.

TAGINE of KNUCKLE of VEAL with ARTICHOKES and PEAS
Tagine Bil Korni Wal Jelban

Ask your butcher to saw the knuckle of veal into rounds, retaining the marrow in the center of the bone (as for Italian osso buco). You can buy very good frozen artichokes, which come from Egypt, from Middle Eastern stores. They come in packages weighing 14 ounces and containing about 9 small artichoke bottoms. If you want to use fresh artichoke hearts or bottoms, see page 8.

Use young fresh peas or frozen petits pois.

SERVES 4

1/2 stick (4 tablespoons) butter or 3 tablespoons sunflower oil

1 onion, chopped

2 garlic cloves, crushed or chopped finely

1/2 teaspoon ground ginger

1/2 teaspoon saffron threads

4 thick rounds cut from the knuckle of veal

salt and black pepper

one 14-ounce package frozen artichoke bottoms, defrosted

juice of 1/2 lemon

peel of 1/2 to 1 preserved lemon (optional) (see page 7)

14 ounces fresh young peas (shelled weight), or frozen *petits pois*, defrosted

2 tablespoons chopped coriander

8 green olives (optional)

Heat the butter or oil in a wide pan or casserole. Put in the onion, garlic, ginger, saffron, and meat. Cook over a low heat for about 5 minutes, turning over the meat.

Cover with water, season with salt and pepper, and simmer, with the lid on, for 1 1/2 to 2 hours, or until the meat is so tender it almost comes away from the bone. If necessary, add water to keep the meat covered, and stir occasionally to make sure it does not stick to the bottom of the pan. Remove the lid toward the end to reduce the sauce.

Add the artichoke bottoms, cut in half or quartered, lemon juice, and preserved lemon peel cut into strips, if using, and cook for 5 minutes. Then add the peas and coriander, and, if you like, the olives. Cook for 5 minutes, or until the vegetables are tender. The sauce should be reduced and thick.

TAGINE *of* KNUCKLE *of* VEAL *with* FENNEL
Tagine Bil Bisbas

Bulb fennel has an attractive intense aniseed flavor. Follow the above recipe for *Tagine* of Knuckle of Veal (page 103) but, instead of artichokes and peas, use 4 medium-size fennel bulbs. Trim the base, cut away the hard ends of the round stalks, and remove the outer layer if it is stringy or bruised. Cut in half or quarters, lengthwise. Add to the meat and cook for 30 minutes, or until very soft.

TAGINE *of* KNUCKLE *of* VEAL *with* EGGPLANTS
Tagine Bil Brania

For this *tagine*, follow the recipe for *Tagine* of Knuckle of Veal with Artichokes and Peas (page 103), but instead of adding the artichokes and peas at the end, serve the meat with a purée of mashed eggplants poured over it.

Roast 2 pounds of eggplants in the hottest oven. Peel, chop, and mash them as described on page 8. Heat 2 tablespoons extra virgin olive oil in a skillet with 4 crushed cloves of garlic. When the aroma rises, add the eggplant purée with a squeeze of lemon and cook for 1 to 2 minutes. Pour over the meat and heat through just before serving.

You can also add a 14-ounce can of chickpeas, drained of their water, to the meat toward the end of the cooking.

LAMB TAGINE with POTATOES and PEAS
Tagine Bil Batata Wal Jelban

The best lamb to use for this tagine is either boned shoulder or neck fillet. Trim away some of the excess fat before cooking. Some supermarkets sell fresh shelled peas, which are young and sweet, but frozen petits pois will also do very well. If the olives are very salty, soak them in water for up to an hour.

SERVES 6

3 tablespoons extra virgin olive oil

1 onion, chopped

2 garlic cloves, crushed

1 teaspoon ground ginger

1/2 teaspoon saffron threads

3 pounds boned shoulder or neck fillet of lamb, cut into 6 to 8 pieces

salt and black pepper

2 pounds new potatoes, peeled

1 pound fresh young peas (shelled weight) or frozen *petits pois*, defrosted

peel of 1 to 1 1/2 preserved lemon (optional) (see page 7)

16 or more green olives

2 tablespoons chopped coriander

2 tablespoons chopped flat-leaf parsley

Heat the oil in a wide pan or casserole. Put in the onion, garlic, ginger, saffron, and meat. Cook on low heat for about 5 minutes, turning over the meat. Cover with water, season with salt and pepper and cook, covered, over low heat, for 1 to 1 1/2 hours, or until the meat is very tender, turning the pieces over once in a while.

Add the potatoes, cutting any large ones in half. Top up the water, if necessary, and cook 20 minutes, or until the potatoes are tender. Then add the peas, preserved lemon peel cut into thin strips, if using, olives, coriander, and parsley, and cook, uncovered, for 5 minutes longer, or until the peas are tender and the sauce reduced and thick.

VARIATION

Young fava beans can be used instead of peas, but they will need to be cooked for at least 10 minutes.

TAGINE *of* LAMB *with* CARAMELIZED BABY ONIONS *and* PEARS
Tagine Bil Bouawid

This is a recipe that is similar to the chicken tagine on page 93, but the result is quite different. The sweetness of the pears goes surprisingly well with the lamb. Choose firm pears; if the fruit is too soft, they tend to collapse during the cooking. Comice and Bosc are good varieties. Use a boned shoulder of lamb or neck fillets, and trim only some—not all—of the fat.

SERVES 6 TO 8
3 pounds boned shoulder of lamb
5 tablespoons sunflower or vegetable oil
1 onion, chopped
salt and plenty of black pepper
1/2 teaspoon ground ginger
1/2 teaspoon ground cinnamon
1/2 teaspoon saffron threads
1 pound (about 2 cups) shallots or baby onions
3 large pears
1/4 stick (2 tablespoons) butter

Cut the meat into 6 or 8 pieces, and put it into a wide pan with 2 tablespoons oil over medium heat; turn to brown the pieces all over. Add the chopped onion and barely cover with water. Stir in salt and pepper, ginger, cinnamon, and saffron, and simmer, covered, over a low heat for 1 1/2 hours, turning the pieces over a few times.

To peel the onions or shallots, blanch them in boiling water for 5 minutes and, when cool enough to handle, peel off the skins and trim the roots. Sauté them in a skillet in 2 tablespoons oil over a low heat for 5 to 10 minutes, shaking the pan, until the onions have slightly colored. Then add them to the meat and cook for a further 30 minutes, until the meat is very tender and the baby onions are so soft that, as they say in Morocco, "you can crush them with your tongue." Toward the end of the cooking time, cook uncovered to reduce the sauce. There should be only a small amount of liquid remaining.

Wash the pears. Quarter and core them but do not peel them. Sauté them in a large skillet in a mixture of butter and the remaining tablespoon of oil over medium heat until their cut sides are slightly brown and caramelized. If they have not softened right through (that depends on their size and degree of ripeness), put them into the pan over

the meat, skin side up, and continue to cook, covered, until they are very tender. It could be 15 minutes, but you must watch them as they can quickly fall apart.

Serve the meat with the pears, arranged skin side up, on top.

VARIATIONS

◇ Stir in 1 to 1 1/2 tablespoons of clear honey when you put in the pears, and adjust the seasoning so that there is enough salt and plenty of pepper to mitigate the sweetness.

◆ Add 1/2 cup blanched almonds to the meat at the start. They will soften during the cooking.

◇ Instead of pears, sharp green apples, such as Granny Smiths, may be used.

◆ Use veal instead of lamb.

TAGINE of LAMB with CARAMELIZED BABY ONIONS and QUINCES
Tagine Bil Sfargal

Follow the recipe for *Tagine* of Lamb with Caramelized Baby Onions and Pears (page 106) but instead of the pears, use 3 quinces, weighing about 2 pounds. Quinces are now available for several months, starting in the fall, as they are imported from various countries, which have different seasons.

Wash and scrub the quinces. Boil them whole for about 1 hour, or until they feel soft. The time varies greatly depending on their size and degree of ripeness, so watch them and do not let them fall apart. Drain them and, when cool enough to handle, cut them into quarters, then cut away the cores but do not peel them.

In a large skillet, sauté the quarters in a little sunflower oil until the cut sides are brown. This gives them a delicious caramelized flavor. Alternatively, for a honeyed version, sauté the quinces in a mixture of 1/4 stick (2 tablespoons) unsalted butter, melted with 1 tablespoon sunflower oil and 1 1/2 tablespoons clear honey. You may also add 3/4 cup walnut halves, which gives a wonderful contrast of texture.

Put the quinces—caramelized or honeyed—in the pan with the meat, skin side down, and cook until they are soft but, again, watch them so that they do not fall apart. If there is not enough room, lift out the meat and put in the fruits, returning the meat to heat through before serving. Serve hot, with the quinces, skin side up, on top of the meat.

TAGINE of LAMB with APRICOTS
Tagine Bil Mashmash

The combination of lamb and apricots has become popular in America, and with good reason—they go beautifully together. Follow the recipe for *Tagine* of Lamb with Caramelized Baby Onions and Pears (page 106) until the meat is very tender and the sauce reduced. Instead of the onions and pears, pit 2 pounds fresh apricots, add them to the meat, and cook for minutes, only until they soften.

Another particularly splendid version (my favorite—which you must try) is with dried apricots. Soak 1 pound dried apricots in water for an hour or longer, drain, and cook for about 1 hour in water to cover (you will need to keep adding water) until they are very soft. Then let the liquid reduce to practically nothing. Add 2 tablespoons clear honey and 1/4 stick (2 tablespoons) unsalted butter, and cook, stirring, until the apricots begin to turn brown and caramelize. Pour them on top of the meat when serving. Sprinkle the dish, if you like, with 1/4 cup blanched almonds fried in 1 tablespoon sunflower oil until lightly browned.

TAGINE of LAMB with DATES and ALMONDS
Tagine Bil Tmar Wal Loz

In an Arab culture born in the desert, dates have something of a sacred character. Considered the "bread of the desert," they symbolize hospitality and are much loved and prestigious. You would find this dish at wedding parties. Some people find it too sweet, so you might prefer it, as I do, without the optional honey. The dates give it a slightly sticky texture. Use the semi-dried moist varieties from California or the Deglet Nour dates from Tunisia.

SERVES 6 TO 8   3 pounds boned shoulder or neck fillet of lamb
1/2 stick (4 tablespoons) butter or 1/2 cup sunflower oil
2 onions, finely chopped
1/2 teaspoon saffron threads
1/2 teaspoon ground ginger
salt and plenty of black pepper
1 cinnamon stick
1 to 2 tablespoons clear honey (optional)
1 teaspoon ground cinnamon
1 3/4 cups dates, pitted
To garnish: 1/2 cup blanched almonds; 3 tablespoons sesame seeds (optional)

Trim any excess fat from the lamb and cut into 6 or 8 pieces. Heat the butter or 3 tablespoons oil in a large pan, put in the meat, and brown it lightly all over. Take out the meat, put in the onions and cook, stirring, until they begin to color. Stir in the saffron and ginger and return the meat to the pan. Add salt and pepper and the cinnamon stick. Cover with water and simmer, covered, for 1½ to 2 hours, or until the meat is very tender, turning the pieces occasionally.

Take out two pieces of meat in order to make room in the pan, stir in the honey, if using, and the ground cinnamon and more pepper (it needs plenty to counterbalance the sweetness). Move the meat around so the honey and cinnamon is spread around and then return the two pieces of meat. Cook until the sauce is reduced, turning the meat over as you do. Add the dates and cook 5 to 10 minutes more.

Fry the almonds in the remaining tablespoon of oil until lightly golden. Leave whole or coarsely chop, and sprinkle over the meat when serving, adding lightly toasted sesame seeds, if you like.

VARIATION

Stuff the pitted dates with walnut halves. In this case, omit the almonds and sesame seeds.

TAGINE of LAMB with PRUNES and ALMONDS
Tagine Bil Barkok Wal Loz

This is the best-known fruit tagine outside Morocco. Restaurants in Paris accompany it with couscous seffa made with fine-ground couscous (see page 28) with plenty of butter, one bowl of boiled chickpeas, and another of stewed raisins. The best prunes to use are the moist Californian ones, which are already pitted.

SERVES 6 TO 8

3 pounds boned shoulder or neck fillet of lamb
4 tablespoons sunflower oil
1 large onion, chopped finely or grated
2 garlic cloves, chopped
1 teaspoon ground ginger
1/2 teaspoon saffron threads
salt and plenty of black pepper
2 teaspoons ground cinnamon
3/4 pound (about 2 cups) prunes (see above)
To garnish: 1/2 cup blanched almonds; 3 tablespoons sesame seeds (optional)

Trim any excess fat from the lamb and cut it into 6 or 8 pieces. Put the meat in a pan with 3 tablespoons of the oil, onion, garlic, ginger, saffron, salt, pepper, and 1 teaspoon cinnamon. Cover with water and simmer gently, with the lid on, for 1 1/2 to 2 hours, until the meat is very tender, adding water to keep it covered.

Add the prunes and the remaining cinnamon. Stir well, adjust the seasoning, and simmer, uncovered, for 30 minutes more, until the sauce is reduced and thickened.

Fry the almonds in the remaining tablespoon of oil until they are lightly colored, and sprinkle these over the meat before serving. If you wish, you can also garnish with lightly toasted sesame seeds.

VARIATIONS

◆ Put the almonds in with the meat from the start of the cooking. They will become soft.

◇ Add 1 to 2 tablespoons clear honey at the same time as the prunes.

TAGINE *of* LAMB *with* CHESTNUTS
Tagine Bil Kastal

Follow the recipe for *Tagine* of Lamb with Prunes and Almonds (page 111) until the meat is very tender and the liquid reduced to a thick sauce. But instead of prunes, add 14 ounces frozen and defrosted, or vacuum-packed, peeled chestnuts and cook for 10 minutes, or until the chestnuts are soft and heated through. You could add 1 tablespoon clear honey with the chestnuts, in which case, adjust the seasoning; you will need quite a bit of pepper to mitigate the sweetness. The sauce should be reduced and creamy. In this version, leave out the almonds and sesame seeds.

PREPARING COUSCOUS— BASIC RECIPE

This is an easy foolproof method of preparing the precooked couscous available in America (see page 28). I make it straight in the round clay dish in which it will be served with its broth and other accompaniments. In Morocco, 500 grams (1.2 pounds) serves 4 people but by standards in America, it is enough for 6. If you are cooking for 8 or 10 people, it is worth making 2.4 pounds, if only because a mountain of couscous looks good.

You need the same volume of salted water as couscous.

Put 2 1/2 cups couscous in an oven dish. Gradually add 2 1/2 cups warm salted water, made with 1/2 to 1 teaspoon salt, stirring vigorously so that it is absorbed evenly. Leave to swell for about 10 minutes, then mix in 2 tablespoons oil and rub the couscous between your hands above the bowl to air it and break up any lumps. That is the important part.

Put the dish in an oven preheated to 400°F and heat through for 20 minutes, or until it is steaming hot (it takes longer for 5 cups couscous). Before serving, work in 3 tablespoons butter cut into small pieces, or 2 to 3 tablespoons oil, and fluff it up again, breaking up any lumps.

COUSCOUS with SPRING VEGETABLES
Kesksou L'Hodra

This aromatic herby couscous with young tender vegetables and no meat makes a lovely main dish. Vegetarians will love it. Use fresh young fava beans and peas (some supermarkets sell them already shelled) or frozen petits pois.

SERVES 6

2 1/2 cups barley couscous or ordinary couscous

2 1/2 cups warm water with 1/2 to 1 teaspoon salt

6 tablespoons mild extra virgin olive oil

4 1/2 cups stock made with 2 vegetable or chicken bouillon cubes

14 ounces young fava beans (shelled weight), or frozen fava beans, defrosted

1/2 pound scallions

14 ounces frozen artichokes or baby artichokes

salt and black pepper

14 ounces young peas (shelled weight), or frozen petits pois, defrosted

large handful of chopped flat-leaf parsley

large handful of chopped coriander

handful of chopped mint

Following the basic recipe (page 112), put the couscous in a wide, ovenproof dish, add the same volume of salted water gradually, stirring so that it gets absorbed evenly. After about 10 minutes, when the couscous has become plump and almost tender, add 3 tablespoons olive oil and rub the couscous between your hands to air it and break up any lumps. This can be done in advance and then heated through 20 to 30 minutes before serving in an oven preheated to 400°F until it is steaming hot. For the broth, bring the stock to boiling point, then add the fava beans; the scallions, trimmed of their green ends and sliced; and the artichokes, cut in half or quartered, and cook for 10 minutes, or until tender. Season with salt and pepper, taking into consideration the saltiness of the bouillon cubes. Add the peas, and cook for 5 minutes, or until they are just tender. Stir in the herbs just before you are ready to serve.

Before serving, fluff up the couscous with a fork, breaking up any lumps, and stir in the remaining olive oil. Arrange the vegetables on top and pass the broth around in a bowl for everyone to help themselves.

You may like to melt into the couscous at the end ^{1}/2 stick (4 tablespoons) of butter and omit the olive oil.

BARLEY COUSCOUS with SEVEN VEGETABLES
Kesksou Seb'Hdati

Traditionally, the Berbers first made couscous with barley, and barley couscous is still very popular, especially in the south of Morocco. It is now available in precooked form from some Middle Eastern stores. You can substitute ordinary couscous.

You can make the broth with lamb, beef, or veal (preferably shoulder, neck fillet, or knuckle) and with a choice of vegetables. According to local lore, seven is a magic number that brings good luck. Onions, tomatoes, and chili peppers count as flavorings, so you must have seven more vegetables. I have listed eight, so drop one. The number of ingredients makes it seem a scary endeavor, but it is only a matter of throwing things into a pot, and it makes a spectacular one-dish meal for a large party. You will need a very big pot.

SERVES 10

FOR THE COUSCOUS

5 cups barley couscous

5 cups warm water

1 to 2 teaspoons salt

1/4 cup sunflower or vegetable oil

1 stick (1/2 cup) butter

FOR THE BROTH

3 pounds meat (see above)

3 large onions

3/4 cup chickpeas, soaked overnight

black pepper

1/2 teaspoon saffron powder or threads

1 teaspoon ground cinnamon

> 1 teaspoon ground ginger
>
> 1 pound tomatoes, peeled and quartered
>
> 1 pound carrots, peeled and cut into strips
>
> 1 pound small turnips, halved
>
> 1 small white cabbage, cut in chunks
>
> 1 pound new potatoes
>
> 2 chili peppers (optional)
>
> salt
>
> 4 stalks celery, halved
>
> 1 pound orange pumpkin, cut in 1-inch pieces
>
> 1 pound zucchini
>
> 1/2 pound young fava beans (shelled weight), or frozen fava beans, defrosted
>
> 1/2 cup chopped coriander
>
> 1/2 cup chopped flat-leaf parsley

Prepare the couscous in a large, round, ovenproof dish as described on page 112, leaving the final heating in the oven to be done 20 to 30 minutes before serving.

Cut the meat into 10 pieces and the onions into quarters, then into thick slices, and put them in a large pan with the drained chickpeas. Cover with about 6 pints of water, bring to the boil, and remove the scum. Add the pepper (no salt is added at this stage since it would stop the chickpeas from softening), saffron, cinnamon, and ginger and simmer, covered, for 1 hour.

Now put in the tomatoes, carrots, turnips, cabbage, potatoes, cut in half or left whole if small, and the whole chilies, if using. Add salt, and cook for 30 minutes, or until the meat is very tender.

Add the celery, pumpkin, zucchini, cut into fat slices or left whole if they are baby ones, fava beans, and herbs. Add more water, if necessary, taste, and adjust the seasoning, and cook 30 minutes more.

About 20 to 30 minutes before the end of the cooking time—when the last vegetables go in—put the couscous into the oven, preheated to 400°F, and heat through until it is steaming hot, taking it out and fluffing it with a fork after about 10 minutes. Before serving, fork the butter, cut into small pieces, into the couscous and fluff up the couscous as it melts in.

To serve, moisten the couscous with a little broth and shape it into a cone with a crater at the top. Arrange some meat in the crater and some vegetables down the sides, then pour a little broth over the mound. Bring the remaining broth, meat, and vegetables to the table in another bowl. Alternatively, bring the couscous to the table in one dish, and the broth with the meat and vegetables in another, and serve them directly into individual bowls or soup plates.

VARIATIONS

◈ Use 2 chickens cut into pieces instead of the meat.

◇ For a peppery sauce, pass around a bowl with 3 to 4 ladles of the hot broth mixed with 1 tablespoon or more *harissa* or 2 tablespoons paprika and 1 teaspoon or more chili pepper. Although this was originally a Tunisian and Algerian custom, not Moroccan, the French like it as do some of us now.

COUSCOUS with LAMB, ONIONS, and RAISINS
Kesksou Tfaya

The special feature of this dish is the exquisite mix of caramelized onions, honey, and raisins called tfaya, which is served as a topping to the long-cooked, deliciously tender meat.

SERVES 4 TO 6

FOR THE COUSCOUS

2 1/2 cups couscous

2 1/2 cups warm water

1/2 to 1 teaspoon salt

3 tablespoons sunflower or vegetable oil

1/2 stick (4 tablespoons) butter

2 pounds boned shoulder or leg of lamb

2 1/2 pounds onions

salt and black pepper

1/2 to 1 teaspoon ground ginger

2 1/2 teaspoons ground cinnamon

4 whole cloves

1/2 teaspoon saffron threads or powder

1/3 stick (2 1/2 tablespoons) butter

1 tablespoon extra virgin olive oil

2 tablespoons clear honey

1 cup raisins, soaked in water for 20 minutes

1 cup blanched almonds

Prepare the couscous in a large, round, ovenproof dish as described on page 112, leaving the final heating in the oven to be done 20 to 30 minutes before serving.

Prepare the meat broth in a large pan. Put in the meat, with about 1/2 pound onions, chopped, and cover with 7 1/2 cups water. Bring to the boil and remove the scum. Add salt and pepper, the ginger, 1 teaspoon cinnamon, and the cloves. Simmer for 1 1/2 hours. At this point, add the saffron and more water, if necessary, and simmer for another 30 minutes, or until the meat is so tender you can pull it apart with your fingers.

At the same time, prepare the honeyed onion tfaya. Cut the remaining onions in half and slice them. Put them in a pan with 1 cup water. Put the lid on and cook over low heat for about 30 minutes, until the onions are very soft. Remove the lid and cook further, until the liquid has evaporated. Add the butter and oil and cook until the onions are golden. Stir in the honey and the remaining 1 1/2 teaspoons cinnamon, the drained raisins, and a pinch of salt. Continue cooking for another 10 minutes, or until the onions caramelize and become brown.

Fry the almonds in a drop of oil until golden, turning them over, then drain on paper towels. Coarsely chop about half of them.

About 20 to 30 minutes before the end of the cooking time, put the couscous in the oven, preheated to 400°F, and heat through until it is steaming hot, fluffing it with a fork after about 10 minutes. Before serving, fork the butter, cut into small pieces, into the couscous and again fluff up the couscous as it melts in.

To serve, moisten the couscous with a ladle of broth and mix in the chopped almonds, and leave it in the baking dish or turn it onto a large, round platter; shape it into a mound and make a wide shallow hollow in the center. Put the meat in the hollow, cover with the onion and raisin tfaya, and sprinkle with the remaining whole, fried almonds. Serve the broth separately.

"BURIED in VERMICELLI"
Shaariya Medfouna

This specialty of Fez—shaariya medfouna, which means "buried in vermicelli"—is a fabulous surprise dish—a chicken tagine hidden under a mountain of vermicelli. It is a grand festive dish, a kind of trompe l'oeil, as the vermicelli is decorated like a sweet dessert couscous (page 124), with alternating lines of confectioners' sugar, cinnamon, and chopped fried almonds. It sounds complex, but it is really worth making for a large party.

You can leave out the confectioners' sugar if you think your guests are likely to prefer it without, and instead pass the sugar around in a little bowl for those who would like to try. The vermicelli is traditionally steamed like couscous, but it is easier to boil it. It is more practical to cook the chickens in 2 large pans and to divide the ingredients for the stew between them.

In Morocco they also cook pigeons and lamb in the same way.

SERVES 10
OR MORE

- 2 large whole chickens
- 4 large onions, chopped coarsely
- 2 teaspoons ground cinnamon
- 1 teaspoon ground ginger
- 1 teaspoon saffron threads or powder
- salt and black pepper
- 1 1/4 stick (1/2 cup plus 2 tablespoons) butter
- 1 tablespoon clear honey
- 2 teaspoons orange blossom water (optional)
- 1/2 cup chopped flat-leaf parsley
- 1/2 cup chopped coriander
- 1 cup blanched almonds
- 1 1/2 tablespoons sunflower or vegetable oil
- 2 pounds vermicelli nests
- To decorate: 2 teaspoons cinnamon; confectioners' sugar (optional)

Use two deep pans and put 1 chicken into each. To each pan, pour in 2 1/4 cups water, bring to the boil, and remove the scum. Add 2 chopped onions, 1 teaspoon cinnamon, 1/2 teaspoon ginger, and 1/2 teaspoon saffron. Add salt and pepper and simmer, covered, for about 1 hour. Turn the chickens occasionally so they are well cooked all over.

Lift out the chickens and, when cool enough to handle, remove the skin and bones and cut the meat into medium-size pieces.

Pour the chicken stock with the onions into one pan only and reduce by boiling it

down until a thick sauce results. Stir in 1/2 stick (4 tablespoons) of butter, the honey, and the orange blossom water, if using, and cook a few minutes more. Taste, and add extra salt and pepper if necessary.

Add the herbs and return the chicken pieces to the sauce. All this can be done in advance and reheated when you are about to serve.

Fry the almonds in the oil until lightly browned, then drain on paper towels. Crush them with a pestle and mortar or coarsely chop them.

Just before serving, break the vermicelli into small pieces by crushing the nests in your hands. Cook in rapidly boiling salted water for 5 minutes, until al dente, stirring vigorously at the start so that the threads do not stick together in lumps. Drain very quickly and then pour it back into the pan. Stir in the remaining butter, cut into small pieces, and some salt.

Put the chicken with its sauce into a very large, deep, round serving dish. Cover with a mountain of vermicelli, and decorate this with lines of cinnamon, confectioners' sugar, if using, and chopped almonds emanating from the center like rays.

VARIATION

For "buried in couscous" (couscous *medfoun*), the fine-ground couscous, *seffa*, is used instead of vermicelli. Prepare 5 cups as described on page 112 and heat it through in the oven. Cover the chicken with a mountain of couscous. As above, make a design by sprinkling thin lines of cinnamon and confectioners' sugar, fanning down like rays from the top, and decorate the bottom of the mound with whole or chopped toasted almonds or walnut halves and raisins or dates.

Desserts

Morocco is a fruit lovers' paradise. In *riads*, traditional Arab houses with interior gardens, there are always fruit trees, and their scents permeate the air. It is from the Persians and their notion that paradise was an orchard that the Arabs adopted and passed on their love of fruit. Bowls of dried fruit and nuts are ready in every home to greet visitors—sometimes the hostess will fill a date or a fig with an almond or a walnut and hand it to you. And the usual way to end a meal is with fruit. For guests, it is served either simply cut up on a plate or as a fruit salad.

Pastries are for special occasions, or for visitors when they drop in. They are filled with almonds, pistachios, or walnuts and with dates and usually soaked in sugar or honey syrup.

SWEET COUSCOUS
Kesksou Seffa

A sweet couscous made with the fine-ground couscous called seffa (see page 28) is served hot, accompanied by a drink of cold buttermilk or milk perfumed with a drop of orange blossom water served in little glasses. The couscous needs quite a bit of butter because there is no broth. See the suggestions below for extra garnishes.

SERVES 6 TO 8   2 1/2 cups fine-ground couscous (*seffa*)

2 1/2 cups warm water

1/2 to 1 teaspoon salt

2 tablespoons sunflower or vegetable oil

1 stick (1/2 cup) or more unsalted butter

2 tablespoons superfine sugar

To decorate: confectioners' sugar and ground cinnamon

To serve: little bowls of confectioners' sugar, ground cinnamon,
   and honey

Prepare the couscous as described in Preparing Couscous on page 112. Before serving, cut the butter into small pieces and work it and the superfine sugar into the hot couscous, fluffing up the grain with a fork and breaking up any lumps.

Shape the couscous into a cone in a round, flat dish. Dust the pointed top with confectioners' sugar and draw lines, fanning down the sides, with confectioners' sugar and cinnamon. Decorate further with one or two of the fruit and nut garnishes listed below.

Serve in bowls and pass around bowls of honey, sugar, and cinnamon and more of the fruit and nuts, for people to help themselves as they wish.

EXTRA GARNISHES TO CHOOSE FROM

Arrange dessert raisins such as Muscatels or Smyrna sultanas with blanched almonds (toasted or fried in a drop of oil until lightly golden), or dates and walnut halves, around the bottom of the cone or between the lines of confectioners' sugar and cinnamon. (The same nuts, coarsely chopped, and small raisins can be mixed with the couscous before it is shaped into a cone.) Sweet seedless grapes or shiny, pink pomegranate seeds are an alternative garnish to sprinkle over the mound of couscous.

FRUIT SALAD with HONEY and ORANGE BLOSSOM WATER
Slada Bil Fawakih

For this delicately scented fruit salad, have a mix of fruit chosen from three or four of the following: peaches, nectarines, apricots, bananas, plums, grapes, apples, pears, strawberries, mangoes, melon, pineapple, dates, pomegranate seeds.

SERVES 4

juice of 1 large orange
2 tablespoons honey
1 teaspoon orange blossom water
1 1/2 pounds mixed fruit
To garnish: a few mint leaves

Mix the orange juice, honey, and orange blossom water straight into a serving bowl. Wash or peel the fruits, core or remove pits, and drop the fruit in the bowl as you cut them up into pieces so that they do not have time to discolor.

Leave in a cool place for an hour or longer before serving. Garnish with the mint leaves.

ORANGE SALAD
Slada Bil Bortokal

This is the most common Moroccan dessert; it is always appealing and perfect to serve after a rich meal.

SERVES 4

6 large oranges
1 tablespoon orange blossom water
2 tablespoons confectioners' sugar (optional)
To decorate: 1 teaspoon ground cinnamon

Peel the oranges, taking care to remove all the white pith. Cut into slices, remove any pips, and arrange in circles on a serving plate. Sprinkle with orange blossom water and confectioners' sugar, if using.

Just before serving, decorate with lines of ground cinnamon.

◈ Sprinkle with $1/3$ cup walnuts, coarsely chopped, and 8 dates, coarsely chopped.

◆ Replace 3 of the oranges with blood oranges.

ALMOND PASTRIES in HONEY SYRUP
Briwat Bi Loz

These exquisite pastries called "the bride's fingers" feature in medieval Arab manuscripts found in Baghdad, fried and sprinkled with syrup and chopped pistachios. In Morocco, they are made with the thin pastry called warka or brick (see page 29) and deep-fried. I prefer to make them with fillo and to bake them. For a large-size version of the pastries, I use a supermarket brand where the sheets are about 12 inches × 7 inches.

I especially recommend you try the dainty little "bride's fingers" (see Variation). I make them for parties and I keep some in a cookie tin to serve with coffee. They are great favorites in our family; my mother always made them and now my children make them, too.

MAKES ABOUT 14 PASTRIES

$1/2$ pound clear honey
$1/2$ cup water
2 cups ground almonds
$1/2$ to $2/3$ cup superfine sugar
1 teaspoon ground cinnamon (optional)
2 tablespoons orange blossom water
14 sheets of fillo
5 tablespoons ($1/3$ cup) unsalted butter, melted

Make the syrup by bringing the honey and water to the boil in a pan and simmering it for half a minute. Then let it cool.

Mix the ground almonds with the sugar, cinnamon, and orange blossom water.

Open the package of fillo only when you are ready to make the pastries (see page 9). Keep them in a pile so that they do not dry out. Lightly brush the top one with melted butter.

Put a line of about 2 to $2\,1/2$ tablespoons of the almond mixture at one of the short ends of the rectangle, into a line about $3/4$ inch from the short and long edges. Roll up loosely into a fat cigar shape. Turn the ends in about one-third of the way along to trap

the filling, then continue to roll with the ends opened out. Continue with the remaining sheets of fillo.

Place the pastries on a baking sheet, brush them with melted butter, and bake them in an oven preheated to 300°F for 30 minutes, or until lightly golden and crisp.

Turn each pastry, while still warm, very quickly in the syrup and arrange on a dish. Serve cold with the remaining syrup poured all over.

VARIATIONS

◆ Instead of the honey syrup, make a sugar syrup by simmering 1 cup water with 2 cups sugar and 1 tablespoon lemon juice for about 5 to 8 minutes, until it is thick enough to coat the back of a spoon, adding 1 tablespoon orange blossom water toward the end.

◇ Instead of rolling the pastries in syrup, sprinkle them with confectioners' sugar. These keep very well for days in an airtight cookie tin.

◆ For the dainty little "bride's fingers," cut sheets of fillo into narrow strips—they can measure from 3 1/2 to 4 1/2 inches wide and be about 12 inches long. You can use larger sheets cut into 3 or 4 strips. Use 1 heaped tablespoon of the filling for each roll. It makes about 28.

WALNUT PASTRIES in HONEY SYRUP
Briwat Bi Joz

Follow the recipe for Almond Pastries in Honey Syrup (page 127) but use the following filling.

Coarsely grind 2 cups shelled walnuts in the food processor. Add 1/3 cup sugar and the finely grated zest of 1 unwaxed orange and mix well.

Add 1 1/2 tablespoons orange blossom water to the syrup.

DATE ROLLS *in* HONEY SYRUP
Briwat Bi Tamr

Follow the recipe for Almond Pastries in Honey Syrup (see page 127), but use the following filling.

    Use a moist variety of dates such as the Tunisian Deglet Nour or the Californian varieties. You will need about 1 1/3 pounds once they have been pitted. Blend them in the food processor, adding a little water, if necessary, by the tablespoon, to achieve a soft paste.

PASTRY CRESCENTS *with* ALMOND FILLING
Kaab El Ghzal

The most famous of Moroccan pastries are best known abroad by their French name, cornes de gazelle, or gazelle's horns. They are stuffed with ground almond paste and curved into horn-shaped crescents. They are ubiquitous wedding party fare.

MAKES 24 TO
26 CRESCENTS

FOR THE PASTRY

3 1/3 cups all-purpose flour
1/2 cup vegetable oil
2 eggs, lightly beaten
about 6 tablespoons fresh orange juice
confectioners' sugar

FOR THE FILLING

3 1/3 cups ground almonds
1 cup superfine sugar
1 egg plus 1 egg yolk, lightly beaten
grated zest of 1 unwaxed lemon or orange
2 to 3 drops of almond or vanilla essence

For the pastry, mix the flour with the oil and the eggs very thoroughly. Bind with just enough orange juice to hold it together, adding it by the tablespoon, then knead into a soft, malleable dough. Wrap the dough in plastic wrap and leave to rest for 30 minutes.

Mix all the filling ingredients together and work with your hands into a soft paste.

Divide the pastry dough into four for easy handling. Then roll it out into thin sheets on a clean surface (it does not need flouring because the dough is very oily and does not stick). Cut the sheets into 4-inch squares. Take a lump of almond paste and shape it into a thin, little sausage 3 1/2 inches long. Place it in the middle of a square, diagonally, on the bias, about 1/2 inch from the corners. Lift the dough up over the filling (a wide-bladed knife helps to lift the dough) and roll up, then very gently curve the roll into a crescent. Pinch the dough to seal the openings at the end. Repeat, making crescents with the remaining dough and filling.

Arrange the crescents on oiled trays. Bake them in an oven preheated to 325°F for 30 minutes. The crescents should not turn brown, but only just begin to color. When cool, dip them in plenty of confectioners' sugar so that they are entirely covered.

VARIATIONS

◇ Another way of making the crescents is to cut the pastry into rounds, place a line of filling on one half and fold the other half of the pastry over the filling to make a half-moon shape. Then pinch the edges together, trim some of the excess rounded edge, and curve the pastries slightly into crescents.

◆ Instead of dusting with confectioners' sugar, dip the pastries in warmed honey mixed with a drop of water to make it runnier (see page 127).

ALMOND "SNAKE"
M'hencha

This splendid Moroccan pastry filled with a ground almond paste is a very long coil, hence the name m'hencha, meaning snake. It is stunning to look at and exquisite to eat. In Morocco, it is made with the pastry called warka or brick (see page 29). This is available vacuum-packed and frozen in North African stores, but turns out tough if it is baked and not fried. It is better to use fillo pastry. I give very large quantities because it is the kind of thing to make for a great festive occasion, but of course you can make it smaller and reduce the quantities accordingly. The finished "snake" will be about 14 inches in diameter. If your oven is not large enough to take it, you can make two small ones. You need large fillo sheets measuring about 19 × 12 inches (and if the fillo is frozen, you will need to allow 3 hours for it to defrost, see page 9).

SERVES 30 TO 40

FOR THE FILLING
7 1/2 cups ground almonds
5 cups superfine sugar
2 tablespoons ground cinnamon
less than 1 cup orange blossom water
a few drops almond essence (optional)

FOR THE PASTRY
1 pound fillo pastry
2 sticks (1 cup) unsalted butter, melted
2 egg yolks for glazing
To decorate: confectioners' sugar, 1 tablespoon ground cinnamon

Mix all the filling ingredients together and work them into a stiff paste with your hands. Use just enough orange blossom water to bind the paste. Put in less than you seem to require, as once you start kneading with your hands, the oil from the almonds will act as an extra bind.

Take the sheets of fillo out of the package only when you are ready to use them and keep them in a pile (so they do not dry out) with one of the longer sides facing you. Lightly brush the top sheet with melted butter. Take lumps of the almond paste and roll into "fingers" about 3/4 inch thick. On the top sheet, place the "fingers" end to end in a line all along the long edge nearest to you, about 3/4 inch from the edge, to make one long rod of paste. Roll the sheet of fillo up over the filling into a long, thin roll, tucking the ends in to stop the filling from oozing out.

Lift up the roll carefully with both hands and place it in the middle of a sheet of foil on the largest possible baking sheet or oven tray. Very gently curve the roll into a tight coil. To do so without tearing the fillo, you have to crease the pastry first like an accordion by pushing the ends of the rolls gently toward the center with both hands.

Do the same with the other sheets until all the filling is used up, rolling them up with the filling inside, and placing one end to the open end of the coil, making it look like a coiled snake.

Brush the top of the pastry with the egg yolks mixed with 2 teaspoons of water and bake in an oven preheated to 325°F for 30 to 40 minutes, until crisp and lightly browned.

Let the pastry cool before you slide it, with its sheet of foil, onto a very large serving platter or tray.

Serve cold, sprinkled with plenty of confectioners' sugar and with lines of cinnamon drawn on like the spokes of a wheel. Cut the pastry as you would a cake, in wedges of varying size. It is very rich and some will want only a small piece.

VARIATION

For a pistachio *m'hencha*, use ground pistachios instead of almonds and rose water instead of orange blossom water. Although less common, this, too, is fabulous!

ALMOND MACAROONS

These are good to serve with coffee or tea.

MAKES ABOUT 20 MACAROONS

4 cups ground almonds
3/4 cup superfine sugar
grated zest of 1 unwaxed lemon
2 to 3 drops almond essence
1 large egg white
confectioners' sugar

Put all the ingredients except the confectioners' sugar in the food processor and blend into a soft, malleable paste.

Put some confectioners' sugar on a small plate. Rub your hands with oil so that the almond paste does not stick to your hands. Take lumps of the paste the size of a large walnut and roll into balls. Now press one side of each ball into the confectioners' sugar, flattening it a little, and place it on a buttered baking sheet, sugared side up. Bake in an oven preheated to 400°F for 15 minutes.

Let the macaroons cool before lifting them off the sheet. They will be lightly colored and crackled and soft inside.

DATES STUFFED *with* ALMOND *or* PISTACHIO PASTE
Tmar Bi Loz

In Morocco, this is the most popular sweetmeat. The almond stuffing is colored green to give the semblance of pistachios, which are considered more prestigious. Use slightly moist dates such as the Tunisian Deglet Nour or Californian varieties.

2 cups ground almonds or pistachios
1/2 cup superfine sugar
2 to 3 tablespoons rose water or orange blossom water
1 pound dates

Mix the ground almonds or pistachios with the sugar, and add just enough rose or orange blossom water to bind them into a firm paste. Put in less than you seem to require, since once you start kneading with your hands, the oil from the almonds will act as an extra bind. Alternatively, you can start with blanched almonds or pistachios and blend all the ingredients except the dates to a paste in the food processor.

Make a slit on one side of each date with a pointed knife and pull out the pit. Take a small lump of almond or pistachio paste, pull the date open wide, press the paste in the opening, and close the date over it only slightly so that the filling is revealed generously.

SUGARED ORANGE SLICES
Mrabbet Bortokal

These orange slices can be served with coffee or tea, or as an improvised sweet at the end of a meal, accompanied by crème fraîche or thick heavy cream. They keep for weeks in the refrigerator so you can bring them out on different occasions. Choose oranges with thick skins, which must be unwaxed.

10 SERVINGS   2 pounds unwaxed oranges
              2 cups sugar

Wash the oranges and cut them in thin slices, removing any pips.

Sprinkle the bottom of a large heavy-bottomed pan with a little of the sugar. Arrange some of the orange slices on top so that they overlap slightly and sprinkle generously with more sugar. Make layers of orange slices, each sprinkled with sugar and finishing with sugar.

Pour cold water over the slices so that they are only just covered. Cut a circle of foil or waxed paper and press it on top of the oranges to prevent evaporation. Cook over low heat for about 2 hours, until the orange slices are very soft and the white pith is translucent. The syrup should have the consistency of liquid honey when cool. Test a little on a plate. If it is too thick and sticky, add a little water and bring to the boil again.

MINT TEA

Pastries are served with mint tea. Spearmint is considered the best for tea, but other varieties can be used. In Morocco, they drink the tea very sweet with a large number of sugar lumps in the teapot, but you can suit your taste.

To make enough for 10 small glasses, you need a teapot that will hold 6 cups. Heat the pot first. Put in 1 1/2 tablespoons Chinese green tea such as Gunpowder tea, a large bunch of fresh spearmint, washed and patted dry, and lump sugar to your taste. Pour in boiling water and allow to infuse for about 5 minutes. Taste a little of the tea in a small glass, and add more sugar, if necessary.

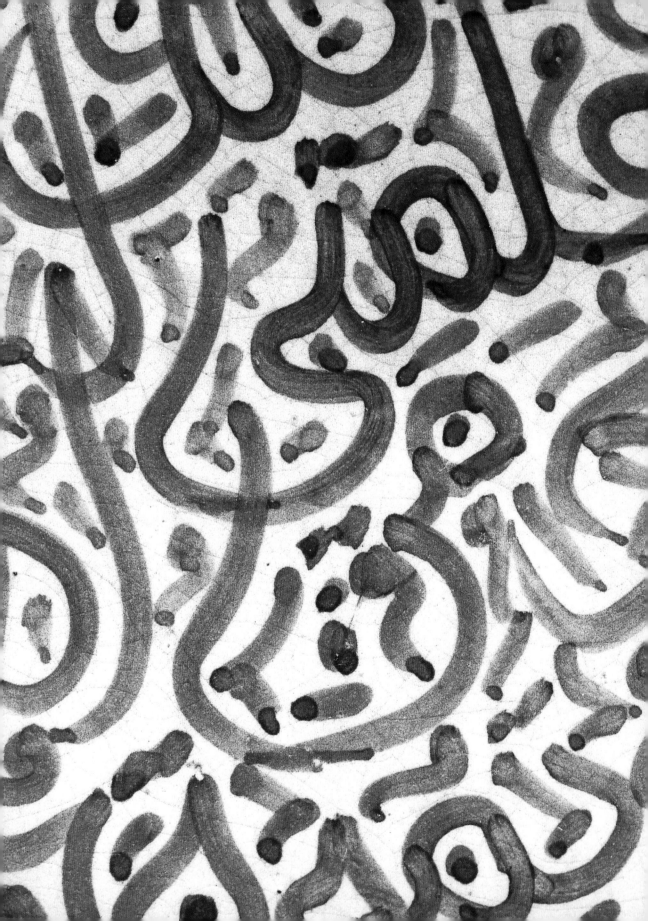

Turkey

A sophisticated, aristocratic cuisine developed in Constantinople—now Istanbul—when it was, for more than 400 years, the glittering capital city of the Ottoman Empire, which spread over most of the Middle East, the Balkans, and parts of North Africa, southern Russia, and the Caucasus. That cuisine came to be considered on a par with those of France and China. While many of the more elaborate dishes have disappeared, what you find in homes in Istanbul today and on the standard menus of Turkish restaurants are simplified adapted versions of that high style.

In Anatolia, which covers much of the landmass of modern Turkey, the cooking reflects the changing geography, climate, and local produce, as well as the diversity of cultures. Regional cuisines were hardly known outside their localities until the arrival, in the last couple of decades, of millions of migrants from rural and eastern Turkey into the big cities. (Istanbul had a population of less than 1 million in the census of 1950 and currently has more than 10 million people.) You can now find regional dishes in restaurants that have opened in the last fifteen years and you can catch a whiff of the cooking in the blocks of tall buildings that have mushroomed clandestinely around the city. That cooking is for the most part spicy, hot, and garlicky. It is not popular with the worldly "Stambouli" bourgeoisie who see themselves as Europeans with a taste for pure, mild, and delicate flavors. For them, the strongly flavored food represents the "Arab" and "Oriental" tastes of the provincials who have swamped their once cosmopolitan, sophisticated city and changed its image in a way they do not like. Istanbul, this dream of the Orient with her cupolas and minarets, hamams (old-style bathhouses), and bazaars, is torn between town and country, East and West, tradition and modernization, but remains attached to her past and her culinary memories and legacies.

Specialties of Istanbul—kebabs and pilafs, fillo pies, yogurt and cucumber salads, eggplant purées and stuffed vegetables, milk puddings, and nutty, syrupy pastries—are common in all the main cities of the countries that were part of the Ottoman Empire. When I lived in Egypt—it was the time of King Farouk and I was there for the revolution in 1953—the royal family was an Ottoman Albanian dynasty, and the aristocracy was Turkish, as was the haute cuisine. The country was annexed to the Ottoman Empire in 1517, and stayed under Turkish rule until 1805 when Mohammed Ali became its governor and established a dynasty that owed only nominal allegiance to the Sultan of Turkey. The food served in the Egyptian palaces was no different than that served to the Ottoman sultans, and the palace cooks were brought over from Constantinople. When Turkey became a republic in 1923, many members of the old Ottoman aristocracy moved to Egypt. In 1995, at the celebration launch of the Royal Club Mohamed-Aly in Cairo, the buffet was prepared by cooks from Istanbul. I have the menu—and most of the dishes listed on it are in this book.

The Story Behind the Cooking

The area that is Anatolia today was successively colonized by the Greeks and Persians and by Alexander the Great before it came under Roman rule. Emperor Constantine established the then Greek city of Byzantium as the new second capital of the Roman Empire in A.D. 330 and it was renamed Constantinople after him. When the empire split into eastern and western sections in A.D. 395, Constantinople became the capital of the Eastern Roman Empire.

The Turks came on the scene many centuries later. They were nomadic people from the steppe lands of Central Asia on the edge of China who migrated west with their flocks. They started to convert to Islam in the eighth century. As slave soldiers in the armies of the caliphs of Baghdad, they were formidable warriors who, by the eleventh century, came to form a number of small, local dynasties of their own in territories they captured from the Byzantines as well as in parts of the disintegrating Arab Empire. One of the most important dynasties, the Seljuks, seized Isfahan in Persia in 1051, and in the twelfth century established a sultanate, which controlled most of Anatolia from its capital, Konya.

Konya became a brilliant center of culture that attracted scholars, poets, artists, and mystics from all over the Islamic world. It was the home of the great Sufi mystic and poet Jalal al-Din Rumi, who was known as Mevlana (the Master). The highly sophisticated culture that developed, including cooking traditions, was influenced by Persia. By the thirteenth century, following the onslaught of Mongol invasion, the great Seljuk dynasty had ended, but their cultural influence continued by means of the establishment of principalities by lesser Seljuk clans throughout Anatolia. Part of their legacy is seen in the many traces of old Persian styles in the Turkish kitchen today, and in Konya in particular.

Another nomadic Turkish branch, the Osmanlis, or Ottomans, who were also warriors, captured Constantinople in 1453 and went on to establish the most powerful Muslim empire ever. The original Ottoman diet consisted mainly of the nomadic staples, yogurt and meat, and the pasta they adopted from the Chinese and Mongols whom they had been fighting for centuries. Shish kebabs are said to have originated on the battlefield when their invading armies camped outdoors in tents. The sultans came to place great importance on their kitchens. When Sultan Mehmet II conquered Constantinople in 1453 and made it his imperial capital, he built the Topkapi Palace with a giant, four-domed kitchen. A century later, Sultan Süleyman the Magnificent added a new kitchen building with six domes, and ten further sections were added by Sultan Selim II

in the sixteenth century. By the following century, on festive occasions, as many as 10,000 people, including the sultan, his harem and eunuchs, palace workers, *vizirs* (ministers), Janissary Corps, the military élite, members of the *divan* (cabinet), and foreign ambassadors and their retinues, were fed from the kitchens in which 1,370 cooks worked.

An extraordinary number and variety of dishes were developed in the court kitchens and the palaces of the aristocracy. Some originated in the cultures—Persian, Arab, Syrian—that had been absorbed into the Islamic world; some were adopted from the Byzantine Empire. Others arose as a result of the unique cosmopolitan character of the early empire and its ruling class whose members entered as the sultan's slaves and remained part of the Ottoman slave household. The profession of public slaves was all-important and glorious. Most were Christians, or the children of Christians, who were converted to Islam. Some were captured in battle or were bought in markets. Many were plucked from Caucasian highlands, from Russian forests and Eurasian steppe lands; others came from western Europe, including some given as gifts by Venetian traders. Some were sold by their parents; wrenched from all family ties and roots, they were expected to serve more loyally. The more able recruits became courtiers. The royal family, the sultan's wives, palace and government officers, *grand vizirs*, the standing army—all were household slaves or their descendants.

In this unique cosmopolitan society, where products arrived from the far corners of the empire and palace cooks learned their trade as slave page boys in the palace cooking school, a wide variety of foods of various origins entered the culinary pool. Cooking was considered one of the most important of the arts. Poets, physicians, and princes all wrote recipes, sang songs, and recited poems about food. The importance of food was especially evident in the Janissaries, the Imperial guard. They received their daily food rations directly from the palace, and their insignia, a pot and spoon, indicated a standard of living higher than that of other troops. The titles of the officers were drawn from the camp kitchen, from "First Maker of Soup" to "First Cook" and "First Carrier of Water," and the massive cauldron in which they cooked became an icon symbolizing their privileged relationship with the sultan. They overturned it to signal dissatisfaction and rebellion. This could happen, for instance, on payment day ceremonies at the palace.

The kitchen also had an important place in the communal life of the Turkish Sufi brotherhoods, the *tarikat*, which ran hospices and soup kitchens, and who were very influential. The *Mevlana* order of Whirling Dervishes in Konya, followers of the mystical philosopher and poet Jalal al-Din Rumi and his descendants, famously elevated food to a particularly high position. Rumi, whose interest in food is legendary, wrote poems celebrating food. He associated it with spirituality and equated cooking with man's path to spiritual knowledge. The order's kitchen served as a place of initiation and training. Many palace cooks were Sufis who cooked instinctively by feel and taste while at the same time observing a strict discipline and organization.

Until the early seventeenth century the palace table, or *sofra*, was characterized by the quantity and variety of dishes. European ambassadors and foreign visitors marveled at their number—up to 300, I have heard—that arrived one after the other at banquets in their honor. By the mid-nineteenth century, when Ottoman cuisine reached its pinnacle, foreign guests extolled its exquisiteness and refinement in their letters and diaries. It was a time of western influence when the Turkish *élites* became fascinated by French cuisine and assimilated French ways as well as the ingredients from the New World that had arrived in western Europe long before.

The Professional Cooks from Bolu

In the latter part of the empire, palace cooks were recruited in the *vilayet* (region) of Bolu near Lake Abant. According to legend, the nobles were so pleased with the young men who cooked their meat for them in the open after they had spent the day hunting in the mountain forests of the Black Sea region that they brought them back to the city. It soon became the tradition that all the young men from Bolu went to serve at the palace and in the homes of the nobility in Constantinople, leaving the women to till the fields and raise the children. At the age of twelve or thirteen, boys were sent to work in the kitchens near their fathers, uncles, and male cousins. They would go back to the village to marry, only to leave their wives and return to their kitchens. This is how the closed society of chefs that still exists today was formed.

In her family chronicle *Three Centuries* (1963), the Turkish writer Emine Foat Tugay wrote about that old generation of cooks who came from Bolu: "Turkish cooking of the past ranked among the great cuisines of the world. Much of it has disappeared together with the excellent chefs, who had learnt their trade as apprentices in *konaks* [grand old-style mansions] and palaces. . . . They gradually worked their way up under the master chef from scullery-boy or apprentice to become third, second, and finally first assistant cook. After ten or twelve years the chef would declare his first assistant capable of working on his own account. The old chefs almost always brought their complete

staffs with them when they were appointed and took them away with them when they left."

When Turkey became a modern, secular republic under President Mustafa Kemal Atatürk in 1923, the huge kitchen staff at the palace lost their jobs. The cooks who worked for the Turkish aristocracy that now moved to Egypt went with their employers. Others opened kebab houses and eateries, offering so-called *saray* (palace) cooking in Istanbul and other Turkish cities, while still others became makers of specialties such as pickles or puddings.

The Turkish Restaurant and Specialty Food Producers

The earliest Turkish word for restaurant, lokanta, comes from the Italian, meaning inn. Today, while a lokanta offers modest homely food in a cafeteria-style environment for workers and shoppers at lunchtime, a restoran is more upmarket and can be very grand. The oldest eating-and-drinking places are the meyhane, the old-style taverns or drinking houses of Istanbul situated near the markets in the old neighborhoods, which were once the preserve of Greek, Armenian, and Jewish minorities, such as Pera (now known as Beyoglu), Galata, Kumpkapi, and Balat. A large number opened in the mid-nineteenth century following a policy of westernization and modernization in the empire. They were formerly owned and run by Christians and some still are. When the secular state was founded, Muslims too were allowed to run them. Meyhanes offer large selections of meze—hot and cold appetizers or hors d'oeuvres—to accompany raki, the anise-flavored spirit, beer, and wine, while itinerant singers and musicians croon nostalgic love songs and play classic Turkish and Gypsy and arabesk music around the tables.

Meze are also a feature of the kebabcis that specialize in grilled meats, and of the fish restaurants along the Bosphorus that have recently become very popular. There is a whole parade of fish restaurants in Ortakoy, the former Jewish quarter in Istanbul where I found my grandmother Eugénie's old home. Many regional restaurants have opened in Istanbul in the last few years, while those in Gaziantep in the south of the country, which offer dishes similar to those from neighboring Syria, have been particularly appreciated. Recently, for the first time, a restaurant opened offering Kurdish specialties. I was taken there by Kurdish friends who could hardly contain their joy.

The high degree of specialization in the food trade is a legacy of the organization in the Ottoman palace kitchens where cooks were entrusted with one type of food only, such as soups, or kebabs, or jams. Now pideci specialize in lahmacun, a Turkish type of meat pizza; börekçi specialize in all kinds of pies; işkembeci are tripe soup eateries; muhallebicis offer a variety of milk puddings, and baklavaci sell baklavas and other pastries. There are also those who specialize in producing cured meats and sausages, cured fish, cheese, pickles, and jams to sell in the bazaars and streets. To protect their trade in the new republic, food makers formed craft guilds that are still important today. But because young men are now not so keen to work as hard as their fathers and are leaving the family businesses to work in other professions, the food trades are no longer jealously guarded and many outsiders have been allowed to join.

As I mentioned earlier, until a few decades ago most professional cooks came from Bolu and many still do, especially from the towns of Gerede and Mengen, where a catering school was opened in 1985. The prestige with which cooks are still regarded in Turkey today has never been equaled anywhere in the Middle East or North Africa. The strict hierarchy that reigns in restaurant kitchens, denoted by different shapes and sizes of cooks' hats, is also a legacy from palace days. And women still never enter a professional kitchen—unless they own the restaurant.

Since the late eighties, a new modern restaurant trade has developed with the growth of tourism. International hotel chains were the first to open grand restaurants offering local cuisine of a high standard. I was there when the Holiday Inn in Istanbul asked my friend, the food writer Nevin Halici, to teach their highly trained, local kitchen staff regional dishes in which they had previously had little interest.

In the early 1990s, a renaissance of "Ottoman Cuisine" began to take place. The first to give new life to the old dishes was the young chef Vedat Basaran, who introduced an Ottoman menu at the Tura Restaurant in the Çiragan Palace—the sumptuous palace in Istanbul where the sultans moved from Topkapi in the nineteenth century—renovated by the Kempinski Hotel chain. The idea was quickly copied by other hotel chains. Travel agents began offering "Ottoman gourmet tours"; companies sponsored the publication of illustrated, coffee-table books featuring translations of nineteenth-century recipes. Vedat Basaran next opened the Feriye Lokantasi in a renovated pavilion in the palatial precinct of the Çiragan Palace. His dishes are Ottoman in the broad sense: they include seventeenth-century recipes from countries that were part of the Ottoman Empire, such as Syria and Egypt, and are inspired by recipes from his huge collection of old cookery books and from manuscripts found in the palace archives. But he interprets them in a modern way. I think his food is exquisite—I experienced a magical evening there.

Istanbul

The Istanbul skyline with its domes and minarets, the call of the *muezzin*, the smells at the bazaar conjure up memories of my childhood in Egypt with a thrilling feeling of exaltation. The city also brings back my maternal grandmother Eugénie's stories of her life in that city. Recently I found hundreds of letters, written by her father, in an archive in Paris. My great-grandfather Joseph Alphandary was a headmaster at the Alliance Israelite Française, an organization that brought French education to Jewish children in Arab and Ottoman countries. He taught in schools in Salonica, Haifa, Tanta in Egypt, and in Istanbul where he was born. His beautifully written letters to the president of the organization in Paris are necessarily official yet also personal. Those from Istanbul bring the city's past alive for me in an incredibly vivid way. In a little synagogue near the mosque in Ortakoy by the Bosphorus, I found him in a group photograph. As I wandered around Istanbul, I very much felt his presence.

In the markets you are aware, by the way shoppers behave, that you are in a country where people love food. The labyrinthlike spice market with the vaulted roof is called *Misir Carsisi*, which means Egyptian Bazaar, because the spices once arrived via Egypt. Amid the carpet shops, jewelers, and leather-goods sellers, food vendors display their wares. Giant chunks of white cheese sit by piles of olives and cured fish. Lamb sausages hang over jumbled mountains of thinly sliced, spiced beef. Syrupy pastries filled with nuts are arranged beside creamy, white, milk puddings. Spice merchants, *baharatci*, sell every kind of aromatic as well as dried fruit and nuts, grains, and dried vegetables such as baby okra, little red chilies, and hollowed eggplants that look like leather bells.

Regional Cooking

In the late 1970s, I was invited by Gulsen Kahraman, then the director of the Turkish Tourist Office in London, to travel through Turkey. Having asked me where I wanted to go, who I wanted to meet, and what I wanted to see and eat, she arranged the most extraordinary trip. One of my stops was Konya, where the local Cultural Association ran the *Mevlana* festivals of Whirling Dervishes; troubadour, folk music, and poetry festivals; rose festivals; horse racing; racing pigeon and javelin throwing, and Koran-reading competitions. They also organized national food symposiums and cookery competitions for the surrounding villages, and I suggested to the Halici family, who was behind all these activities, that they should put on an international food event.

Enthusiastically, they asked for a list of people who might like to attend such an event, and the following year found many of us at their international congress. It was organized by Feyzi Halici, a poet and one-time senator, and his sister Nevin, who had made a study of Turkish regional cooking by going from village to village and knocking on doors. We traveled around the country with them and tasted all kinds of foods, some unknown even to the Turkish gastronomes traveling with us. We heard scholarly lectures ranging from the history of Turkish food to nutrition, visited palace kitchens and food bazaars, and went to see artisans at work. In one town, we visited a factory where the workers brought dishes they had cooked at home, producing a great banquet for us. We were invited into people's homes and one family cooked several lambs for us in a pit. We ate in their garden, sitting on cushions around low tables consisting of large trays set on small wooden trestles.

In Turkey, entertaining guests is a central part of social customs. Sharing food is a strict rule of almost religious importance; indeed, it is a command of the prophet. Sayings such as "Guests are the blessing of the house" and "Eat together since communal meals are blessed" attest to this. For outsiders like us, their hospitality was an overwhelming experience.

Biennial congresses followed until they stopped due to lack of funds. A good deal of what I know about Turkish food I owe to Nevin Halici, who has accompanied me on many research trips, and to one of her friends, the much-loved gastronome Tuğrul Şavkay who sadly died in 2003, far too young.

About Alcoholic Drinks

Alcoholic drinks are prohibited by Islam, but Turkey is a secular state and tolerant about alcoholic prohibition. *Raki*, a powerful spirit made from the distilled, fermented juice of white grapes flavored with aniseed, is the national drink for all but the very religious. It is drunk neat or with iced water, which turns it milky-white, with or without ice. It is produced by the state, as are many of the local wines. The government also encourages a privately owned, quality-wine trade. *Boza* is a rich, thick drink made from fermented millet. It is of ancient, nomadic origin and has a very distinctive flavor.

One of my most amusing and exciting memories of Turkey is the inaugural evening to celebrate the formation of the Turkish wine-lovers' branch of the Chevaliers du Tastevin. I happened to be in Istanbul and my friend the late Tuğrul Şavkay invited me to the ceremony and dinner. The venue was the grand ballroom of a yet to be opened five-star hotel. An enormous banqueting table was set in the middle of the empty ballroom. With Ottoman lavishness, course upon course of modern nouvelle cuisine–style Turkish delicacies were served, accompanied by a succession of local and foreign wines, while toasts were proposed in an atmosphere of convivial jollity. The scene was enchantingly fairylike, with an added cloak-and-dagger feel. The event had been secretly arranged to foil Islamic fundamentalists (there were whispers of a possible bomb). Velvet cloaks, hats, gold chains, and a great sword had been promised by the Chevaliers' Californian branch, which was renovating its wardrobes. The regalia arrived an hour late, which created some anxiety. In due course, however, the women were seated in rows to watch the "knighting by the sword" of their dressed-up men while classical music created an elevated feeling of ceremony. As each man knelt on a velvet cushion to be knighted, the women giggled helplessly.

About Tea, Coffee, and Other Beverages

Coffee made with pulverized grounds and sugar in a *cezve* (a small pot with a wide base, narrower neck, and long handle) and served in tiny cups has an important place in Turkish cultural identity. It is a symbol of hospitality and is highly esteemed, but in the last twenty-five years its consumption has waned in favor of tea, and it is reserved now for drinking after main meals and for special occasions.

Tea became the favored all-day beverage at a time of economic crisis because it was cheaper than coffee, and it has remained so. It is served in tulip-shaped glasses without milk and with lumps of sugar. Herbal infusions such as sage, thyme, mint, and melissa (lemon balm) as well as apple tea and cinnamon tea are also popular. *Salep* is a hot drink of milk thickened with the ground root of an orchid flavored with rose water and served with a sprinkling of cinnamon and ground pistachios. In winter it is sold by street vendors.

In summer, fresh fruit juices—in particular cherry, apricot, and orange—are fashionable. A wonderfully refreshing and very popular drink that is served at mealtimes is *ayran*: this is yogurt beaten with the same amount of water or soda water and just a touch of salt. In Islamic culture, water has symbolic importance. It is seen as a divine gift, a purifier, and saintly. Springwater is much appreciated: people pride themselves in recognizing where it comes from, and it is sometimes served with a slice of lemon or perfumed with rose petals.

Starters and Meze

In Turkey *meze*—hot and cold appetizers or hors d'oeuvres—are traditionally served with *raki* to counteract the effect of the strong spirit while delighting the palate. Palace cooks are said to have been familiar with at least two hundred different types. The *meyhanes*, the old-style taverns where women were rarely seen until recently, and the little fish restaurants by the sea, have made them a specialty. In the past, when families entertained at home, *meze* were served before the meal at a separate "raki table" where men alone gathered. Now, although *raki* is still considered a virile drink, women have joined the men at the *raki* table and enjoy the *meze* with them.

A well-chosen selection makes a great start to a meal but they should not fill you up. They should be light and tasty, varied and colorful. Serve them with pita bread (*pide* in Turkey) or with Turkish breads you find in Middle Eastern stores: there are crusty, white loaves; very large, spongy flat breads like the Italian *focaccia*; very thin ones called *lavas*; and bread rings covered with sesame seeds called *simit*.

The salads and vegetable dishes in this chapter can also be served to accompany main dishes. Also included are dishes, such as soups and pies, a cold pilaf, and pastas, which make good first courses in their own right as opposed to being part of a *meze*. In Turkey, meals at home often begin with soup, which is regarded as a symbol of happiness. Seasonal vegetables cooked in olive oil, served as a first course or on their own after the main meat dish, are an important feature of traditional home cooking.

Yogurt in Turkey is the best in the world—the one made with buffaloes' milk is sensational—and they use it lavishly in so many of their dishes that it is ubiquitous.

EGGPLANT PURÉE
Patlican Salatasi

The Turkish people claim to have a hundred ways of preparing eggplants. For them, it is the king and queen of vegetables. This is the classic purée that is also found in all the countries around the Mediterranean with a variety of different flavorings and trimmings. Serve it as a dip with bread or with crudités such as carrot, cucumber, and celery sticks.

SERVES 4

2 eggplants (weighing about 1¹/₂ pounds)
4 tablespoons extra virgin olive oil
juice of ¹/₂ lemon, or more to taste
salt

Prick the eggplants with a pointed knife to prevent them from bursting in the oven. Place them on a large piece of foil on a baking sheet and roast them in a hot oven preheated to 475°F for about 45 to 55 minutes, or until they feel very soft when you press them and the skins are wrinkled. When cool enough to handle, peel and drop them into a strainer or colander with small holes. Press out as much of the water and juices as possible. Still in the colander, chop the flesh with a pointed knife, then mash it with a fork or wooden spoon, letting the juices escape through the holes.

Transfer the purée to a serving bowl and beat in the oil and lemon juice and a little salt.

VARIATIONS

◈ For a spicy Moroccan version, add 1 crushed garlic clove, a pinch of cayenne, ¹/₂ teaspoon paprika, ¹/₂ teaspoon ground cumin, and 1 tablespoon chopped cilantro leaves.

◈ For a Lebanese version, mix in 1 to 2 tablespoons of pomegranate molasses (see page 7), plus 2 crushed garlic cloves and 3 tablespoons chopped flat-leaf parsley.

EGGPLANT PURÉE *with* YOGURT
Yoğurtlu Patlican Salatasi

Yogurt softens the flavors and adds to the creamy texture of this refreshing purée.

SERVES 6 TO 8

2 or 3 eggplants (weighing about 1½ pounds)
juice of ½ to 1 lemon
2 tablespoons extra virgin olive oil
1 cup strained Greek-style yogurt
2 to 3 garlic cloves, crushed (optional)
salt
To garnish: 1 to 2 tablespoons finely chopped flat-leaf parsley or mint (optional)

Prick the eggplants with a pointed knife to prevent them from bursting in the oven. Place them on a large piece of foil on a baking sheet and roast them in a hot oven preheated to 475°F for about 45 to 55 minutes, or until they feel very soft when you press them and the skins are wrinkled. When cool enough to handle, peel and drop them into a strainer or colander with small holes. Press out as much of the water and juices as possible. Still in the colander, chop the flesh with a pointed knife, then mash it with a fork or wooden spoon, letting the juices escape through the holes.

Beat in the lemon juice, olive oil, yogurt, garlic, if using, and a little salt. Serve garnished, if you like, with parsley or mint.

TARAMA

Gray mullet roe was originally used in Turkey for this famous dip (also known under the Greek name taramasalata) but smoked cod's roe has now generally replaced it. This is a world away from what you can buy ready-prepared and is really worth making. Serve it with Turkish or pita bread.

SERVES 6 TO 8   1 slice of white bread, crusts removed

7 ounces smoked cod's roe

juice of 1 lemon

3 tablespoons sunflower oil

2 tablespoons extra virgin olive oil

Soak the bread in water. Skin the smoked cod's roe and blend in the food processor. Add the bread, squeezed dry, the lemon juice, sunflower oil, and olive oil and blend to a creamy consistency that should still be a little rough, adding 1 or 2 tablespoons of water, if necessary.

CUCUMBER and YOGURT SALAD
Cacik

This salad is popular throughout the Middle East. Unless it is to be eaten as soon as it is made, it is best to salt the cucumber and let the juices drain before mixing with the yogurt; otherwise it gets very watery. If possible, use the small cucumbers sold in Middle Eastern and Asian stores—they have a finer flavor than the large ones. Cacik is served as part of a meze and also as a side dish—to be eaten with spoons from little individual side bowls—to accompany pies, meat dishes, and rice. It even makes a lovely cold summer soup. Use plain whole-milk yogurt.

SERVES 4 TO 6   4 small cucumbers or 1 large one

salt

2 cups plain whole-milk yogurt

2 garlic cloves, crushed (optional)

2 sprigs of finely chopped mint or dill, or 2 teaspoons dried,
    crushed mint

Peel and dice or grate the cucumbers, or cut them in half lengthwise, and then into half-moon slices. Unless the salad is to be served immediately, sprinkle with salt and leave for 1/2 to 1 hour in a colander for the juices to drain.

Beat the yogurt in a serving bowl with the crushed garlic, if using, and the mint or dill, and fold in the cucumber. Add a little salt, taking into account the saltiness of the cucumber if you have salted it, although most of the salt will have gone with the drained juices.

EGGPLANT SLICES *with* WALNUTS *and* GARLIC
Cevizli Patlican

This strongly flavored version of a very common meze originates in Georgia, where walnut trees abound. There is plenty of garlic, but it is not overpowering because it is fried. The eggplant slices can be deep-fried, but I prefer them roasted in the oven. They should be served cold, and they can be made in advance.

SERVES 6

2 pounds eggplants
extra virgin olive oil
2 to 3 tablespoons wine vinegar
salt
6 to 7 garlic cloves, crushed
1/3 cup walnuts
handful of chopped flat-leaf parsley

Wash the eggplants and cut them lengthwise into slices a little more than a quarter of an inch thick. Place them on a well-oiled piece of foil on an oven tray and brush them with olive oil on both sides. Cook in an oven preheated to 475°F for about 20 minutes, or until lightly browned and soft, turning them over once.

Arrange them on flat serving plates, then brush with vinegar and sprinkle lightly with salt.

Soften the garlic in 1 tablespoon of olive oil over medium heat until the aroma rises, but do not let it color. Finely chop the walnuts in a food processor and mix with the chopped parsley in a bowl. Add the garlic with another tablespoon of olive oil and a sprinkling of salt, mix well, and spread this paste on the eggplant slices.

PEPPERY BULGUR SALAD
Kisir

Kisir is a salad from Gaziantep. You need the fine-ground (not medium) bulgur, which you can find in Middle Eastern stores. The chili pepper gives it a thrilling zing but you can leave it out. Serve the salad with little lettuce leaves that can be used as scoops.

SERVES 6

1 cup fine bulgur
1/2 cup boiling water
1 tablespoon tomato paste
juice of 1 1/2 lemons
5 tablespoons extra virgin olive oil
1/2 to 1 fresh red or green chili pepper, finely chopped
salt
5 to 7 scallions
3 tomatoes (about 11 ounces), diced
1/4 cup chopped flat-leaf parsley
2 tablespoons chopped mint leaves
To serve: 2 Little Gem (baby romaine) lettuces

Put the bulgur into a bowl, pour the boiling water over it, stir, and leave for 15 to 20 minutes, until the grain is tender. Don't be tempted to add more water since the juice from the lemons and tomatoes will soften it further.

Add the tomato paste, lemon juice, olive oil, chili pepper, and some salt and mix thoroughly. Trim the green tops off the scallions, then slice them finely. Add them and the diced tomatoes to the bulgur mixture, together with the parsley and mint and mix well.

Serve with the small lettuce leaves stuck around the edges of the salad. Another way is to roll the bulgur mixture into oval balls the size of a small egg and to place each one in the hollow of a lettuce leaf.

VARIATION
Add 1 to 2 tablespoons of pomegranate molasses (see page 7) to the dressing. This gives the grain a sweet-and-sour flavor.

LEEKS with EGG and LEMON SAUCE
Terbiyeli Pirasa

An egg and lemon sauce is one of Turkey's culinary signature tunes. A touch of sugar gives it a slight sweet-and-sour taste. I like making this dish, which can be served hot or cold, with baby leeks, but larger ones can be used instead.

SERVES 4 TO 6
1 1/4 pounds baby leeks
salt
2 egg yolks
juice of 1 1/2 lemons
1 teaspoon sugar

Wash the leeks in running water, making sure you remove any dirt trapped between the leaves. Trim the root ends and the tough tops of the green leaves.

Boil the leeks in salted water until tender, then drain, reserving 1 cup of the cooking water. Pour this cooking water back into the pan and bring to the boil.

In a small bowl, beat the egg yolks and lemon juice with the sugar. Pour in a little of the hot cooking water and beat well, then pour the egg and lemon mixture into the pan, beating vigorously, for seconds only until the sauce thickens slightly. Be careful not to let it boil or it will curdle. Add a little salt, if necessary, to taste.

Serve the leeks hot or cold with the sauce poured over.

CELERIAC with EGG and LEMON SAUCE
Terbiyeli Kereviz

Celeriac is a popular winter vegetable in Turkey. The creamy, gently sweet-and-sour sauce enhances its delicate flavor. It is as good cold as it is hot.

SERVES 4
1 celeriac (weighing about 2 pounds)
juice of 1 lemon
salt
1 teaspoon sugar
2 egg yolks

Cut away the knobbly skin of the celeriac and cut the flesh into 3/4-inch cubes. (It is a very hard root and you will need to use a big strong knife and quite a bit of force.)

Put the celeriac cubes in a pan and barely cover with water. Add the juice of 1/2 lemon, some salt, and the sugar, and simmer, covered, for 15 to 20 minutes, or until just tender.

Just before serving, beat the egg yolks with the remaining lemon juice in a little bowl. Beat in 2 to 3 tablespoons of the cooking water, then pour the egg and lemon mixture into the pan, stirring vigorously. Heat through, stirring constantly, but do not let it boil or the egg will curdle.

Serve hot or cold with the sauce poured on top.

ROASTED EGGPLANTS and BELL PEPPERS with YOGURT and PINE NUTS

This is one of my favorites. It makes a good first course as well as a vegetarian main dish. The vegetables can be served hot or cold and the yogurt should be at room temperature. I mix the two kinds of yogurt—plain whole-milk and strained Greek-style yogurt—to get a thick creamy texture that still pours well.

SERVES 6

4 small eggplants (about 2 pounds)
3 large red bell peppers
1 tablespoon lemon juice
4 tablespoons extra virgin olive oil
salt and black pepper
1/2 cup plain whole-milk yogurt
1/2 cup strained Greek-style yogurt
2 garlic cloves, crushed
1/4 cup pine nuts

Prick the eggplants with a pointed knife to prevent them exploding in the oven. Place them and the peppers on a large piece of foil on a baking sheet and roast in an oven preheated to 425°F for about 45 to 60 minutes, until the eggplants feel soft when you press them. Turn the peppers one half turn after 25 minutes and take them out before the eggplants when they are soft and their skins are blackened in places.

As the peppers come out of the oven, drop them in a strong plastic bag and twist to seal it closed. When cool enough to handle, peel them, remove and discard the stems and seeds, and cut them in half or in 4 lengthwise.

When they are cool enough to handle, peel the eggplants and drop into a colander. Press the flesh gently to let the juices run out. Cut each into 4 pieces and turn them in a little lemon juice to prevent them from discoloring.

Put the eggplants and peppers on one side of a shallow serving plate. Dress with 3 tablespoons olive oil, salt, and pepper and mix gently. Mix the two types of yogurt together, beat in the garlic and some salt, and pour onto the other side of the plate.

Just before serving, fry the pine nuts in the remaining oil, stirring, until very lightly browned, and sprinkle over the yogurt. Pass the dish round for people to help themselves.

ROASTED VEGETABLES *with* YOGURT *and* FRESH TOMATO SAUCE

A very traditional meze is fried eggplants served with yogurt and tomato sauce. I like to do the same with a mix of roasted vegetables, and I serve them either hot or cold. It is the kind of thing you can do easily in large quantities for a party. It can be done a day in advance, cooking the vegetables in batches, if necessary, and reheating them, if you wish, on the day. The yogurt should be at room temperature. The tomato sauce has a sweet-and-sour flavor and is served cold.

SERVES 6

2 medium eggplants
3 fleshy red or green bell peppers
3 fat zucchini
4 medium red or white onions
extra virgin olive oil
salt
2 cups plain whole-milk yogurt
2 teaspoons dried mint
1 to 2 garlic cloves, crushed (optional)

FOR THE TOMATO SAUCE
3 garlic cloves, chopped
1 to 2 tablespoons extra virgin olive oil
1 1/2 pounds tomatoes, peeled and chopped
1 tablespoon sugar
salt
good pinch of ground chili pepper or flakes
2 tablespoons wine vinegar

Cut the eggplants in half lengthwise and then into 1/2-inch-thick slices. Cut the peppers in half through the stem end, remove the seeds, and cut them in half again, lengthwise. Cut the zucchini into 1/2-inch slices crosswise. Cut the onions into quarters.

Each type of vegetable should be placed on separate pieces of foil on baking trays since they take different times to cook. Sprinkle the vegetable pieces generously with olive oil and with a little salt and turn them around with your hand so that they are lightly oiled all over.

Roast them in your hottest preheated oven for about 25 minutes, or until the vegetables are tender and lightly browned, taking each type of vegetable out as they are done.

Serve the roasted vegetables hot or cold. They should be placed on a large serving dish and passed around with a bowl of yogurt into which you have beaten a little salt, dried mint, and, if you like, crushed garlic, and a bowl of the following tomato sauce.

Heat the chopped garlic in the oil for a few seconds only, stirring, until the aroma rises. Add the tomatoes, sugar, salt, and chili pepper and cook, stirring occasionally, for about 20 minutes, until reduced and thick. Add the vinegar toward the end.

ZUCCHINI FRITTERS
Kabak Mücveri

Fried onions, feta cheese, and herbs lift what is otherwise a bland vegetable. These little fritters can be served hot or cold. They can be made in advance and reheated.

SERVES 4

1 large onion, coarsely chopped

3 tablespoons vegetable or sunflower oil, plus more for frying

1 pound zucchini, finely chopped

3 eggs

3 tablespoons all-purpose flour

black pepper

2 to 3 sprigs of mint, chopped

2 to 3 sprigs of dill, chopped

7 ounces feta cheese, mashed with a fork

Fry the onion in 3 tablespoons oil over medium heat until it is soft and lightly colored. Add the zucchini and sauté, stirring, until they, too, are soft.

In a bowl, beat the eggs with the flour until well blended. Add pepper (there is no need of salt because the feta cheese is very salty) and the chopped herbs, and mix well. Fold the mashed feta into the eggs, together with the cooked onions and zucchini.

Film the bottom of a preferably nonstick frying pan with oil and pour in the mixture by the half ladle (or 2 tablespoons) to make a few fritters at a time. Turn each over once, and cook until both sides are browned a little. Drain on paper towels.

BEETS with YOGURT
Pancar Salatasi

Beets may be boiled or roasted, but I think roasting, which takes much longer, gives them a deliciously intense flavor. It is best to buy small ones because they take less time to cook. Or, of course, you can buy them already cooked.

SERVES 6 TO 8
- 2 pounds beets
- 2 garlic cloves, crushed (optional)
- 2 cups strained Greek-style yogurt
- 2 tablespoons lemon juice
- 6 tablespoons extra virgin olive oil
- salt
- handful of chopped mint or flat-leaf parsley

Cut the stems and leaves about 3/4 of an inch above the beets. To boil them, cook them in plenty of boiling salted water until tender—small ones will take about 30 minutes, larger ones about 1 1/2 hours. To roast them, put them on a sheet of foil on a baking sheet, cover them with foil, and roast in the oven at 400°F for 2 to 3 hours, depending on their size, until one feels tender when you cut right through with a pointed knife. You could cut them in half (lay them cut side down) and reduce the cooking time considerably.

When cool enough to handle, peel and cut the beets into less than 1/2-inch-thick rounds or half-moon slices. Wear rubber gloves to avoid staining your hands.

Beat the crushed garlic, if using, into the yogurt and spread the mixture on a serving plate. Arrange the beet slices on top. Beat the lemon juice with the oil and a little salt, stir in the chopped mint or parsley, and spoon over the beet slices.

VARIATION

A Lebanese version uses 1 1/2 tablespoons *tahina* (see page 7) beaten into the yogurt. This, too, is delicious.

MASHED POTATOES *with* OLIVE OIL, SCALLIONS, *and* PARSLEY
Patates Salatasi

This is as good hot as it is cold and can be served as part of a meze or as a side dish.

SERVES 6

1 1/2 pounds baking potatoes
6 tablespoons extra virgin olive oil
salt and pepper
about 6 scallions, chopped
handful of chopped flat-leaf parsley

Peel and boil the potatoes in salted water until soft. Drain, keeping about 1/2 cup of the cooking water.

Mash the potatoes and beat in the olive oil. Add salt and pepper to taste and a little of the cooking water—enough to make a soft, slightly moist texture. Then stir in the scallions and the chopped parsley.

EGGPLANTS STUFFED *with* ONIONS *and* TOMATOES
Imam Bayildy

Imam Bayildi is one of the most famous Turkish dishes. Conflicting stories are told about the origin of its name, which means "the Imam fainted." Some say it came about when an Imam (Muslim priest) fainted with pleasure when it was served to him by his wife. Others believe that the Imam fainted when he heard how much of his expensive olive oil had gone into its making. It is best cooked in a saucepan, but you may find it easier in the oven. Serve it cold.

Small, elongated eggplants—at most 5 1/2 inches long, each weighing about 4 to 4 1/2 ounces—are best for this dish. You will find them in Asian and Middle Eastern stores.

FOR THE FILLING

1 1/2 large onions, sliced thinly

2 to 3 tablespoons extra virgin olive oil

5 garlic cloves, chopped

4 tomatoes, peeled and chopped

3 tablespoons chopped flat-leaf parsley

salt

6 small eggplants (see above)

1 cup good-quality tomato juice

1 teaspoon sugar, or more to taste

salt

juice of 1 lemon

2/3 cup extra virgin olive oil

Make the filling first. Soften the sliced onions gently in the oil, but do not let them color. Add the chopped garlic and stir for a moment or two until the aroma rises. Remove the pan from the heat and stir in the tomatoes and the chopped parsley. Season to taste with salt, and mix well.

Trim the caps from the ends of the eggplants (you may leave the stalks on). Peel off 1/3-inch-wide strips of skin lengthwise, leaving alternate strips of peel and bare flesh. Make a deep cut on one side of each eggplant lengthwise, from one end to the other, but not right through, in order to make a pocket.

Stuff the pocket of each eggplant with the filling and place them tightly side by side, with the opening face up, in a wide shallow pan. Mix the tomato juice with a little sugar, salt, and the lemon juice and pour this and the oil over the eggplants. Cover the pan and simmer gently for about 45 minutes, or until the eggplants are soft and the liquid much reduced.

Alternatively, you can cook the stuffed eggplants in the oven. Arrange them, cut side up, in a baking dish, with the rest of the ingredients poured over. Cover with foil and cook in the oven preheated to 400°F for 1 hour, or until soft. Allow to cool before arranging on a serving dish.

EGGPLANT PILAF
Patlicanli Pilav

This is a cold pilaf to serve as a first course. It has an exciting combination of ingredients and flavors, while a mix of cinnamon and allspice lend a beautiful light brown color.

SERVES 4

1 pound eggplants

salt

about 1/3 cup extra virgin olive oil

1 medium onion, chopped

3 tablespoons pine nuts

1 cup long-grain rice

2 medium tomatoes, peeled and chopped

1 1/2 teaspoons sugar

2 tablespoons currants or small black raisins

salt and black pepper

1 teaspoon ground cinnamon

1/2 teaspoon ground allspice

4 tablespoons chopped dill

Peel the eggplants and cut them into 1-inch cubes. Place them on a sheet of foil on a baking tray. Sprinkle with salt and pour over enough olive oil so that when the eggplant pieces are turned, they are well covered with oil. Preheat the oven to its highest temperature, and bake the eggplants for 25 minutes, or until they are soft and lightly browned.

Fry the onion in 2 tablespoons olive oil until it is soft and golden. Add the pine nuts and when they begin to color, add the rice and stir until it is well coated with oil. Add the tomatoes and the sugar and simmer for 5 minutes.

Add the currants or raisins and 1 1/2 cups water. Season with salt, pepper, cinnamon, and allspice and stir gently. Cook, covered, over a low heat until the liquid is absorbed and the rice is tender. It can take up to 20 minutes. (Some brands that claim not to be parboiled or precooked now take as little as 8 to 10 minutes, so read the information on the package.) Remove the lid toward the end if it is too moist.

Stir in 4 to 5 tablespoons olive oil and the chopped dill. Very gently fold in the eggplants and serve cold.

GRAPE LEAVES STUFFED with RICE, RAISINS, and PINE NUTS
Zeytinyağli Yaprak Dolmasi

Stuffed grape leaves were served at the court of King Khusrow II in Persia in the early seventh century. Their popularity spread through the Muslim world when the caliphs of Baghdad adopted Persian cooking traditions, while the Ottomans introduced them throughout their empire. There are numerous versions of this delicacy today, which is popular in every country throughout the Middle East. The following, with raisins and pine nuts, is a Turkish version. It is served cold.

Short-grain or risotto rice is used because the grains stick together. Grape leaves can be bought preserved in brine and vacuum-packed, but if you can get hold of young fresh tender ones, do use them. They freeze well raw, wrapped in foil.

SERVES 8 OR MORE

1/2 pound grape leaves
2 large onions, finely chopped
2/3 cup extra virgin olive oil
2 tablespoons pine nuts
1 1/2 teaspoons tomato paste
1 cup short-grain or risotto rice
2 tablespoons currants or tiny black raisins
salt and black pepper
1 teaspoon ground allspice
2 to 3 tablespoons chopped mint
2 to 3 tablespoons chopped dill
2 tomatoes, sliced
1 teaspoon sugar
juice of 1 lemon, or to taste

If using grape leaves preserved in brine, remove the salt by putting them in a bowl and pouring boiling water over them. Make sure that the water penetrates well between the layers. Leave them to soak for 20 minutes, then rinse in fresh, cold water and drain. If using fresh leaves, plunge a few at a time in boiling water for a couple of seconds only, until they become limp, then lift them out. Cut off and discard the stalks.

For the filling, fry the onions in 3 tablespoons of the oil until soft. Add the pine nuts and stir until they are golden. Stir in the tomato paste, then add all the rest of the ingredients down to and including the chopped dill. Mix well.

On a plate, place the first leaf, vein side up, with the stem end facing you. Put one heaped teaspoonful of filling in the center of the leaf near the stem end. Fold that end up over the filling, then fold both sides toward the middle and roll up like a small cigar. Squeeze the filled roll lightly in the palm of your hand. Fill the rest of the leaves in the same way. This process will become very easy after you have rolled a few.

Line the bottom of a large, heavy-bottomed pan with tomato slices and any left-over, torn, or imperfect grape leaves, then pack the stuffed grape leaves tightly on top.

Mix the remaining olive oil with 2/3 cup water, add the sugar and lemon juice, and pour over the stuffed leaves. Put a small plate on top of the leaves to prevent them from unrolling, cover the pan, and simmer very gently for about 1 hour, until the rolls are thoroughly cooked, adding more water occasionally, a small coffee cupful at a time, as the liquid in the pan becomes absorbed. Let the stuffed grape leaves cool in the pan before turning them out.

BELL PEPPERS STUFFED
with RICE, RAISINS, *and* PINE NUTS
Zeytinyağli Biber Dolmasi

This is the classic Turkish rice filling for vegetables to be served cold. Choose plump bell peppers that can stand on their base. I prefer to use red peppers because they are sweeter and for the color, but in Turkey green ones are more often used.

SERVES 6

1 large onion, finely chopped
6 tablespoons extra virgin olive oil
1 1/4 cups short-grain or risotto rice
salt and pepper
1 to 2 teaspoons sugar
3 tablespoons pine nuts
3 tablespoons currants or tiny black raisins
1 large tomato, peeled and chopped
1 teaspoon ground cinnamon
1/2 teaspoon ground allspice
2 tablespoons chopped mint
2 tablespoons chopped dill

2 tablespoons chopped flat-leaf parsley

juice of 1 lemon

6 medium green or red bell peppers

To serve: 1 cup plain whole-milk yogurt mixed with 1 garlic clove,
crushed (optional)

For the filling, fry the onion in 3 tablespoons oil until soft. Add the rice and stir until thoroughly coated and translucent. Pour in 2 cups water and add salt, pepper, and sugar. Stir well and cook for 15 minutes, or until the water has been absorbed but the rice is still a little underdone. Stir in the pine nuts, currants or raisins, tomato, cinnamon, allspice, mint, dill, parsley, and lemon juice, as well as the rest of the oil.

Retaining the stalk, cut a circle around the stalk end of the peppers and set to one side to use as caps. Remove the cores and seeds with a spoon and discard. Fill the peppers with the rice mixture, and replace the caps.

Arrange the peppers side by side in a shallow baking dish, pour about 1/2 inch water into the bottom, and bake in the oven preheated to 375°F for 45 to 55 minutes, or until the peppers are tender. Be careful that they do not fall apart.

Serve cold, accompanied, if you like, by a bowl of yogurt beaten with or without crushed garlic.

TOMATOES STUFFED with RICE, RAISINS, and PINE NUTS
Zeytinyağli Domates Dolmasi

Use the same filling as above for 6 firm, large tomatoes (beefsteak tomatoes are best) or 12 medium ones. Cut a small circle around the stem end and cut out a cap from each tomato. Remove and discard the center and seeds with a pointed teaspoon. Fill with the rice stuffing given in Bell Peppers Stuffed with Rice, Raisins, and Pine Nuts above and replace the caps.

Arrange the tomatoes in a shallow baking dish and bake in an oven preheated to 350°F for 20 to 30 minutes, until the tomatoes are soft. Watch them carefully, and remove them if they start to fall apart.

Serve cold, accompanied by yogurt flavored, if you like, with the crushed garlic.

ARTICHOKES STEWED in OIL
with PEAS and CARROTS
Zeytinyağli Enginar

This classic Turkish combination is gently flavored with dill, lemon, garlic, and a tiny bit of sugar. It looks wonderful on the serving dish.

I use the frozen artichoke bottoms from Egypt, which I get in Middle Eastern stores, and fresh young peas that I am lucky enough to find already podded from my supermarket; however, frozen petits pois will do very well. If you want to use fresh artichokes, see page 8 on how to prepare them.

SERVES 6

1/2 pound carrots, peeled and diced
2 garlic cloves, chopped
4 tablespoons extra virgin olive oil
one 14-ounce package artichoke bottoms, defrosted
salt and pepper
7 ounces young peas (shelled weight) or frozen *petit pois*, defrosted
juice of 1 lemon, or to taste
1 teaspoon sugar
3 tablespoons chopped dill

Put the diced carrots in a pan wide enough, if possible, to hold the artichoke bottoms in one layer. Add the chopped garlic, 3 tablespoons oil, and about 1 3/4 cups cold water. Bring to the boil and simmer for 5 minutes.

Put in the artichoke bottoms, season with salt and pepper, and simmer for 7 to 10 minutes, until they are just tender, turning them over once. Then add the peas, lemon juice, sugar, and dill, and cook 2 to 5 minutes more (less if they are the tiny *petits pois*), or until the peas are cooked.

Place the artichoke bottoms on a serving plate, and spoon some of the carrots and peas into each. Pour the remaining reduced sauce around them. Serve cold with a drizzle of the remaining olive oil over the top.

VARIATIONS

⊚ Instead of peas use fava beans. Although it depends on how young they are, they usually need cooking a little longer, so put them in at the same time as the artichokes.

⊚ To add body to the sauce, put a diced potato in 5 minutes before the carrots. It will fall apart by the end of the cooking and thicken the sauce.

BAKED PASTA with CHEESE
Peynirli Erişte

A pasta like tagliatelle called erişte is a traditional Turkish food that is still made by hand in rural areas. This recipe, with feta cheese, eggs, and milk is easy-to-make comfort food. It can be served as a first or main course and can be made in advance and heated through before serving.

SERVES 4

2 1/4 cups milk

4 eggs

7 ounces feta cheese, mashed with a fork

salt

10 ounces dry tagliatelle nests

Bring the milk to the boil. Lightly beat the eggs in a bowl, then beat in the milk. Add the mashed feta to the milk and eggs with some salt (it still needs some despite the saltiness of the cheese).

Crush the tagliatelle nests into small pieces with your hands. Throw them into plenty of boiling, salted water and cook until done al dente, about 5 to 8 minutes. Drain and turn into a greased baking dish. Pour the milk, egg, and cheese mixture over the pasta and mix well.

Bake in an oven preheated to 350°F for 45 to 60 minutes, until the creamy mixture has set.

VARIATION

Another, quicker dish is the same pasta tossed with melted butter and topped with plenty of crumbled feta cheese, and a generous amount of chopped flat-leaf parsley.

LITTLE CHEESE FILLO ROLLS
Peynirli Sigara Böreği

These dainty little rolls, or "cigars," make ideal appetizers and canapés. The cheese used is beyaz peynir, or "white cheese," which is salty and much like feta cheese. Use large sheets of fillo measuring about 19 inches × 12 inches, cut into strips, but if the fillo sheets are too thin, the pastry is liable to tear and the filling to burst out during the cooking. In that case, use 2 strips together, brushing with butter in between. You will then need to double the number of sheets. I prefer using only one strip if possible, as it makes for a lighter pastry. (See page 9 for information about fillo.) Serve the rolls hot. They can be made in advance and reheated.

MAKES
16 ROLLS

7 ounces feta cheese, mashed with a fork
1 egg, lightly beaten
3 tablespoons chopped mint or dill
8 large sheets of fillo
1 stick (8 tablespoons) butter, melted

For the filling, mix the mashed feta with the egg and chopped mint or dill.

Take out the sheets of fillo only when you are ready to use them since they dry out quickly. Cut them into 4 rectangles measuring about 12 inches × 4 1/2 to 5 inches and put them in a pile on top of each other. Brush the top strip lightly with melted butter. Take a tablespoon of filling. Place it at one short end of the strip in a thin sausage shape along the edge, about 3/4 inch from it and 3/4 inch from the side edges. Roll up the fillo with the filling inside, like a cigar. Fold in the ends about one-third of the way along to trap the filling, and then continue to roll.

Do the same with the remaining strips of fillo and cheese filling. Place the cigars, seam side down, on a baking sheet and brush the tops with melted butter. Bake at 300°F for 30 minutes, or until crisp and golden.

LAYERED CHEESE PIE
Peynirli Börek

This pie, made with fillo pastry, can be served hot as a first course, a tea-time savory, or as a snack. Milk sprinkled between the sheets gives it a lovely soft, moist texture. The most common cheese used in these pies is beyaz peynir, or "white cheese," which is salty and much like feta cheese. Another cheese called lor is like our cottage cheese. I like to use a mixture of the two. For this recipe, you will need large sheets of fillo; I used sheets measuring 19 inches × 12 inches. These are usually sold frozen and need to be defrosted for 2 to 3 hours (see page 9 for information about fillo).

SERVES
ABOUT 8

7 ounces feta cheese, mashed with a fork
8 ounces cottage cheese
2 eggs, lightly beaten
black pepper
large bunch of flat-leaf parsley (2 1/2 to 3 ounces), chopped
1 stick (1/2 cup) butter, melted, or 1/3 cup vegetable oil
14 ounces large fillo sheets
1/2 cup milk
1 egg yolk

For the filling, mix the mashed feta, cottage cheese, and eggs thoroughly until well blended. Add pepper and stir in the chopped parsley.

Use a large rectangular or round pie dish, a little smaller than the sheets of fillo, and brush it with melted butter or oil. Place half the package of fillo (about 7 sheets), one on top of the other, at the bottom of the dish, brushing each sheet with melted butter or oil and sprinkling each with about a tablespoon of milk. Let the sheets hang over the sides of the dish and press them into the corners with the pastry brush. If you are using a round dish, place the sheets so that the corners hang over in different places around the edge.

Spread the filling evenly on top. Then cover with the remaining sheets, brushing each, including the top one, with melted butter or oil, and sprinkling all except the last two with a tablespoon of milk.

With a sharp, pointed knife trim the fillo around the edges, and score the top into 16 squares or diamonds with parallel lines, cutting only down to the filling, not right through to the bottom. Brush the top with egg yolk mixed with a drop of water.

Bake in the oven preheated to 350°F for 30 to 45 minutes, or until crisp and golden. Serve hot, cutting along the scored lines, this time right through to the bottom.

CREAMY FILLO SPINACH PIE
Ispanakli Tepsi Böreği

This wonderful, creamy pie is somewhere between a savory flan and a spinach lasagne. The fillo turns into a soft, very thin pasta, so don't expect it to be crisp and papery. It sounds complicated, but it is quite easy and really worth the labor. I am sure you will be delighted by the result. It can be made in advance and reheated. The pie is excellent when cut up into small pieces and served at a party.

Use a package of fillo containing large-size sheets. (I used a 14-ounce package of sheets measuring 19 inches × 12 inches, minus 2 sheets.) The large sheets are usually sold frozen and you need to defrost them for 2 to 3 hours before using (see page 9 for information about fillo). The Turkish kasar, a sharp hard cheese, can be found in Turkish stores but mature Cheddar is equally good for the dish. From the supermarket, you can now buy packages of young spinach leaves, washed and ready to use, but you can also use not-so-young spinach and remove any thick stems, or use frozen leaf spinach.

SERVES 8   1 pound young spinach leaves

7 ounces feta cheese, mashed with a fork

4 eggs

2/3 stick (or 5 1/2 tablespoons) butter

2 1/4 cups milk

12 ounces large fillo sheets

7 ounces Turkish *kasar* cheese or mature Cheddar, grated

To make the filling, wash the spinach, removing stems only if they are thick and tough. Put them to steam in a large pan with 4 to 5 tablespoons water over medium heat, with the lid on. Within very few minutes they will have crumpled into a soft mass, so keep your eye on them. Strain well, then, when cool enough to handle, squeeze them dry, pressing all the water out with your hands. Still using your hands, mix the spinach into the mashed feta.

Beat the eggs with a fork in a large bowl. Heat the butter in a pan. When it has melted, pour in the milk and heat until it is warm, then gradually beat this into the eggs.

Grease a rectangular or square baking dish a little smaller than the sheets of fillo. Open the sheets only when you are ready to use them and keep them in a pile so that they do not dry out.

Lay a sheet in the greased baking dish, pressing it into the corners with a pastry brush and letting the edges come up the sides of the dish. Pour a little of the milk-butter-egg mixture—about 4 to 5 tablespoons or a little less than a standard ladleful—all over the sheet. (You will need a similar amount to pour between each sheet and a larger amount for the last one on top.) Sprinkle on a little of the grated *kasar* or Cheddar. Lay a second sheet on top and repeat with the milk-butter-egg mixture and then the grated cheese.

Continue until you have used about half the sheets, then spread the spinach filling evenly on top. To do this, press lumps of the spinach and feta mixture between the palms of your hands to flatten them and lay them side by side.

Continue laying sheets of fillo, pouring over each the milk mixture and sprinkling with cheese until you are left with 2 last sheets. With a sharp or fine, serrated knife, trim the edges of pastry around the sides of the dish. Lay the remaining 2 sheets on top of the pie, sprinkling the milk mixture and cheese between them and tucking them down the sides of the dish. If there is too much to tuck in, trim with scissors. Pour any remaining milk mixture over the top.

Bake the pie in the oven preheated to 350°F for 30 to 45 minutes, until the top is golden brown—it puffs up and falls again. Serve hot, cut into pieces.

For an all-cheese filling instead of the spinach, blend 7 ounces feta cheese with 7 ounces cottage cheese and mix in about 4 tablespoons chopped parsley or dill.

PUFF PASTRY SPINACH ROLL
Ispanakli Börek

For 6 to 8 people, use the same filling of spinach and feta cheese as in the Creamy Fillo Spinach Pie (page 179).

Cut 10 ounces puff pastry in half and roll each half into a long rectangle about 9 inches × 12 inches. Roll it out on a floured surface with a floured rolling pin. Keep turning the sheet of pastry over and over, dusting it with flour each time until it is very thin. Spread the filling in the middle in a band 9 to 9 1/2 inches wide to about 1 inch from the short ends at the top and bottom. Fold one side of the pastry over the filling, then fold the other side over the first, making a long parcel. Press the ends firmly to seal them. Place the two parcels on a greased baking dish, folded side down, brush with an egg yolk mixed with a drop of water, and bake in the oven preheated to 375°F for 35 minutes, until puffed up and golden. Serve hot.

COLD YOGURT SOUP with CHICKPEAS and BULGUR
Yoğurtlu Nohut Çorbasi

I made notes about this recipe and a few others at Haci Abdullah's restaurant in Istanbul. It is a cool summer soup using rural staples, and it takes only minutes to make.

SERVES 6

3/4 cup bulgur
salt
4 cups plain whole-milk yogurt
2 tablespoons crushed, dried mint
2 garlic cloves, crushed (optional)
one 14-ounce can chickpeas, drained

Put the bulgur in a pan with 1 cup water and a little salt. Bring to the boil and cook, covered, over very low heat for about 10 minutes, until the water has been absorbed and the grain is tender. Let it cool.

Pour the yogurt into a serving bowl, beat in 1 cup cold water, and add the crushed mint and garlic, if using. Season with salt, and mix well. Stir in the drained chickpeas and the bulgur and serve.

BARLEY SOUP with YOGURT
Yoğurtlu Çorbasi

This Anatolian peasant soup with the delicate flavor of mint and saffron is magnificent. I make it when I have a roast chicken carcass or, better still, when I have two and have remembered to retain the cooking juices and melted fat.

SERVES 8	1 or 2 chicken carcasses
OR MORE	salt and white pepper
	1 large onion, chopped
	2 tablespoons vegetable oil
	2/3 cup pearl barley
	good pinch of saffron threads
	2 tablespoons chopped flat-leaf parsley
	4 tablespoons chopped mint
	2 cups plain whole-milk yogurt

Put the chicken carcasses in a large pan with about 5 1/2 pints (11 cups) water. Add salt and pepper and boil for 1 hour or longer. Strain, and put back any little bits of chicken into the stock.

In the washed and dried pan, fry the onion in the oil until soft. Add the stock and any cooking juices and melted fat left over from the original roasting of the chicken. Bring to the boil, then add the barley. Crush the saffron threads with the back of a spoon on a little plate and stir them in. Simmer over low heat for about 30 minutes, or until the barley is swollen and tender. Add the chopped parsley and mint and adjust the seasoning, but remember the yogurt will add a little needed sharpness.

Just before serving, beat the yogurt in a bowl with a few ladles of the soup. Then pour the yogurt mixture into the soup, beating vigorously, and heat to just below boiling, stirring constantly. Do not allow the soup to boil, or it will curdle.

TOMATO and RICE SOUP
Domatesli Pirinç Çorbasi

For this fresh-tasting soup, I blend the tomatoes to a cream in the food processor without peeling them and cook them only a little. The egg and lemon finish gives it a creamy texture. The rice should be cooked separately and added just before serving as it goes mushy if it stays too long in the soup. Spearmint is commonly used but you can use other types of mint.

SERVES 4 TO 6
1/3 cup basmati or long-grain rice
2 chicken bouillon cubes
2 pounds ripe tomatoes
salt and black pepper
3 teaspoons sugar, or to taste
2 sprigs of spearmint, finely chopped
1 egg
juice of 1/2 lemon

First, cook the rice. If using basmati rice, wash it in a bowl of cold water, then drain and rinse under cold running water. Pour it into plenty of boiling salted water and cook for about 20 minutes, until just tender. (Some brands that claim not to be parboiled or pre-cooked now take as little as 8 to 10 minutes, so read the information on the package.) Drain and keep it to one side until you are ready to serve.

In a large pan bring to the boil 1 1/4 cups water with the crumbled chicken bouillon cubes.

Without peeling them, cut the tomatoes into quarters and remove the hard white bits near the stem end. Blend to a light cream in the food processor and add to the pan. Season with salt, pepper, and sugar and add the chopped mint. Mix well and simmer for 5 minutes.

Just before serving, stir in the rice, adding a little water if the soup is too thick, and bring to the boil. In a little bowl, beat the egg with the lemon juice. Add a ladle of the soup to the egg, beat well, pour it into the soup, stirring vigorously for a few seconds, only until it becomes creamy, then quickly take it off the heat. Do not let it boil again, or the egg will set.

PUMPKIN SOUP
Kabak Çorbasi

This is the simplest ever pumpkin soup where the pure, sweet taste of pumpkin is married with the slightly sharp one of yogurt. The large orange-fleshed pumpkins are winter vegetables, but you can find them throughout the year in Asian and Middle Eastern stores, sold by the slice, with their seeds and fibers removed, and wrapped in plastic wrap.

SERVES 4

2 1/2 pounds pumpkin
4 1/2 cups chicken stock (or use 2 bouillon cubes)
1 to 2 teaspoons sugar
salt and black pepper
To serve: 1 cup plain whole-milk or strained Greek-style yogurt, at
    room temperature

Remove the peel and any seeds and fiber from the pumpkin and cut the flesh into pieces. The peel is extremely hard and you have to cut it away by laying the slices or chunks flat on a board, cut side down, and then pressing down with a large heavy knife to cut the skin off.

Put the pieces in a large pan with only about 1 1/2 cups stock (it will not cover the pieces), and simmer, covered, for 15 minutes, or until the pumpkin is tender.

Blend to a purée in the food processor, or mash it with a potato masher, and return to the pan. Add the remaining stock, the sugar, and a little salt and pepper, and cook for a few minutes more, adding water to thin the soup, if necessary.

Serve the soup hot, and pass around the yogurt in a bowl for people to help themselves.

Main Courses

Meat—lamb or mutton—cooked in a variety of ways, is the prestige food of Turkey. Chicken comes second. Fish and seafood were always appreciated in the coastal cities, especially in Istanbul and Izmir, but, apart from a few esteemed fish, they were considered poor man's food and were bought from vendors and eaten in the street. At night at the top of the Bosphorus, a thousand lights glittered on the sea from the little boats of menfolk fishing for their families. It is only in the last twenty years, since fish restaurants have proliferated in response to demand by foreign tourists, that they have become enormously popular with the local population. It seems surprising in a country surrounded by three large seas—the Black Sea, the Aegean, and the Mediterranean, as well as the smaller Sea of Marmara—that fish does not enjoy equal status to meat, even though it is more expensive. One suggestion is that for a people with atavistic tastes born in the steppe lands of Central Asia, it was not easy to incorporate the produce of the sea in their culinary traditions.

Many years ago I asked the head of the Association of Turkish Chefs why meat was so important in Turkey. He replied that in Ottoman times, Islamic law allowed men to have four wives, and they were obliged to satisfy them all equally and that required a great deal of strength and energy so they had to eat a lot of meat! A certain sultan, he said, was reputed to have habitually eaten a whole lamb at one sitting. I suspect he was pulling my leg.

Meat is the food cooked when people entertain, but the majority of the population can rarely afford it and lives mainly on bulgur, rice, pulses, and vegetables. Rice pilaf is eaten almost every day in the cities, sometimes for both lunch and supper, either as an accompaniment or as a substantial main course. As well as being a staple meal, it has always been considered a grand dish of celebration. There is no wedding without a rice pilaf. Bulgur pilaf is more common than rice in rural homes since Anatolia is wheat country.

SMOKED MACKEREL with WALNUT SAUCE
Taratorlu Uskumru

This can be served as a first course or as a cold main course with pickles, sliced red onions, and a green salad. Cold-smoked mackerel is soft and moist and more of a delicacy than the hot-smoked variety. Hazelnuts, almonds, or pine nuts can be used as an alternative to walnuts for this classic sauce, which is called tarator. In that case, white bread should be used. The sauce can also be served with poached or grilled fish or with cold vegetables cooked in olive oil.

SERVES 4

FOR THE SAUCE
1 cup walnut halves
3 slices whole wheat bread, crusts removed
2 garlic cloves, crushed
6 tablespoons extra virgin olive oil
3 tablespoons white wine vinegar
salt

2 cold-smoked mackerel
1 lemon, cut in quarters

Make the sauce first. Grind the walnuts in the food processor, then add the bread, previously soaked in water and squeezed dry, and the garlic, and blend together. Add the oil and vinegar, a little salt, and blend with just enough water (about 4 tablespoons) to produce a creamy consistency.

Skin and fillet the fish and serve with the sauce and lemon quarters.

DEEP-FRIED RED MULLET with GARLIC AND PARSLEY
Barbunya Tavasi

Deep-frying is the most popular way of cooking small- to medium-size whole fish, and red mullet (barbunya) are among the most prized. Garlic and parsley enhance their sweet flesh. Ask the fishmonger to clean the fish, but to leave the head on. Serve them with salad or Mashed Potatoes with Olive Oil, Scallions, and Parsley (see page 168).

SERVES 4   4 red mullet (weighing about 9 to 12 ounces each)
5 garlic cloves, crushed
salt and black pepper
6 tablespoons chopped flat-leaf parsley
flour
olive oil, for frying
To serve: 1 lemon, cut in quarters

Rub the fish with about a quarter of the crushed garlic mixed with salt and pepper, then stuff them with 5 tablespoons of chopped parsley mixed with the remaining garlic and a little salt and pepper.

Roll the fish in flour until they are well covered and deep-fry in sizzling olive oil for about 4 to 5 minutes. Then lift them out and drain on paper towels.

Serve sprinkled with the remaining parsley, accompanied by lemon quarters.

GRILLED SEA BASS FLAMBÉED
with RAKI
Raki Soslu Levrek

Raki, the Turkish national spirit, gives the grilled sea bass a faint anise aroma. Arak, ouzo, and even Pernod can be used instead. Other fish such as bream, turbot, and red mullet can be prepared in the same way.

SERVES 4
- 4 fillets sea bass (weighing about 2 pounds), skin on
- 4 tablespoons extra virgin olive oil
- salt and black pepper
- 4 tablespoons raki

Brush both sides of the fillets with 2 tablespoons of the oil and season lightly with salt and pepper. Arrange the fish on a piece of foil in a heat-proof dish, skin side up, and place them under a preheated broiler. Cook for about 4 minutes, or until the skin is crisp and brown and the flesh just beginning to flake when you cut into the thickest part with a pointed knife.

Take the fish from under the broiler, pour over the *raki*, and set light to it. Serve immediately when all the flames have died down, sprinkling on the remaining olive oil.

SEARED TUNA *with* LEMON DRESSING
Izgara Orkinoz

Olive oil and lemon with parsley or dill is the standard dressing in Turkey for all grilled and fried fish. The best way to eat tuna is rare—simply seared, with the flesh inside still pink, and almost raw. Serve it with a salad or Mashed Potatoes with Olive Oil, Scallions, and Parsley (see page 168).

SERVES 4

juice of 1 lemon
salt and black pepper
6 tablespoons extra virgin olive oil
2 tablespoons finely chopped flat-leaf parsley or dill
4 thick tuna steaks

For the dressing, mix the lemon juice, salt and pepper, and 4 tablespoons olive oil, then stir in the chopped parsley or dill.

Heat the remaining 2 tablespoons oil in a large, preferably nonstick, skillet. Put in the tuna steaks and cook them over high heat for less than 1 minute on each side, sprinkling them lightly with salt. To test for doneness, cut into one with a pointed knife; the time depends on the thickness of the steak. It should be uncooked and red inside. If you prefer it less rare, cook it only a tiny bit longer. You can easily spoil tuna by overcooking it.

Serve the tuna steaks with the dressing poured over.

CHICKEN with PLUMS
Erikli Tavuk

This is a dish of Georgian origin. Georgia, which borders on northwest Turkey, is famous for its plum trees and plum sauces. Our slightly sour, dark red plums will do well.

SERVES 6

6 boneless, skinless chicken pieces, breasts or thighs
2 to 3 garlic cloves, chopped
2 to 3 tablespoons butter
1 tablespoon sunflower oil
salt and pepper
9 dark red plums

FOR THE SAUCE
4 tablespoons plum jam
1 tablespoon red or white wine vinegar
1 garlic clove, crushed
pinch of chili pepper flakes or ground chili pepper

In a large skillet, sauté the chicken pieces with the garlic in a mixture of butter and oil, over low heat. Cook them for about 10 to 15 minutes, or until they are no longer pink inside when you cut in with a pointed knife. Season with salt and pepper, and turn the pieces over at least once.

Just before serving, cut the plums in half and ease out the pits. Lift out the chicken pieces and put them on one side while you sauté the plums. Cook them for 7 to 10 minutes, turning them over once, until they soften. Return the chicken pieces to the pan and heat through.

For the sauce, heat the plum jam with the vinegar in a small saucepan, stir in the garlic and chili flakes or ground chili pepper and cook for a few moments longer.

Serve the chicken pieces with the sauce poured over, and garnish with the plums.

RICE PILAF
Pilav

This is the basic recipe for the rice that accompanies grills and stews. Although long-grain rice is more commonly used, basmati is today preferred by gourmets. It is my preferred rice for pilaf. It has an appealing taste and aroma, and the grains stay light, fluffy, and separate. You can use water or stock. It is best to use real chicken stock, if possible, but stock made with bouillon cubes will do very well, too; use 1 1/2 cubes with 3 1/2 cups water.

SERVES 6 TO 8   2 1/2 cups basmati or long-grain rice
3 1/2 cups water or chicken stock
2/3 stick (5 1/2 tablespoons) butter
salt

Wash the rice (American long-grain does not need washing). Pour cold water over it in a bowl, stir well, and leave it to soak for a few minutes, then strain and rinse under cold running water.

Bring the water or stock to the boil in a pan. Put in the butter, cut into pieces, and when it has melted, pour in the drained rice. Stir well, bring to the boil, and cook gently over very low heat, tightly covered and undisturbed, for 18 to 20 minutes, until the rice is tender, the water has been absorbed, and little holes have appeared on the surface. Add a little extra water if it becomes too dry. (Some brands that claim not to be parboiled or precooked now take as little as 8 to 10 minutes, so read the information on the package.) Turn out and fluff up the grains with a fork. If you need to reheat the rice, put it, covered, in the oven for 15 minutes, or until it is really hot.

VARIATION

For rice with chickpeas, *nohutlu pilav*, prepare the rice as above. Fry 1 chopped onion in 2 tablespoons sunflower oil until soft. Add the drained chickpeas from a 14-ounce can and heat through, then mix them into the rice.

This dish has a place in Ottoman folklore. At the Topkapi Palace, in the time of Sultan Mehmet the Conqueror (he captured Constantinople in 1453), a little gold ball in the shape of a chickpea would be hidden in the rice, creating excitement with the guests, each hoping to find it on their plate.

CHICKEN with TOMATO PILAF
Tavuk Ve Domatesli Pilav

Sautéed chicken kebabs are more tender and juicy than the grilled ones on skewers, which are served in kebab houses. Accompany these with tomato pilaf and a Cucumber and Yogurt Salad (see page 156). The dark, wine-red spice called sumac (see page 7) lends a sharp lemony taste to the chicken.

SERVES 4

FOR THE TOMATO PILAF

1 1/2 cups basmati or long-grain rice
1 pound ripe tomatoes, peeled
1 chicken bouillon cube
2 teaspoons sugar
salt and black pepper
1/2 stick (4 tablespoons) butter, cut in small pieces

4 boneless, skinless chicken pieces, breasts or thighs
1 tablespoon sunflower oil
2 tablespoons butter
salt and black pepper
2 tablespoons chopped flat-leaf parsley
To garnish: 1 lemon, quartered, or sumac

Start by making the tomato pilaf. If using basmati, wash the rice by pouring cold water over it in a bowl, stir well, and leave to soak for a few minutes, then strain and rinse under cold water.

Quarter the tomatoes, remove the hard white bits near the stem end, then liquefy the tomatoes in the food processor. Measure the resulting tomato juice and add enough water to make it up to 2 2/3 cups. Pour it into a pan, add the crumbled stock cube, the sugar, and a little salt and pepper and bring to the boil.

Add the rice and stir well. Simmer, covered, over low heat, for 18 to 20 minutes, until the rice is tender and the liquid absorbed. (Some brands that claim not to be par-boiled or precooked now take as little as 8 to 10 minutes, so read the information on the package.) Do not stir during the cooking, but add a little extra water if it becomes too dry. Fold in the butter pieces. Taste and add salt and pepper if necessary.

While the rice is cooking, cut the chicken into 1 1/2-inch pieces. Heat the oil and butter in a skillet and sauté the chicken for 6 to 8 minutes, until lightly browned, adding salt and pepper, turning the pieces over once. Sprinkle the chicken with parsley and serve with lemon quarters or with sumac to sprinkle over, accompanied by the rice.

ROAST CHICKEN with PINE NUT and RAISIN PILAF
Pilavli Ve Tavuk Firinda

Many of the dishes popular in the court kitchens in Constantinople during the Ottoman period spread throughout the empire. This pilaf is one of the classics that you find in all the cities that were once the outposts of the empire. It goes particularly well as an accompaniment to roast chicken and it also often forms a stuffing for the bird.

SERVES 4 TO 6

1 large chicken
2 tablespoons extra virgin olive oil
salt and pepper

FOR THE PILAF

2 cups basmati or long-grain rice
1 large onion, chopped
3 tablespoons sunflower oil
1/2 cup pine nuts
3 cups chicken stock (or use 1 1/2 bouillon cubes)
1/2 teaspoon ground allspice
1 teaspoon ground cinnamon
salt and pepper
3 tablespoons currants or tiny black raisins
1/2 to 2/3 stick (4 to 5 1/2 tablespoons) butter, cut into small pieces

Rub the chicken with a mixture of olive oil, salt, and pepper. Put it breast side down in a roasting pan so that the fat runs down, which prevents the breasts from drying out. Add 4 tablespoons of water to the bottom of the pan. Roast for 1 hour in an oven preheated to 400°F, then turn the chicken breast side up and continue to cook for about 30 minutes (the time depends on the size of the chicken), or until it is well done and the skin is crisp and brown.

While the chicken is cooking, prepare the pilaf. Wash the rice if it is basmati. Pour cold water over it, stir well, and leave to soak for a few minutes. Strain and rinse under cold running water.

In a large pan, fry the onion in the oil until soft and golden. Add the pine nuts and stir until lightly colored. Add the rice and stir over a moderate heat until it is well coated with the oil. Then add the hot stock and stir in the allspice, cinnamon, salt (you need to take into consideration the saltiness of the stock), pepper, and the currants or raisins.

Bring to the boil, then simmer, covered and undisturbed, over low heat for 20 minutes, or until the rice is tender and the water absorbed. Add a little extra water if it looks necessary.

Stir in the butter, check the seasoning, and add salt, if necessary. Serve hot with the chicken.

ROAST CHICKEN with BULGUR and WALNUT PILAF
Tavuk Firinda Ve Bulgur Pilav

Bulgur pilaf is an everyday dish in rural Turkey. Bulgur is whole wheat kernels that have been boiled, then dried and ground. In the old days in rural areas, before mechanization, and still today in some parts, it is made collectively. The men harvest the wheat, then the women separate the grain from the chaff. They wash the grain and boil it for hours in huge pots until it splits. It is then dried in the sun, spread out on large sheets laid out on the flat roofs of houses or in the fields. When it is dry and hard, it is taken to be ground in a stone mill. Three types of grind—coarse, medium, and fine—can be found in Middle Eastern stores in this country. The coarse-ground one is the best for pilaf, but the medium-ground one, which is the most widely available, will also do.

The amount of bulgur here is quite large and enough for 2 chickens. You can make it in advance and reheat it in the oven before serving.

SERVES 8

2 chickens
3 to 4 tablespoons extra virgin olive oil
salt and pepper

FOR THE BULGUR PILAF
3 cups coarse or medium bulgur
1 large onion, chopped
2 tablespoons sunflower oil
4 1/2 cups chicken stock (or use 1 1/2 bouillon cubes)
salt and pepper
1 1/2 teaspoons ground cinnamon
1 teaspoon ground allspice
1 1/2 cups walnuts, coarsely chopped
2/3 to 1 stick (5 1/2 to 8 tablespoons) butter, cut into
    small pieces

Rub the chickens with a mixture of olive oil, salt, and pepper. Put them breast side down in a roasting pan so that the fat runs down, which prevents the breasts from drying out. Add 1/4 cup of water to the bottom of the pan. Roast for 1 hour in an oven preheated to 400°F, then turn the chickens breast side up and continue to cook for about 30 minutes, depending on their size, until they are well done and the skin is crisp and brown.

While the chickens are cooking, prepare the pilaf. Wash the bulgur—although I find that with the processed qualities of bulgur today, this is not strictly necessary. Pour cold water over it, stir well, and then rinse under cold running water. Fry the onion in the oil until it is soft and golden. Add the bulgur, stir well, then pour in the hot stock. Add salt (taking into consideration the saltiness of the stock), pepper, cinnamon, and allspice. Stir and cook, covered and undisturbed, over very low heat for about 15 minutes, or until the liquid is absorbed and the grain is tender. Check the seasoning and add salt if necessary. Finally, fold in the walnuts and the butter pieces.

Carve the chicken and serve with the bulgur pilaf.

CHICKEN PILAF in a PIE
Perdeli Pilav

Perdeli pilav means "veiled pilaf." The veil is a pastry crust in the shape of a dome. It takes time and care, but if you like artistry and dramatic effects, it is very worth making. Much of it can be made in advance, but the last bit—encasing the chicken and rice in puff pastry—must be done as close as possible to serving.

SERVES 6

1 chicken

2 tablespoons sunflower oil

salt and black pepper

1 medium onion, quartered

1 1/2 cups basmati or long-grain rice

1 1/2 chicken bouillon cubes

1/2 stick (4 tablespoons) butter, cut into small pieces

1/3 cup pistachio nuts, very coarsely chopped

1/3 cup blanched almonds, very coarsely chopped

1 pound puff pastry

1 egg, separated

The chicken is roasted and the carcass is used to make a broth that is served to accompany the pie. Rub the chicken with the oil, salt, and pepper. Put it breast side down in a roasting pan so that the fat runs down, which prevents the breasts from drying out. Add 4 tablespoons of water to the bottom of the pan. Roast for 45 minutes in an oven preheated to 400°F, then turn the chicken breast side up and continue to cook for 20 minutes more; it should be a little underdone.

When the chicken is cool enough to handle, cut it up into 6 large pieces and remove the skin and bones, which should be kept for the broth. Cut any remaining meat from the carcass into small pieces. Keep all this covered with plastic wrap so it does not dry out. Keep the chicken juices and the fat from the roasting pan for the rice.

Put the skin, bones, and carcass into a pan with the onion, cover with water, add a little salt, and simmer for 1 hour, until the broth is reduced and concentrated, then strain it. This will be the "sauce" to accompany the pie.

Wash the rice, if using basmati. Pour cold water over it, stir, and leave to soak for a few minutes, then strain and rinse in cold running water. Bring 2¼ cups water to the boil with the crumbled bouillon cubes, add the rice, and stir well. Add salt, taking into consideration the saltiness of the bouillon cubes. Cook, covered and undisturbed, over very low heat for about 18 minutes, until the rice is only just tender. (Some brands that claim not to be parboiled or precooked now take as little as 8 to 10 minutes, so read the information on the package.)

Pour in the chicken juices and the fat from the roasting pan, and add the reserved small pieces of chicken. Fold in the butter, pistachios, and almonds. Taste to see that there is enough salt because rice needs quite a bit. The rice, too, can be prepared in advance.

Assemble the pie not too long before your guests arrive. Roll out the puff pastry so that it is a large rectangle measuring 14 inches × 16 inches on a floured surface with a floured rolling pin, turning the sheet of pastry often and dusting it with flour. Lift it onto a large, flat baking dish or sheet. Put the rice in the center and shape it into a dome, with a base about 10 inches in diameter. Arrange the 6 large chicken pieces on top. Bring the pastry up over the rice and chicken mound, bringing up the four corners to meet at the top, and twisting them together. Now comes the artful part—you have to make it look like an Ottoman dome!

Bring the edges of the pastry together to close the side openings, right up to the top of the dome, hugging the filling. Cut away the excess dough, and seal the four openings by pinching them firmly together. A little egg white brushed along the edges makes them stick better. By pinching and twisting all the way along the edges, produce a scalloped effect (like the hem of women's lingerie). It is the kind of edging you find along many Middle Eastern pies. Cut a little round about 1½ inches in diameter from the off-cuts and stick it on the top of the dome, with a little egg white, to cover up the joins.

Brush the whole pastry with the egg yolk mixed with a drop of water, and bake in an oven preheated to 350°F for 45 minutes, or until the pastry is crisp and golden brown.

Serve with the strained and reheated chicken broth.

VARIATION

If you want the chicken pilaf but do not want to bother with a pastry crust, press the pilaf in a ring- or dome-shaped mold and heat it through in the oven. Turn it out and surround it with the chicken pieces.

PUFF PASTRY MEAT PIES with RAISINS and PINE NUTS
Talaş Böreği

These individual pies are tasty, elegant, and very easy to prepare. They make a perfect light meal, accompanied by a salad.

SERVES 4

1 large onion, chopped

2 tablespoons sunflower oil

1 pound ground lamb or beef

salt and black pepper

1/2 teaspoon ground cinnamon

1/2 teaspoon ground allspice

3 tablespoons pine nuts

2 tablespoons currants or small black raisins

3 to 4 tablespoons chopped flat-leaf parsley

14 ounces puff pastry

1 egg, separated

First, make the filling. Fry the onion in the oil until soft and golden. Add the ground meat, the seasoning, and spices. Turn the meat over, and crush it with a fork to break up any lumps. Cook for about 8 to 10 minutes, until the meat is no longer pink and the juices have been absorbed. Stir in the pine nuts, currants or raisins, and chopped parsley, then let it cool.

Cut the puff pastry into 4 pieces. Roll each piece out into a square or rectangle, large enough to make an eventual flat parcel of about 7 inches × 4 inches. Roll out the pastry on a floured surface with a floured rolling pin, turning the sheets often and dusting them each time with flour. Spread a quarter of the meat filling onto one half of one of the pieces of pastry, leaving a 1/2-inch margin around the three edges. Brush the edges with egg white to make them stick better. Fold the pastry over to cover the filling. Trim any superfluous pastry from around the pie with a knife and pinch firmly to seal. Place the pies, turned over with the smooth side up, on an oiled baking sheet and brush the tops with the egg yolk mixed with a drop of water.

Bake in an oven preheated to 350°F for 25 to 30 minutes, until puffed up and golden.

SHISH KEBAB
Şiş Kebabi

Meats grilled on skewers over the dying embers of a fire are a symbol of Turkish cuisine. They are said to be a legacy of nomadic times, perfected in the conquering era of the Ottomans, when soldiers camping out in tents skewered their meats on swords and cooked them on the campfire.

Years ago, I went on a tour of kebab houses in Istanbul. It was a grand eating marathon. At the fifth establishment they opened the refrigeration room and showed me all the prize cuts, which were later presented to me straight from the fire on a huge platter. As well as lamb kebabs and ground meat kebabs on skewers, there were small lamb chops, kidneys, slices of calf's liver, beef steaks, sucuk (spicy beef sausages), and pieces of chicken. It was a gourmand's dream, but for me at the time, afraid to give offence by not eating everything, it was a nightmare.

Serve the kebabs with pita bread or with other bread from a Middle Eastern store, such as Turkish flat bread like an Italian focaccia or a sesame bread, and with one or more of the garnishes below.

SERVES 6

2 pounds boned leg of lamb

2 large onions, quartered

6 tablespoons mild extra virgin olive oil

salt and black pepper

Cut the meat into 1- to 1¼-inch cubes. Liquefy the onions in the food processor and prepare a marinade by mixing the onion juice with the oil, salt, and pepper. Leave the meat in this for 1 hour in the refrigerator, keeping it covered with plastic wrap, and turning the pieces over at least once.

Thread the pieces of meat onto 6 skewers. These need to be the type with a flat, wide blade so that the meat does not slide. Grill them over charcoal or wood embers, on a well-oiled grill. Or cook them under a preheated gas or electric broiler. Cook them for about 7 to 10 minutes, turning them over once, until the meat is well browned on the outside but still pink and juicy inside.

For an alternative marinade: Blend 1 onion to a purée, then add 1¼ cups yogurt, salt, and pepper.

GARNISHES AND ACCOMPANIMENTS

Thread 1 piece of onion, 1 piece of tomato, and 1 piece of sweet pepper—cut to the same size as the meat—between each piece of meat. Alternatively, put quartered onions and peppers and small whole tomatoes separately onto the grill to be served at the same time.

⊙ Serve with an onion relish made by slicing 4 medium onions as thinly as possible using a food processor. Sprinkle the slices generously with salt, and leave them in a bowl for at least an hour. Rinse and drain them and mix with 4 tablespoons chopped parsley and, if you like, 1 tablespoon of the sharp, red spice called sumac (see page 71).

⊙ Serve with a salad of diced tomato, cucumber, and red onion with chopped mint and parsley, dressed with olive oil and lemon juice.

⊙ Serve the kebabs with a yogurt sauce made by beating 2 cups yogurt with 1 or 2 crushed garlic cloves and 1 tablespoon dried crushed mint.

⊙ Grill whole, small eggplants at the same time as the kebabs, turning them until they are soft inside, and serve them cut open with a sprinkling of salt and pepper, a drizzle of olive oil, and a squeeze of lemon juice.

KOFTE KEBAB with TOMATO SAUCE and YOGURT
Yoğurtlu Köfte Kebabi

This is a mainstay of Turkish kebab houses, where it is often dramatically served in a dish with a dome-shaped copper lid, the type that was once used at the sultan's palace. I serve it in a large, round, clay dish, which can be warmed in the oven.

This is a multilayered extravaganza. There is toasted pita bread at the bottom with tomato sauce poured over. This is topped with yogurt and sprinkled with fried pine nuts. Grilled ground meat kebabs or shish kebab (see above), or both, are laid on top. It requires organization and must be assembled at the last minute as the pita should remain a little crisp. The tomato sauce and meat should be very hot while the yogurt should be at room temperature.

SERVES 4 TO 6   FOR THE TOMATO SAUCE

   1 small onion, chopped
   2 tablespoons extra virgin olive oil
   2 garlic cloves, chopped
   1 chili pepper, seeded and chopped
   1 1/2 pounds tomatoes, peeled and chopped
   salt and black pepper
   1 to 2 teaspoons sugar

   2 pita breads
   1 1/2 pounds ground beef or lamb
   salt and black pepper

1 medium onion, finely chopped (optional)

1/4 to 1/3 cup finely chopped flat-leaf parsley

1 teaspoon sumac, plus a pinch more (see page 7)

2 cups plain whole-milk yogurt

2 tablespoons butter or extra virgin olive oil

2 to 3 tablespoons pine nuts

Make the tomato sauce first. Fry the onion in the oil until soft. Add the garlic and chili pepper, and stir for a moment or two. Put in the tomatoes, season with salt, pepper, and sugar, and cook over a medium heat for 10 minutes, until they soften and the sauce is reduced.

Open out the pita and toast them until they are crisp, then break them into small pieces in your hands.

For the *kofta* kebabs, season the ground beef or lamb with salt and pepper, and work it into a soft dough with your hands. Add the onion, if using, and the parsley, and work into the meat. Shape into sausages about 3/4 inch thick and 23/4 inches long. Arrange them on an oiled sheet of foil on a baking sheet and cook them under a pre-heated broiler for about 8 minutes, turning them over once, until well browned outside but still pink and moist inside.

Spread the pieces of toasted pita at the bottom of the serving dish and sprinkle over a pinch of sumac. Pour the hot tomato sauce all over and top with a layer of the yogurt beaten with a fork.

Heat the butter or oil with the pine nuts and stir in the remaining teaspoon of sumac. When the butter or oil sizzles, sprinkle it all over the yogurt. Arrange the meat on top and serve at once.

VARIATION

For a rural *yoğurtlu* kebab, sauté small pieces of lamb in butter or oil with chopped onion, salt, and pepper. Serve on a bed of toasted and broken pita bread and pour warmed yogurt over the top. Mix a little paprika in sizzling butter and drizzle over the yogurt.

LAMB STEW *with* EGGPLANT SAUCE
Hünkâr Beğendi

One legend surrounding the name of the sauce, hünkâr beğendi, which means "Her Majesty's delight," places it in 1869 when the Sultan Abdul Aziz entertained Empress Eugénie (my Istanbul grandmother was named after her), wife of Napoleon III, in his white rococo palace of Beylerbey on the Asian side of the Bosphorus. The empress was so enchanted by the pale, creamy, eggplant purée that she asked for the recipe to be given to her cooks. The sultan's cook explained that he could not pass on the recipe because he "cooked with his eyes and his nose."

In Turkey, they use mature kaşar, a hard yellow cheese, or Gruyère in the sauce, but mature Cheddar can be used too. Serve it with rice pilaf (page 193).

SERVES 6

1 large onion, chopped

3 tablespoons sunflower oil

2 pounds boned leg or neck fillet of lamb

1 pound tomatoes, peeled and chopped

1 teaspoon sugar, or to taste

salt and black pepper

FOR THE EGGPLANT SAUCE

3 pounds eggplants

3/4 stick (6 tablespoons) butter

3 tablespoons flour

2 1/4 cups milk

salt

good pinch of nutmeg

1/2 cup grated cheese (see above)

For the stew, fry the onion in the oil until soft. Cut the meat into 1-inch cubes, add them to the pan, and cook, turning to brown lightly all over. Add the tomatoes, sugar, salt, and pepper. Cover with water and simmer, with the lid on, for 1 hour, until the meat is very tender, adding water if it becomes dry, but letting the sauce reduce at the end.

For the eggplant sauce, prick the eggplants with a pointed knife to prevent them from bursting in the oven. Place them on a large piece of foil on a baking sheet and roast them in a hot oven preheated to 475°F for about 45 to 55 minutes, or until they feel very soft when you press them and the skins are wrinkled. When cool enough to handle, peel and drop them into a strainer or colander with small holes. Press out as much of the water and juices as possible. Still in the colander, chop the flesh with a pointed knife, then mash it into a purée with a fork or wooden spoon, letting the juices escape through the holes.

Make a béchamel sauce by melting the butter in a saucepan, add the flour, and stir over low heat for about 2 minutes, until it is well blended. Take the pan off the heat and add the milk gradually, beating vigorously all the time to avoid lumps forming. Add salt and nutmeg, and cook over low heat, stirring constantly for about 15 minutes, until the sauce thickens.

Off the heat, mix the eggplant purée into the béchamel sauce, then return to the heat, beating vigorously until it is well blended. Add the grated cheese and stir until it has melted. Add a little salt if necessary.

Serve the meat stew in a wide shallow dish with the eggplant sauce in a circle around it.

LAMB STEW with SHALLOTS and CHESTNUTS
Kestaneli Kuzu

This is a dish you can prepare well in advance. In Turkey, they may add a little grape molasses called pekmez, which you can buy in Turkish stores, but, for me, the dish is sweet enough as it is with the onions, chestnuts, and sugar.

Serve it hot with plain rice or rice with chickpeas (see Variation page 193).

SERVES 6 TO 8
- 1 1/2 pounds shallots or baby onions
- 3 pounds boned shoulder or neck fillet of lamb
- 1/4 cup sunflower oil
- 1 teaspoon ground cinnamon
- 1/2 teaspoon ground allspice
- 1 teaspoon sugar
- salt and black pepper
- 1 pound frozen or vacuum-packed peeled chestnuts

To peel the shallots or baby onions more easily, blanch them in boiling water for 5 minutes. This loosens their skins. When they are cool enough to handle, peel them and trim the roots.

Cut the meat into 6 to 8 pieces. Remove any skin, and trim some but not all of the fat.

In a large saucepan, fry the shallots or onions in the oil over a medium heat, turning them, until they are brown all over. Then lift them out and put in the meat. Turn the pieces to brown them on all sides.

Add water to barely cover the meat. Bring it to the boil, remove any scum, then add the cinnamon, allspice, sugar, salt, and pepper. Simmer, covered, for about 1 1/2 hours, until the meat is very tender, turning it over and adding a little water so that it does not dry out. Put back the onions and cook for 15 minutes more. Finally, add the chestnuts and cook for 10 minutes more.

LAMB SHANKS COOKED
in YOGURT
Yoğurtlu Kuzu

The dish can be made with small lamb shanks or with knuckle of veal (osso buco) or slightly fatty, cubed meat. I have used lamb shanks, a cut not normally available in supermarkets. But butchers sell fresh ones from the foreleg weighing about 10 ounces and frozen ones from New Zealand from the back leg weighing from 14 to 16 ounces. Serve it with plain or Vermicelli Rice (see page 304). The yogurt makes a wonderful, soupy sauce so provide spoons, too.

SERVES 6

6 small or 4 large lamb shanks
salt and white pepper
1 pound shallots or baby onions
8 cups plain whole-milk yogurt
2 tablespoons cornstarch
3 garlic cloves (optional)
To serve: crushed dried mint

Put the lamb shanks in a large pan and cover them with water. Bring to the boil, remove any scum, and add salt and pepper. Cook them with the lid on for 2 hours, adding water to keep them covered. Peel the shallots or baby onions; drop them in boiling water and poach them for 5 minutes to loosen the skins, then drain and peel them while still warm. Add them to the meat and cook for 30 minutes more, until they are soft and the meat is so tender that it falls off the bone.

You need to prepare or stabilize the yogurt to prevent it from curdling during cooking. Pour it into a large saucepan and beat well until it is liquid. Mix the cornstarch to a light paste with 3 to 4 tablespoons water and add this to the yogurt, beating vigorously until well mixed. Now bring the yogurt to the boil slowly, stirring constantly *in one direction only*, then reduce the heat to as low as possible and let it barely simmer, uncovered, for about 10 minutes. Do not cover the pan with a lid: they say that a drop of steam falling back into the yogurt could ruin it. I am not sure that is true.

Drain the cooked shanks—you can remove the bones or not, as you wish—and the onions and add them to the yogurt. Stir in a little salt and the garlic, if using, and simmer gently, uncovered, for 10 to 15 minutes.

When serving, pass around a little bowl of dried mint so people can stir a teaspoonful or so into their sauce, if they wish.

LAMB SHANKS *with* EGG
and LEMON SAUCE
Terbiyeli Kuzu Incik

This dish can be made with lamb shanks, knuckle of veal (osso buco), or with cubed meat such as shoulder of lamb. Butchers sell fresh lamb shanks from the foreleg weighing about 10 ounces and frozen ones from New Zealand from the back leg weighing from 14 to 16 ounces. Lamb shanks cooked for a long time have a wonderful tenderness and texture without being stringy, and they produce a rich stock. Although they take a long time to cook, they don't need any attention. The sauce is the classic Turkish egg and lemon terbiyeli sauce.

SERVES 6

4 large or 6 small lamb shanks
3 garlic cloves, peeled
salt and black pepper
14 ounces baby onions or shallots
3 large carrots, sliced
1 celeriac, peeled and cubed
3 medium new potatoes, quartered
2 tablespoons chopped flat-leaf parsley
2 tablespoons chopped dill
2 egg yolks
juice of 1 lemon
1 teaspoon sugar

Put the lamb shanks in a large pan and cover with water. Bring them to the boil, remove any scum, and add the garlic cloves, salt, and pepper. Cook, with the lid on, over very low heat for 2 to 2 1/2 hours, adding water if necessary to keep the meat covered, until the meat is so tender it can be pulled off the bone. Lift out the shanks and when cold enough to handle, remove the meat from the bones and set it aside in a bowl with a little stock to keep it moist. Ladle off as much fat as you can. If you are left with too much stock (you need only enough to cover the meat and vegetables), reduce it by boiling it down.

Put the vegetables into the stock (to peel the shallots or baby onions more easily, place them in boiling water and poach for a few minutes to loosen their skins; then peel them while still warm) and cook for 20 minutes, until all the vegetables are very tender. Return the meat to the pan and stir in the parsley and dill.

Just before serving, beat the egg yolks with the lemon juice and sugar in a bowl.

Pour in a ladle of boiling stock from the stew, beating vigorously. Return this mixture to the stew, stirring constantly, and heat through for a moment or two, without letting the liquid boil again or the eggs will curdle.

NOTE

It sometimes makes sense to start the dish a day ahead because of the time the shanks take to boil. In that case, let them simmer for the 2 to 2¹/2 hours, then let them cool in their broth and refrigerate. Remove the solid fat, which collects on the surface, before heating through and continuing as above.

STUFFED EGGPLANTS
with MEAT
Karniyarik

These eggplants stuffed with ground meat—their name, karniyarik, means "slashed belly"—are served as a hot main dish with rice pilaf (page 193). Use a good-quality tomato juice.

SERVES 6

6 thin and long medium-size eggplants
salt
sunflower oil, for frying
2 onions, chopped
14 ounces ground beef or lamb
1 tablespoon tomato paste
2 large tomatoes
1 teaspoon ground cinnamon
1/2 teaspoon ground allspice
black pepper
1/3 cup chopped flat-leaf parsley
1 cup tomato juice

Trim the caps but leave the stems on the eggplants. Peel 1/2-inch-wide strips off the skins lengthwise, leaving alternate 1/2-inch strips of peel. Soak the eggplants in water mixed with 1 tablespoon of salt for 30 minutes, then drain and dry them. Fry them very briefly in hot shallow oil, 2 or 3 in the skillet at a time, turning to brown them lightly all over. Drain them on paper towels.

For the filling, fry the onion in another pan in 2 to 3 tablespoons oil until it is soft. Add the meat and cook for about 5 minutes, crushing it with a fork and turning it over until it changes color. Add the tomato paste and one of the tomatoes, peeled and chopped, and the cinnamon, allspice, salt, pepper, and chopped parsley. Stir well and simmer for about 10 minutes, until the liquid is reduced.

Place the eggplants side by side in a single layer in a baking dish. With a sharp pointed knife, make a slit in each one, lengthwise, along one of the bare strips on the top until about 1 inch from each end. Carefully open the slits and, with a dessertspoon, press against the flesh on the insides to make a hollow pocket.

Fill each of the eggplants with some of the filling, and place a slice of the remaining tomato on top. Pour the tomato juice into the dish, cover with foil, and bake in an oven preheated to 350°F for about 40 minutes, or until the eggplants are soft.

STUFFED QUINCES
Ayva Dolmasi

This is truly exquisite. Quinces are now available for quite a long period in Middle Eastern and Asian stores. In this recipe, the fruits are stuffed with a meat filling and served hot. Quinces are hard and take a long time to cook in the oven before you can cut them up and stuff them, but you can do this in advance—even the day before. I used very large quinces because those were the ones available at the time, but you can use 4 smaller ones, in which case the baking time will be less.

    Serve hot with rice pilaf (page 193) or rice with chickpeas (Variation page 193).

SERVES 4

2 large quinces (each weighing about 1 pound)
1 medium onion, chopped
1 1/2 tablespoons vegetable oil
3 tablespoons pine nuts
7 ounces lean ground lamb or beef
1 teaspoon ground cinnamon
1/2 teaspoon ground allspice
salt and black pepper

Wash the quinces and rub off the light down that covers their skin in patches. Put them on a piece of foil on a baking sheet and bake in an oven preheated to 325° F for 1 to 2 hours (the time varies considerably), until they feel soft when you press them.

    For the stuffing, fry the onion in the oil until soft. Add the pine nuts and stir, turning them over, until golden. Put the ground meat in a bowl and add the cinnamon, allspice, salt, and pepper. Mix and work well to a smooth paste with your hands. Add the fried onions and pine nuts and work them into the paste.

    When the quinces are cool enough to handle, cut them open lengthwise through the stem end. Remove the cores with a pointed knife and discard them. With a pointed spoon, scoop out about one-third of the pulp and mix it into the meat mixture. Heap a quarter of this mixture into each quince half and press it down.

    Return the 4 stuffed quince halves to the baking sheet and bake at 350°F for 30 minutes.

Desserts

A wide range of nutty, syrupy pastries, milk puddings, and fruit compotes are the most typical and essential part of Ottoman gastronomy. Traditionally served at every festive event, be it a wedding, the birth of a baby, a circumcision, or the inauguration of a new home, sweets are the first item of food that is decided upon when a celebration is planned. They symbolize the hope that a marriage will be happy, that a child will be healthy, that a family will prosper. They also signal that a guest is welcome. Some sweets are famously attached to particular religious festivals.

APRICOTS STUFFED with CREAM
Kaymakli Kayisi Tatlisi

Use large dried apricots for this famous Turkish sweet. You need to soak them in water overnight (even if you are using a semi-dried moist variety). The cream used in Turkey is the thick kaymak made from water-buffaloes' milk. The best alternatives in this country are clotted cream or mascarpone.

SERVES 4 TO 6
- 1/2 pound (1 1/4 cups) large dried and pitted apricots, soaked in water overnight
- 1 1/4 cups water
- 1 1/4 cups sugar
- 1 tablespoon lemon juice
- 1 cup clotted cream or mascarpone
- 3 tablespoons pistachios, finely chopped

Drain the apricots. Make a syrup by boiling the water with the sugar and lemon juice. Add the apricots and simmer for 20 minutes, or until the apricots are soft and the syrup is reduced and thick enough to coat the back of a spoon. Leave to cool.

Enlarge the slit along one side of each apricot and stuff with a little cream or mascarpone. Arrange the apricots on a dish and serve, sprinkled with the chopped pistachios.

COMPOTE of FRESH APRICOTS
Kayisi Compostosu

Compotes of dried or fresh fruits in syrup are popular desserts. At parties in Turkey, they are the last thing to be served, signaling that there is nothing more to follow. This sharp-tasting compote with fresh apricots is especially delicious. I add pistachios for their color as well as for their taste, and they should be peeled for this dish. To do this most easily, poach them in water for 1 to 2 minutes and drain; when they are cool enough to handle, pull off or squeeze away the skins.

SERVES 6
OR MORE
- 2 pounds apricots, washed and pits removed
- 2 1/4 cups water
- 1 cup sugar

1/4 cup blanched almonds or pistachios
1/4 cup pine nuts
To serve: 1 cup plain whole-milk yogurt or heavy cream (optional)

Put the apricots in a wide pan with the water and sugar. Bring to the boil and simmer for a few minutes, until the apricots soften, turning them once if the water does not entirely cover them. Lift them out and put them to one side while you reduce the syrup by simmering it until it is thick enough to coat the back of a spoon. Return the apricots to the pan, add the almonds or pistachios and pine nuts and cook 1 to 2 minutes more. Serve cold, with yogurt or cream, if you wish.

ORANGE PUDDING
Portakali Tatlisi

This orange jelly with orange slices can also be made with the juice of freshly squeezed blood oranges or clementines. Many supermarkets and stores now sell these juices freshly squeezed, which makes it an easy pudding to prepare. It is set with cornstarch and is not as firm as a jelly set with gelatine.

SERVES 8
4 1/2 cups orange or tangerine juice, freshly squeezed
1/2 cup sugar
1/3 cup cornstarch
3 large oranges
seeds of 1 pomegranate
To serve: 1 cup whipping or heavy cream, whipped

Bring the orange or tangerine juice to the boil with the sugar. Dissolve the cornstarch in 1 cup water and pour it into the simmering juice, stirring vigorously. Continue to stir, in one direction only, until the mixture thickens, then cook over a low heat for about 15 minutes.

Peel the oranges, taking care to remove all the white pith. Cut each orange into thick slices and each slice into 4 pieces. Remove the pips.

Let the orange mixture cool and pour into a glass serving bowl. Stir in the pieces of orange, cover with plastic wrap, and chill in the refrigerator for a few hours.

Sprinkle the pomegranate seeds over the pudding and serve with whipped cream.

ROAST QUINCES
Ayva Tatlisi

I love these roast quinces even more than the famous quinces in syrup that I have written about in other books, because here the fruits keep their natural and unique taste and perfume. Quinces can be small like an apple, and they can be huge and weigh up to 1 pound each. You need about 1/2 pound per person so a large one is enough for two. Cooking times vary depending on their size and degree of ripeness. Quinces are available in farmers' markets and in Middle Eastern stores.

Kaymak (see page 218) is the cream served with it in Turkey, but clotted cream or mascarpone will do very well.

SERVES 6

3 large or 6 small quinces (weighing about 3 pounds)
1/3 stick (2 1/2 tablespoons) unsalted butter
6 tablespoons sugar
To serve: 2/3 cup clotted cream or mascarpone

Wash the quinces, rubbing their skins to remove the light down that sometimes covers them in patches. Roast them whole, in an oven preheated to 375°F, until they feel soft. Depending on their size and ripeness, it can take from 1 hour up to 2 hours for the largest, so watch them carefully. (The three I cooked, weighing 2 pounds, took 1 1/2 hours.)

When they are cool enough to handle, cut them in half through the core, and cut away the blackened ends and the cores with a pointed knife. Place them, cut side up, on a baking sheet. Put a sliver of butter on top of each half and sprinkle each with 1 tablespoon sugar.

Put them back in the oven for 1/2 to 1 hour, until they are very soft and have turned a rich burgundy color. If you like, put them under the broiler for moments only, until the sugar just begins to caramelize. It fills the kitchen with a sweet smell.

Serve hot with clotted cream or mascarpone.

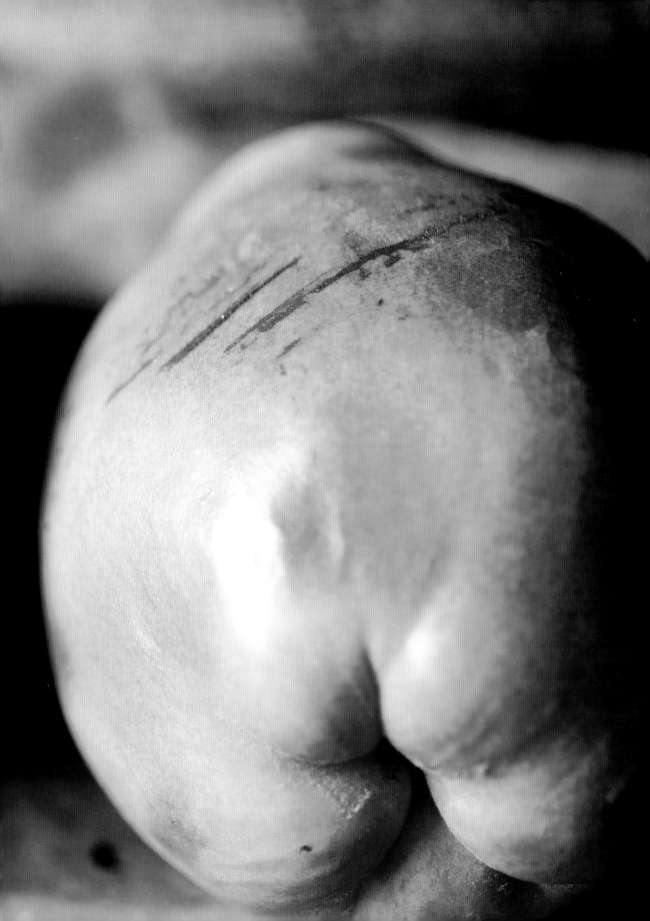

PUMPKIN DESSERT
Kabak Tatlisi

Pumpkin is frequently used in Turkey in sweet as well as savory dishes. This is a "cheese" with an unusual, delicious flavor. It is best made the night before and keeps very well for days in the refrigerator. You need the large pumpkins with the sweet orange flesh. They are winter vegetables, but you can now buy them most of the year in Asian and Middle Eastern stores, where they are sold by the slice, weighing between 1 pound and 2 pounds, the seeds and stringy fibers removed. Some greengrocers also sell them by the slice.

In Turkey, this dessert is served with the very thick cream call kaymak (see page 218) but clotted cream or mascarpone will do very well. It is very rich, so serve small portions.

SERVES 10

4 to 4 1/2 pounds pumpkin slices
2 cups sugar
1 1/2 cups walnuts, finely chopped
To serve: 1 cup clotted cream or mascarpone

Prepare the pumpkin. Scrape away any remaining seeds or stringy bits. The rind is very thin and hard. It is more easily removed if you first cut the slices into chunks. Lay the chunks, skin side facing you, and cut it away, pressing down with force with a large, heavy knife.

Cut the flesh into pieces of about 1 1/4 to 1 1/2 inches. Put them in a wide saucepan with 1 cup water, and cook, tightly covered so that they steam, over low heat for about 20 minutes, or until the flesh is very tender. Drain and mash the flesh with a potato masher. Continue to cook, now uncovered, so that most of the liquid evaporates.

Stir in the sugar and continue to cook until all the water is absorbed, stirring often and making sure that the purée doesn't burn.

Spread the paste on a serving plate, cover with plastic wrap, and leave in the refrigerator overnight. Serve cold, sprinkled all over with walnuts, and accompanied by the cream or mascarpone.

RICE PUDDING with ROSE WATER
Sütlaç

Egg yolks give this version of rice pudding a wonderful creamy texture. It has a delicate taste of rose water and mastic. The mastic—unfortunately labeled "gum mastic"—has nothing at all to do with the waterproof filler called mastic, nor with the glue called "gum arabic" sold in the building trades. It is an aromatic resin from trees that grow on the Greek island of Chios. It comes in tiny translucent grains. Be careful not to use too much as it results in a bitter taste. You must pound and grind the grains with a teaspoon of sugar to a fine powder in a pestle with a mortar. A few drops of vanilla essence are an alternative flavoring if you cannot get gum mastic.

The pudding is addictive, homely, comfort food. A brittle caramel topping turns it into a more glamorous option.

SERVES 6

3/4 cup Italian short-grain or risotto rice

1 1/2 cups water

5 cups whole milk

3/4 cup sugar

1 to 1 1/2 tablespoons rose water

1/4 teaspoon pulverized gum mastic or 3 drops vanilla essence

4 egg yolks

For the caramel topping: 4 tablespoons superfine sugar (optional)

Put the rice in a large pan with the water. Bring it to the boil and simmer for 8 minutes, or until the water is absorbed. Add the milk and simmer on very low heat for 30 to 40 minutes, or until the rice is very soft but there is still quite a bit of liquid left. Stir occasionally with a wooden spoon so that the rice does not stick to the bottom of the pan.

Put in the sugar and stir until it has dissolved. Add the rose water, turn off the heat, and sprinkle on the gum mastic, stirring vigorously. If you are using vanilla essence, put it in at the same time as the sugar.

Beat the egg yolks in a small bowl, then beat in a ladleful of the simmering pudding. Add this mixture to the pan, stirring constantly for a few moments only, until the liquid thickens a little (it becomes creamy), but do not let it boil or the yolks will curdle. Pour the pudding into a serving dish—use a heatproof one if you are making the caramel topping—let it cool, and then refrigerate, covered in plastic wrap.

If you are going to add the caramel topping, the pudding must be chilled before you add the sugar. Sprinkle the top with the 4 tablespoons sugar and put under a preheated broiler. The sugar will bubble and gradually turn into dark caramel. If it is too near the broiler, burnt spots will appear. If that happens, you can just lift them off when the caramel has cooled and hardened. Refrigerate before serving.

MILK and ALMOND PUDDING
Keşkül

Turkey has a very wide range of milk puddings. I once spent much of one night watching specialist milk pudding–makers at work, endlessly stirring creams in giant copper cauldrons. They said they had to work at night because that was when the milk arrived, which was why, they complained, they could not recruit young people to do the job. I don't blame them. This pudding, made with ground almonds, is my favorite.

SERVES 6

1/2 cup blanched almonds
4 cups whole milk
1/4 cup rice flour
1/2 cup sugar
2 to 3 drops of almond essence
To garnish: 2 tablespoons finely chopped or pounded pistachios

Grind the almonds finely in the food processor. Bring the milk to the boil, preferably in a nonstick pan, which prevents the cream sticking and burning at the bottom, then take it off the heat.

In a small bowl, mix the rice flour to a paste with 4 to 5 tablespoons of water, making sure there are no lumps. Add this to the milk, stirring vigorously with a wooden spoon, and cook over low heat, stirring constantly, and always in the same direction, to avoid lumps forming, for about 15 minutes, or until the mixture begins to thicken. (If lumps form, you can save the cream by beating it with an electric beater.)

Add the ground almonds and continue to cook on the lowest possible heat, stirring occasionally, for 20 minutes, or until the consistency is that of a thin porridge. Then add the sugar and continue to cook, stirring, until it has dissolved. Always stir in the same direction. Do not scrape the bottom of the pan (in case it sticks and burns a little, you don't want to scrape up any burnt bits).

Stir in the almond essence, let the pudding cool, then pour it into a glass serving bowl or individual bowls. Serve chilled, sprinkled with the chopped pistachios.

NOTE

In Turkey, it is a traditional option to serve this with a heaped teaspoonful of *kaymak* (see page 218) but here you can use clotted cream. Make a little slit in the skin of each portion, and slip through it a heaped teaspoon of clotted cream.

YOGURT CAKE
Yoğurtlu Tatlisi

There are many versions of Turkish yogurt cake. This one is like a light, airy, fresh-tasting cheese-cake. If you wish, you can make a syrup, which should be passed around in a jug for people to help themselves. I prefer the cake pure and simple, without the syrup.

SERVES 6

4 large eggs, separated
1/2 cup superfine sugar
3 tablespoons all-purpose flour
1 2/3 cups strained Greek-style yogurt
grated zest of 1 unwaxed lemon
juice of 1 lemon

FOR THE OPTIONAL SYRUP
2/3 cup water
1 1/4 cups sugar
1 tablespoon lemon juice
grated zest of 1 unwaxed orange

Beat the egg yolks with the sugar to a thick, pale cream. Beat in the flour, then the yogurt, lemon zest, and lemon juice until it is thoroughly blended.

Whisk the egg whites until stiff and fold them into the yogurt mixture. Pour this into a round, nonstick baking tin (about 9 inches in diameter), greased with butter. Bake in an oven preheated to 350°F for 50 to 60 minutes, until the top is brown. It will puff up like a soufflé and then subside.

Turn out onto a serving plate, and serve warm or cold.

If you are making the syrup, boil the water with the sugar, lemon juice, and grated orange zest for 3 to 5 minutes. Let it cool, then chill in the refrigerator.

PISTACHIO CAKE

This moist, nutty cake soaked in syrup is a modern pastry. Make it at least two hours before you are ready to serve it so that the syrup has time to soak in. You can buy unsalted, shelled pistachios in Middle Eastern and Asian stores.

SERVES
10 TO 12

FOR THE SYRUP

1 1/2 cups sugar

3/4 cup water

1 tablespoon lemon juice

2 tablespoons rose water

5 eggs, separated

1 cup superfine sugar

1 1/2 cups pistachios, ground finely

1/3 cup pistachios, chopped very coarsely

To serve: 3/4 cup clotted or heavy cream (optional)

Make the syrup first. Bring the sugar, water, and lemon juice to the boil and simmer until the sugar is dissolved, then stir in the rose water. Let the syrup cool, then chill it in the refrigerator.

Beat the egg yolks with the sugar to a pale cream, then add the ground pistachios and mix very well. Beat the egg whites until stiff and fold them in gently. Pour into a greased and floured nonstick cake tin 9 to 10 inches in diameter and sprinkle the coarsely chopped pistachios on top. Bake in an oven preheated to 350°F for about 45 minutes.

Turn the cake out into a deep serving dish. Make little holes over the top with a fork and pour over the syrup. The holes will let it soak in quickly.

Serve, if you like, with clotted or heavy cream.

TEL KADAYIF with CLOTTED CREAM and PISTACHIOS

For this luscious sweet, you need to buy the soft, white vermicelli-like pastry called kadayif by the Turks and knafe by the Lebanese from a Turkish or Lebanese store. In Egypt we called it konafa. I saw this pastry being prepared in a large frying pan in a restaurant in Istanbul, but it is easier to bake it in the oven. It is scrumptious both hot and cold. I even like it days after, when the syrup has soaked and softened the pastry—it keeps well in the refrigerator. You can buy unsalted, shelled pistachios in the same stores as kadayif.

In Turkey they use the cream called kaymak (see page 218) but clotted cream is a very good alternative.

SERVES 12

FOR THE SYRUP

2 1/2 cups sugar
1 1/4 cups water
1 tablespoon lemon juice
2 tablespoons orange blossom water (optional)

1 pound *kadayif* or *knafe* pastry
2 sticks (1/2 pound) unsalted butter, melted
1 3/4 to 2 cups thick clotted cream
3/4 to 1 cup pistachios, chopped medium fine

Make the syrup first. Bring to the boil the sugar, water, and lemon juice and simmer for about 5 minutes, or until it is thick enough to coat the back of a spoon, then add the orange blossom water, if using. Let the syrup cool, then chill it in the refrigerator.

Put the pastry in a large bowl and pull out and separate the strands as much as possible with your fingers. Pour the melted butter over them and work it in very thoroughly with your fingers, pulling out and separating the strands and turning them over so that they do not stick together and are entirely coated with butter.

Spread the greased pastry all over the bottom of a large, round pie pan measuring 10 1/2 to 12 inches in diameter (or in two smaller pans). Press it down and flatten it with the palms of your hands. Bake it in an oven preheated to 350°F for about 40 to 45 minutes, or until it is golden. Then place the pan on the stove top over a medium flame and move it around for a moment or two so that the bottom of the pastry browns slightly.

Run a sharp knife around the pan to loosen the sides of the pastry, and turn it out, bottom side up, onto a large serving dish. Pour the cold syrup all over the hot pastry.

Spread the thick clotted cream all over the top and sprinkle generously with chopped pistachios.

Alternatively, you can pour over only half the syrup before serving and pass the rest around in a jug for everyone to help themselves to more.

Lebanon

When I was a child in Egypt, Beirut was the Paris of the Middle East, and the mountain resorts of Lebanon were our Switzerland. People went there to "recuperate"—at least that was the reason members of my extended family gave—and they came back with fantastic stories of the unending assortments of *mezze* (appetizers) they were offered in the resort cafés. My family was from Aleppo in Syria, which was considered the pearl of the Arab kitchen, so praise from them was special. Today, Lebanese restaurants, with their typical menus, have come to represent Arab food everywhere around the world. So big is their reputation that when a Syrian restaurant opens in London, it calls itself "Lebanese," and when hotels in Egypt put on a special Egyptian buffet, the dishes are Lebanese. How did that come about? One reason is that the Lebanese are famously *bons viveurs* who know how to make the best of their culinary heritage. They are also great entrepreneurs and they were the first in the Middle East to develop a restaurant trade. That trade spread to Europe and elsewhere when the civil war forced many to seek their fortunes abroad in the 1970s and '80s.

A Cuisine That Reflects the Past

The cooking of Lebanon has much in common with that of Turkey, and is also similar to that of Syria, Palestine, and Jordan, countries that share with it a long history of constant change of foreign rule. These countries were all part of the Ottoman Empire until the early twentieth century, when Lebanon was part of historic Syria. National borders here are recent—since the 1940s when the countries became independent nation states—but the culture Lebanon shares with her neighbors is very old and has absorbed a wide range of influences.

The Lebanese like to attribute their famous worldliness and entrepreneurial acumen to the Phoenicians, who dominated the Mediterranean and colonized their coast around 2500 B.C., creating cities along the shore and opening trade routes across the sea. Egyptian, Persian, Greek, and Roman civilizations have left their traces in the form of monuments and artifacts. In the fourth century, the area became part of the Byzantine Empire, and Hellenic culture and strict Christian religious orthodoxy were introduced. The influence of Christian religion on the food today can be felt through a wide repertoire of meatless vegetarian and Lenten dishes.

A distinctive Levantine Muslim cuisine began to develop with the arrival of Islam and the establishment of the first great dynasty of the Muslim Empire, the Umayyads, in Damascus in 658. The Umayyads were overthrown after a hundred years, and a new dynasty, the Abbasids, moved their capital to Baghdad, where Persian cooking traditions dominated in the court kitchens. By the ninth century, historic Syria, including the part which is now Lebanon, was ruled by a succession of small Egyptian-based dynasties. In 1095 the Crusaders joined the Byzantine army in a thrust to liberate the Holy Land and established themselves on the Syrian and Lebanese coasts. They were finally pushed out in the late thirteenth century. The Mameluks, originally slave soldiers who took over from their masters based in Egypt, ruled Syria and Egypt for 300 years, until the Ottoman Turks seized the area in the sixteenth century.

Each occupation left a legacy in architecture—there are palaces, mosques, *khans* (caravanserais), and *hamams* (baths)—and each also brought something to the kitchen. A few of the dishes in this book, such as the meat cooked in vinegar with onions and eggplants, could have come out of a thirteenth-century Baghdad culinary manuscript. Falafel and broad bean salad came through the early association with Egypt. The Ottoman Turks kept control of the region by co-opting local feudal lords (*emirs*) as governors, but their influence was powerful, and in the kitchen it was also lasting. After the collapse of the Ottoman Empire, the League of Nations awarded France the mandate for Syria and Mount Lebanon in 1920, and in 1946 Lebanon became an independent state. European missionary schools in the mountains and the American University in Beirut had already, by the late nineteenth century, opened Lebanon up to Western cultural influences; the French added a certain style and elegance to the table.

Extraordinary Culinary Diversity in a Tiny Country

The standard Lebanese restaurant menu is set in stone with items that never change, but at home in the cities and villages there is extraordinary culinary diversity. You might wonder how in a tiny country less than half the size of Wales the cooking could be so varied, but when you visit Lebanon it becomes clear. It is a land of high mountains and a long, narrow seacoast with three different climate zones. Roads into the previously inaccessible interior are as recent as the 1960s, and access is still difficult so villages nestling in the mountains and valleys have remained isolated from each other, retaining the individuality of their cooking, which is based on local produce. Communities have been further separated in this Muslim-Christian country by their division into many religious and sectarian groups, most of them living in their own villages or in separate quarters in the cities. There are Shiite, Sunni, and Druze Muslims. The Maronites are the largest Christian group—theirs is a Roman Catholic church of Eastern origin. It is followed by Greek Orthodox, Greek Catholic, Syrian Catholic, Chaldean Catholic, Protestant, and Armenian churches.

I am, nevertheless, forever surprised and fascinated when I discover a new dish or variation of a dish. When I was invited by my friends Mai Ghoussoub and her husband, Hazim Saghie, to watch Hazim's mother cook for a party when she came to stay with them in London, every dish she made was new to me, and each one was delicious. Khalida Saghie comes from the village of Beino, in the region of Akkar, which is close to the Syrian border; originally all the people in the village were Greek Orthodox but now they have been joined by a few Maronite and Muslim families. Khalida had arrived with her homemade pomegranate syrup, her fermented cheese, and her freshly milled, fine-ground bulgur (called *burghul* in Lebanon). She went to work and never stopped until all the guests had arrived and then she quickly went to change into beautiful silks.

Hazim, a columnist for *Al Hayat*, the Arabic daily newspaper, gave me a little background to the food in Lebanon. The country is extremely fertile—together with Syria, Palestine, Jordan, and Iraq, it is known as "The Fertile Crescent"—and most of the population used to live off the land. It is a peculiarity of Lebanon that it is the only place in the Middle East where a classic type of feudalism exists. Elsewhere, it is a case of absentee landlords, but in Lebanon, from the Middle Ages onward, the land was divided into fiefs, and the feudal lords lived among their peasants. Families like the Maan and the Chehabs established feudal principalities and built themselves palaces in the mountains. This has meant that the countryside was sustainable and that a rich rural culinary tradition developed in the mountain villages. They grew wheat in the valleys, and olive trees, vines, mulberry trees for silk worms, and fruit trees on terraces. Some of the villages, such as Zahlé, Beit Chehab, and Mashgara, grew into towns and cities.

Beginning in the late nineteenth century, when Beirut became a mini cosmopolitan city and a commercial and intellectual center, there was a Christian migration from the mountains to Beirut and the coastal cities where the inhabitants were mainly Sunni Muslims and Greek Orthodox. (Christians, like other minorities, had moved high up into the mountains to ensure their survival and independence.) It is through the meeting of the Ottoman cooking of the main cities along the coast and the cooking of the mountains, between the urban rice culture and the rural *burghul* (bulgur) culture, that the classic Lebanese cuisine of today took shape.

An all-important part of rural tradition is the preservation of food. The provisions made in the summer to last over the winter form the basis of Lebanese cooking and provide its distinctive flavors. These traditions, called the *mune*, were originally a means of survival in a country whose seasons alternated dramatically with short periods of great abundance and long ones of scarcity. Figs, apricots, and tomatoes were laid out on trays in the fields to dry in the sun. Grains, pulses, and nuts were dried on rooftops. Meats were slowly cooked and preserved in their fat. The juice of sour pomegranates was boiled down to syrupy molasses; tomatoes were reduced to paste. Yogurt was drained to make a soft cheese, which was rolled into balls and preserved in olive oil. Butter was clarified to last. Fruit and vegetables were made into jams and pickles. Olives were preserved in salt or crushed for their oil. Distilled rose and orange blossom waters were produced by boiling petals in alembics. Nowadays, all these things are made commercially, and in the cities they are considered delicacies, but there are still those who make them at home, and peasants in their rural hinterland still live off their produce. Every country dwelling once had a special storeroom for the *mune* (many still do), and the woman of the house held the key to the supplies she had labored to produce, usually with the help of neighbors. During the last, long, civil war when routes were barred and people were afraid to travel, the *mune* became important again.

The Lebanese are famously great immigrants and immigration abroad, mainly to Africa and the Americas, was a Christian phenomenon that began in the late nineteenth century. It is said that there are more Lebanese living abroad than in Lebanon—but many of them return home. When families returned, they brought with them the quality of life to which they had grown accustomed. They built beautiful houses (you can see big cars outside) and began to spend money on eating well. They were no longer cooking like the local "peasants" with clarified butter and sheep's-tail fat, but took to lighter cooking

with fresh butter and oil. They saw themselves as neither mountain nor coastal people, but in the middle, and having a touch of worldliness.

Social and economic contrasts have also contributed, along with the country's geography, to culinary diversity and are a reason why you can find many versions of every dish. Prosperity is concentrated in Beirut and on the coast. Apart from the mountain "aristocracies" and the rich villages of returnees from Africa, Latin America, and elsewhere, the hinterland is, in the main, poor and has traditionally subsisted on agriculture.

The Mezze Tradition

One important factor in the development of a sophisticated Lebanese cuisine was that drinking was not banned in this pluralistic country. The Church owned vineyards, and monasteries produced wine. The role of wine and especially *arak*, a powerful distilled spirit made from sweet, white grapes flavored with aniseed, was crucial in refining Lebanese food.

The drinking of *arak* (it is *raki* in Turkey and *ouzo* in Greece) is behind the whole philosophy and practice of the *mezze* tradition. The *mezze*, a national institution, represents an art of living where socializing is all-important. The tradition developed as a way of soaking up the national drink, affectionately called "lion's milk" because it turns cloudy when water is added. It is mixed with cold water (one part *arak* to two of water, but this can vary) and served with a large piece of ice.

According to legend, the special character of the Lebanese *mezze* was born in the Bekaa Valley, where *arak* is produced and where the Lebanese vineyards such as Kefraya and Ksara are situated. The Bekaa Valley is a high valley, cradled between two parallel high mountain ranges, the Mount Lebanon and the Anti-Lebanon. Renowned for its fresh air, its natural springs, and the Bardaouni River, which cascades down the mountain, it is a major agricultural region. It is also the stopping place for travelers on their way from Damascus in Syria.

Zahlé, the resort where Lebanon's favorite riverside restaurants are situated, acquired a mythical reputation for gastronomy. In 1920, the first two cafés opened by the river. They gave away assorted nuts, seeds, olives, bits of cheese, and raw vegetables with the local *arak*. Gradually, the entire valley became filled with open-air cafés, each larger and more luxurious than the next, each vying to attract customers who flocked from all over the Middle East with ever more varied *mezze*. The reputation of the local mountain village

foods they offered spread far and wide, both at home and abroad. It is on these *mezze* that the ubiquitous menu of Lebanese restaurants around the world is based. While in the countryside, hands cross amicably over the table to pick at the foods even when individual plates are offered, in the cities you are given plates to help yourself and you select foods only from your corner of the table. That, Hazim says, is a less sociable way, not quite in the original spirit of the *mezze*.

Whereas restaurant food is based on *mezze* and grilled meats, family meals in the home revolve around a main dish, usually a meat and vegetable stew, or stuffed vegetables such as zucchini, served with *burghul* or rice and sometimes also yogurt. It is accompanied by radishes, little cucumbers, scallions, and pickled turnips or by a salad, and followed by fruit, and it ends with Turkish coffee. Desserts and pastries are not always served at the end of the meal but to visitors who may turn up during the afternoon.

Hospitality and convivial social life are an all-important part of Lebanese life. I am used to high Middle Eastern standards of hospitality, but I have never experienced anything like the gracious, warm, and joyful way in which I was entertained in Lebanon. Everybody is always out and about, meeting friends and enjoying themselves. I wondered how they could ever get any work done in this famously entrepreneurial part of the Middle East. People entertain constantly and *mezze* are the favorite way of entertaining. If you visit a home unexpectedly, you are invariably asked to stay for a drink, and a colorful assortment of *mezze* appears as if by magic. A modest assortment may comprise such items as roasted pumpkin seeds or chickpeas, pistachios, olives, pickled turnips and cucumbers, tomatoes, baby romaine lettuce hearts, radishes, scallions, *labne* (yogurt cheese), feta, and haloumi cheese.

Extended family reunions always turn into gargantuan feasts that begin with *mezze*. There will be *kibbeh* (see page 311), small savory pies, little meat pizzas, a variety of stuffed vegetables, tiny omelettes, grilled quails, *bottarga*, and a variety of dips and salads. They will be served with Arab flat breads or pieces of the very thin large Lebanese *markouk* (see page 245), used for picking up morsels of food. The *mezze* is followed by main dishes and pastries.

It was during the 1960s, between the civil war of 1958 and that of 1975, during the seventeen years of relative calm, when roads were built and communications became easy, that a unified Lebanese cuisine came into its own and the restaurant trade flourished. Unlike some other Middle Eastern countries at that time, such as Syria and Egypt, Lebanon did not have a socialist or military regime. It encouraged private enterprise and attracted money and investment, creating a prosperity unprecedented in that part of the Middle East. The opportunities also created the broadest middle class in the region that could patronize a restaurant trade. Many restaurants were opened during this time, and when the last civil war broke out, many restaurateurs left and opened establishments abroad. That is when Lebanese restaurants mushroomed in Britain, France, the United States, and elsewhere.

The Important Role of Vegetables

Vegetables and pulses are extremely popular in Lebanon and appear in both everyday and celebratory dishes—mezze, pickles, salads, and main and side dishes. The Arabs introduced the cultivation of certain vegetables such as spinach and eggplants to the country at an early point, while the crops from the New World of the Americas arrived late in the Arab world—some as late as the nineteenth century. The tomato, for instance, was introduced in Syria in 1851 when it was labeled "franji," which means French, as everything that came from Europe was then called.

Vegetables are always considered important in areas where much of the population is composed of peasants who can rarely afford meat, but in Lebanon they have a particularly vital role. Many vegetarian dishes are associated with the Christian communities because of the fasts prescribed by the Eastern Orthodox, Catholic, and Armenian Churches. Until a few decades ago, Christians from these churches felt compelled to abide by the strict rules that obliged them to either partial abstinence, when meat could be taken only once a day at the principal meal, or complete abstinence from meat. All foods derived from animals, sometimes including eggs and dairy products, were prohibited for forty days before Christmas, fifteen days before the Assumption of the Virgin Mary, during Lent, which begins seven weeks before Easter, as well as on every Wednesday and Friday in the year. Nowadays, although restrictions have generally been dropped, many of the traditional, meatless dishes of grains, vegetables, and pulses have been adopted by the general population in the cities where they represent the trendy healthy diet that city people now aspire to.

On a recent visit to Lebanon, I spent much time in the kitchen with someone who is a genius with vegetables. Kamal Mouzawak, a food writer and TV chef, teaches vegetarian and gourmet healthy eating. He is the Lebanese coordinator of the Slow Food movement and has started a farmers' market in Beirut. He lives with his fashion-designer partner, Rabih Kayrouz. They are celebrated for their dinner parties (Rabih is in charge of the dramatic décor) that they hold in their fabulous, old-style apartment and on their roof garden. On one occasion, I helped with the cooking when they were entertaining sixty people. Kamal also took me to meet his mother, Fariba, at her village. Several of the dishes in this book are inspired by him and by his mother.

I was a guest on the Lebanese TV program presented by Kamal and Mariam Nour, which is popular all over the Arab world. Mariam is famously dedicated to spreading her ideas on the healing power of vegetarian and macrobiotic foods, which she intermingles with ideas about spirituality, philosophy, the art of living, self-knowledge, identity, medita-

tion, and similar therapies. We were joined by two women who brought baskets full of produce such a lentils still on the plant, and wild endive and herbs from their peasants' cooperative in the south of the country. They made for us a salad of *burghul* and tomato paste and a porridge of wheat and yogurt.

About Bread

Bread is used for picking up morsels of food, for dipping into purées, or soaking up a sauce. People also roll up pieces into small cornets and fill them with food. A common Lebanese bread is like a very thin, round pita, called *khobz halabi* (Aleppo bread), which comes in varying sizes. Another more typical bread, called *markouk*, is made on a curved metal *saj* and is like a very large, very thin giant pancake. There is also a sesame bread called *ka'ak bil semsum*, which is sold in the street and looks like a handbag with a ring handle. It is eaten with *za'tar*, a mix of dried thyme, sumac, sesame seeds, and salt.

About Beverages

Beverages are much like those in Turkey—the cool yogurt drink *ayran*; the heartwarming thick, milky drink *sahlab* (*salep* in Turkey—see page 151), Turkish coffee; mint and cinnamon tea; infusions such as *karkade* (made with hibiscus); syrups such as apricot, date, tamarind, and licorice. A typically Lebanese after-dinner drink that is offered as an alternative to Turkish coffee is "white" coffee, which is boiling water with a drop of orange blossom water. You should try it.

Starters and Mezze

The tradition of the *mezze*—the little appetizers and hors d'oeuvres served with drinks—goes right across the Mediterranean, but Lebanon beats every country by the sheer quantity and variety that is offered in restaurants, with some serving as many as forty and even fifty different ones. At home, some of these little dishes appear on the Sunday lunch tables when extended families get together (everybody goes to visit their parents in the mountain villages on Sunday) and no buffet table could be without a familiar selection.

I went to Zahlé, the "world capital" of the Arab *mezze* (see page 240). My father and many of my cousins in Egypt had been regular visitors to the mountain resort and their descriptions were the basis of an idyllic, rural image I had formed in my imagination. It is now the main city of the Bekaa Valley, full of concrete housing and, in season, a tourist trap of the Arab world. But the rows of open-air restaurants along the river are still immensely appealing with their *mezze* menus rooted in the local rural traditions.

Mezze are the best part of a Lebanese meal. Picking at a variety of delicious foods with different flavors and textures is a wonderful way to eat. But the convivial aspect of the tradition is equally important. The highlight of a recent stay in Lebanon was a wedding party near the ancient city of Baalbek in the Bekaa Valley. Nadim Khattar, an architect based in London, and Andrea Kowalski, a Venezuelan working at the BBC, had organized a sumptuous feast for their guests who came from all over the world; it was held in a field in the middle of the countryside. The lunch went on for hours as little dish upon little dish arrived at the long tables, one more exquisite than the other, each jostling for space, while baby lambs roasted on fires and musicians played. It was pure joy—better than the scenes imagined in my childhood. The wedding party went on for two days. The spirit of fun and conviviality attached to the lingering over *mezze* is something everyone should try to emulate.

Start a dinner party with a carefully chosen variety of *mezze* (it could be just two or three). Serve them with warm bread—the thin round Lebanese pita-like bread called *khobz halabi* or the very thin sheets called *markouk* (see page 245) or with pita bread, and put olives and raw vegetables—radishes, tomatoes, cucumbers, scallions—on the table.

All the dishes in this chapter, except the soups, can be served as part of a *mezze* selection. Some make good finger food and, with the dips, can be served with drinks at a party. Some can make a wonderful first course on their own.

EGGPLANT and TAHINI DIP
Baba Ghanouj

This version of the famous dip—an unusual one with added yogurt—is particularly delicious and creamy. Serve with pita or Lebanese bread.

SERVES 6 TO 8
2 eggplants (about 1 1/2 pounds)
3 tablespoons tahini
juice of 2 lemons
3/4 to 4/5 cup strained Greek-style yogurt
2 garlic cloves, crushed
salt
2 tablespoons extra virgin olive oil
2 tablespoons chopped flat-leaf parsley

Prick the eggplants in a few places with a pointed knife to prevent them from exploding. Turn them over the flame of the gas burner or a hot barbecue, or under the broiler, until the skin is charred all over (this gives them a distinctive smoky flavor) and they feel very soft when you press them. Alternatively, place them on a sheet of foil on an oven tray and roast them in the hottest preheated oven for 45 to 55 minutes until the skins are wrinkled and they are very soft.

When cool enough to handle, peel and drop them into a strainer or colander with small holes. Press out as much of the water and juices as possible. Still in the colander, chop the flesh with a pointed knife, then mash it with a fork or wooden spoon, letting the juices escape through the holes. Adding a tiny squeeze of lemon juice helps to keep the purée looking pale and appetizing.

In a bowl, beat the tahini with the lemon juice (the tahini stiffens at first then softens), then beat in the yogurt. Add the mashed eggplants, garlic to taste, and some salt. Beat vigorously and taste to adjust the flavoring.

Spread the purée onto a flat serving dish and garnish with a drizzle of olive oil and a sprinkling of parsley.

VARIATION

My friend Kamal, whom I watched in his kitchen in Beirut, adds the juice of a bitter orange. In this case, omit the yogurt.

HUMMUS—CHICKPEA and TAHINI DIP
Hummus Bi Tehine

Hummus is popular in America now. It is the kind of thing you make to taste, adding a little more garlic, salt, or tahini as you go along. Serve it with warmed pita bread.

SERVES 6
1 1/4 cups chickpeas, soaked in water overnight
3 to 4 tablespoons tahini
juice of 2 lemons
3 garlic cloves, crushed
salt
4 tablespoons extra virgin olive oil

Drain the soaked chickpeas and put them in a pan with plenty of fresh water. Bring to the boil, remove the scum, and simmer for 1 1/2 hours, until they are very soft. Drain, reserving the cooking water.

Blend the chickpeas to a purée in the food processor. Add the remaining ingredients, except the oil, and a little of the cooking water—just enough to blend it to a soft, creamy paste. Taste and adjust the seasoning.

Pour the *hummus* into a shallow dish and drizzle over the olive oil.

OPTIONAL GARNISHES

Sprinkle on plenty of finely chopped parsley; or make a star design with lines of paprika and ground cumin; or sprinkle with ground sumac (see page 7) and a little chopped flat-leaf parsley; or garnish with a few whole boiled chickpeas, or with pine nuts lightly fried in butter.

VARIATIONS

✻ For a hot version, pour the *hummus* into a shallow baking dish and bake for 15 to 20 minutes in an oven preheated to 400°F. Lightly fry 1/2 cup pine nuts in 4 tablespoons of butter or extra virgin olive oil and sprinkle them, with the melted butter or oil, over the dish.

✻ *Balila* is a warm chickpea salad. Boil the soaked and drained chickpeas in plenty of water for 1 1/2 hours. Turn them out into a serving bowl with just a little of their reduced cooking water and crush them only slightly with a fork. Stir in, to taste, plenty of extra virgin olive oil, a generous amount of crushed garlic, a pinch of chili pepper (optional), and some finely chopped mint.

CHEESE and YOGURT DIP
Jibne Wa Labneh

This dip is quick to make. Serve it with crisp toasted flat bread and, if you like, black olives, cucumbers cut into little sticks, plum tomatoes cut in wedges, and scallions. You can now find labneh, the very thick Lebanese strained yogurt, in Middle Eastern stores.

SERVES 6 TO 8
1/2 pound feta cheese
1 cup thick Lebanese or strained Greek-style yogurt
1/4 cup extra virgin olive oil

Crush the feta cheese with a fork, then add the yogurt and mash together. Spread the dip in a shallow serving dish and drizzle over the olive oil.

WALNUT and POMEGRANATE SALAD
Muhammara

This is a version of a surprising paste that you also find in Turkey. Pomegranate molasses (or concentrate) gives it an intriguing sweet-and-sour flavor (see page 7). Some like it peppery-hot with chili flakes or purée (see Variation below); personally, I like it with only a touch of ground chili pepper.

SERVES 6
1 cup shelled walnuts
1 thick slice of whole wheat bread, crusts off
1 tablespoon pomegranate molasses
1/4 to 1/2 teaspoon ground cumin
pinch of ground chili pepper
salt
4 tablespoons extra virgin olive oil
3 tablespoons pine nuts (optional)

Grind the walnuts in the food processor. Soak the bread in water, squeeze it dry, and put it in the processor with the walnuts. Add the pomegranate molasses, cumin, chili pepper, a little salt, the olive oil, and 3 tablespoons of water and blend to a soft paste. If it is too stiff, add another tablespoon or so of water.

Serve spread on a flat plate, sprinkled, if you like, with the pine nuts fried in a drop of oil until they only just begin to color.

VARIATIONS

 If you want it hot, add 1 teaspoon or more of *harissa*, the North African chili purée that you can buy in jars or tubes in Middle Eastern and North African stores. A few stores sell an "artisan" quality that is particularly good.

 Another version of *muhammara* is a 50/50 blend of walnuts and pine nuts.

TABBOULEH

There is a mystique around the preparation of this famous salad. I watched my friend Kamal make it in Beirut, and his main tip was that you must slice, not chop, the parsley, so that it does not get crushed and mushy. Use the fine-ground bulgur, which is available in Middle Eastern stores. These stores and Asian ones also sell parsley in tied bunches that weigh between 7 ounces and 10 ounces with stems. Mix and dress the salad only when you are ready to serve.

SERVES 6

large bunch of flat-leaf parsley (about 1/2 pound) (3 to 4 cups of leaves, loosely packed)
bunch of mint (about 3 ounces) (1 1/2 cups of leaves, loosely packed)
1/3 cup fine-ground bulgur
juice of 2 lemons
14 ounces firm ripe tomatoes, finely diced
6 scallions, thinly sliced
5 tablespoons extra virgin olive oil
salt and black pepper
1 romaine or 2 Little Gem (baby romaine) lettuces

Keeping the parsley in its bunch, wash it by holding the stems and plunging the leaves in a bowl of water. Shake the water out and leave it to dry on a cloth. Holding the bunch tightly with one hand on a chopping board, slice the leaves with a very sharp knife as finely as you possibly can. Wash and slice the mint leaves in the same way and add them to the parsley.

Rinse the bulgur very briefly in a strainer under cold running water, then press out the excess water. About 20 minutes before you are ready to serve, mix the bulgur with the lemon juice and chopped tomatoes so that it softens in their juices.

Just before serving, mix all the ingredients gently together. The traditional way of eating tabbouleh is to scoop it up with romaine lettuce leaves cut in half or the leaves of Little Gem lettuces. Serve the leaves separately, or stick them in the bowl around the salad.

NOTE

If you cannot get fine-ground bulgur you can use the usual medium-ground one, in which case it will need to soak in water for 20 minutes.

BREAD SALAD with SUMAC
Fattoush

This bread salad is the favorite everyday, Lebanese salad. Sumac (see page 7) gives it a distinctive sharp flavor. The old traditional way was to moisten the toasted bread with water and a little lemon juice before soaking it further with the dressing, which made it deliciously soft and soggy. Nowadays, the toasted bread is broken into pieces and added to the salad at the last minute while it is crisp. You can buy purslane and small cucumbers (they have a better flavor than our large ones) in Middle Eastern stores.

SERVES 6 TO 8
1 1/2 pita breads
1 romaine lettuce, cut into 1/2-inch ribbons
about 2 cups purslane leaves or lamb's lettuce (mâche)
4 firm ripe tomatoes, cut into medium pieces
4 small cucumbers, peeled and cut into thick slices
1 green bell pepper, seeded and cut into small slices
1 1/2 mild onions or 8 scallions, chopped
large handful of chopped flat-leaf parsley
4 to 5 sprigs of mint, shredded
1/3 to 1/2 cup extra virgin olive oil
juice of 1 lemon
salt and black pepper
1 tablespoon ground sumac

Cut around the pita and open them out. Toast them under the broiler or in the oven until they are crisp; turn them over once. Break them into small pieces in your hands.

Put all the vegetables and herbs in a large bowl. For the dressing, mix the olive oil with the lemon juice, salt, pepper, and sumac.

Just before serving, sprinkle the toasted pita pieces over the salad and toss the salad well with the dressing.

BULGUR and CHICKPEA SALAD
Safsouf

This rustic salad from the Bekaa Valley does not feature on the standard restaurant menu. It began originally as the leftover, meatless filling for vine leaves. Make it with fine-ground bulgur.

SERVES 6

1 cup fine- or medium-ground bulgur
2 garlic cloves, crushed
juice of 2 1/2 to 3 lemons
salt and black pepper
7 tablespoons extra virgin olive oil
one 14-ounce can chickpeas, drained
3 1/2 cups loosely packed finely chopped flat-leaf parsley
1 cup loosely packed finely chopped mint leaves

Soak the bulgur in plenty of cold water for 20 minutes, until tender, then drain and squeeze out the excess water. In a bowl, mix the garlic, lemon juice, salt, pepper, and olive oil. Soak the drained chickpeas in this for 10 minutes, then stir in the bulgur.

Mix in the chopped herbs when you are ready to serve.

MINT and PARSLEY SALAD
with RICE
Tabbouleh Bi Roz

This is a very green and appealing herby salad, also born as the leftover filling of vegetables cooked in oil. It is meant to be very sharp, but start with the juice of one lemon and add more, if you wish, after tasting.

SERVES 4
1 cup basmati rice
salt
2 cups loosely packed chopped flat-leaf parsley
5 sprigs mint, chopped
7 scallions, thinly sliced
juice of 1 to 1 1/2 lemons
5 tablespoons extra virgin olive oil
black pepper
5 ripe and firm tomatoes, finely diced
1 Little Gem (baby romaine) lettuce (optional)

Wash and rinse the basmati rice. Cook the rice in plenty of boiling salted water for about 10 to 20 minutes. (Some brands that claim not to be parboiled or precooked now take as little as 8 to 10 minutes, so read the information on the package and watch the rice carefully so it does not overcook.) When it is just tender, drain quickly and leave to cool.

Just before serving, mix the rice with the parsley, mint, and scallions. Dress with a mixture of lemon juice, olive oil, salt, and pepper and mix well. Serve on a flat plate, topped with the diced tomato lightly seasoned with salt.

Garnish, if you like, with a ring of lettuce leaves stuck around the edges of the salad.

EGGPLANT and TOMATO SALAD
Batinjan Raheb

This is beautiful to look at and delicious.

SERVES 6 TO 8   2 to 3 eggplants (weighing about 2 pounds)
juice of 1/2 to 1 lemon
3 garlic cloves, crushed
4 tablespoons extra virgin olive oil
salt and black pepper
large handful of chopped flat-leaf parsley
4 sprigs of mint, chopped
4 scallions, finely sliced
4 plum tomatoes, unpeeled, diced
handful of fresh pomegranate seeds (optional)

Prick the eggplants in a few places with a pointed knife to prevent them from exploding. Turn them over the flame of the gas burner or a hot barbecue, or under the broiler, until the skin is charred all over (this gives them a distinctive smoky flavor) and they feel very soft when you press them. Alternatively, place them on a sheet of foil on an oven tray and roast them in the hottest preheated oven for 45 to 55 minutes, until the skins are wrinkled and they are very soft.

When cool enough to handle, peel and drop them into a strainer or colander with small holes. Press out as much of the water and juices as possible. Still in the colander, chop the flesh with a pointed knife, then mash it with a fork or wooden spoon, letting the juices escape through the holes.

Mix the eggplant purée with the lemon juice, garlic, olive oil, salt, pepper, chopped parsley, and mint. Spread the purée on a large, flat serving plate. Sprinkle all over with the finely sliced scallions, diced tomatoes, and pomegranate seeds, if using.

EGGPLANT with POMEGRANATE MOLASSES
Batinjan Bil Rumman

This dish is traditionally made with fried eggplants, but I like to roast them whole and then peel them and cut them into pieces. Serve them hot or cold.

SERVES 4 TO 6
2 to 3 eggplants (weighing about 2 pounds)
juice of 1 lemon
1 tablespoon pomegranate molasses
1 to 2 garlic cloves, crushed
salt and black pepper
3 tablespoons extra virgin olive oil
2 tablespoons chopped flat-leaf parsley
seeds of 1/2 pomegranate (optional)

Prick the eggplants in a few places with a pointed knife to prevent them from exploding. Place them on a sheet of foil on an oven tray and roast them in an oven preheated to 475°F for 45 to 55 minutes, until the skins are wrinkled and they are very soft.

When cool enough to handle, peel and drop them into a colander or strainer with small holes. Press them very gently to allow their juices to run out. Then, on a serving plate, cut them up into large pieces and dress them quickly so that the flesh does not have time to discolor.

Mix the lemon juice, pomegranate molasses, garlic, salt, pepper, and olive oil, pour over the eggplants, and turn them to coat them all over with the dressing.

Serve sprinkled with chopped parsley and, if you like, pomegranate seeds.

EGGPLANTS with YOGURT and TAHINI
Batinjan Bil Laban Wal Tehine

Prepare the recipe on the previous page. Instead of sprinkling the eggplants with parsley and pomegranate seeds, pour over 2 cups plain whole-milk yogurt beaten with 2 tablespoons tahini. Serve sprinkled with 1/4 cup pine nuts fried until golden in 1 tablespoon olive oil. This is marvelous.

EGGPLANTS with VINEGAR and GARLIC
Batinjan Bi Khal

Roast, peel, and cut up the eggplants as in the recipe on the preceding page for Eggplant with Pomegranate Molasses and marinate overnight in the following dressing:

Fry 6 chopped garlic cloves in about 1 1/2 tablespoons extra virgin olive oil, stirring it over low heat for moments only, until the aroma rises, without letting it brown. Mix in 2 tablespoons white or red wine vinegar, 3 more tablespoons of olive oil, salt, and black pepper. Serve sprinkled with chopped parsley.

EGGPLANTS with PEPPERY TOMATO SAUCE

Roast, peel, and cut up the eggplants as in the recipe for Eggplant with Pomegranate Molasses (page 258). Turn the pieces in the juice of 1/2 lemon to prevent them from discoloring.

Heat 2 or 3 crushed garlic cloves in 2 tablespoons extra virgin olive oil, stirring them over a medium heat for seconds only, until the aroma rises. Add 1 pound peeled and chopped tomatoes, 2 teaspoons sugar, 1 1/2 tablespoons red or white wine vinegar, salt, and 1/2 teaspoon ground chili pepper, or to taste. Cook for 10 to 15 minutes, until the mixture is reduced to a thick sauce. Toward the end, add 2 to 3 tablespoons chopped mint leaves. Let the sauce cool and pour over the eggplants. Serve cold.

EGGPLANT SLICES *with* POMEGRANATE, YOGURT, *and* TAHINI
Batinjan Bil Rumman Wal Laban

The dressing of pomegranate molasses and vinegar gives the eggplant slices a sweet-and-sour flavor. Serve them hot or cold, with the yogurt and tahini topping at room temperature.

SERVES 6 TO 8
4 eggplants (about 2 1/2 pounds)
extra virgin olive oil
salt
1 1/2 tablespoons pomegranate molasses
1 1/2 tablespoons red or white wine vinegar
2 cups plain whole-milk yogurt
1 garlic clove, crushed
2 tablespoons tahini
1/4 cup pine nuts

Cut the eggplants, lengthwise or crosswise, into slices about 1/2 inch thick. Place them on an oiled sheet of foil on a baking sheet or tray. Brush both sides of the eggplant slices with oil and sprinkle lightly with salt. Place in a very hot oven preheated to 475°F for about 30 minutes, until they are soft and browned, turning the slices over once. Arrange on a shallow serving dish.

Mix the pomegranate molasses, vinegar, and 2 tablespoons olive oil, and brush the eggplant slices with the dressing. Beat the yogurt with the garlic and tahini and pour over the slices. Fry the pine nuts very briefly in 1/2 tablespoon olive oil, stirring to brown them very lightly all over, and sprinkle over the yogurt.

VARIATION
Instead of the pine nuts, garnish with the shiny pink seeds of a fresh pomegranate.

EGGPLANTS with TOMATOES and CHICKPEAS
Moussaka'a Menazzaleh

This dish can be served cold as a salad or hot as a side dish to accompany meat or chicken. It has a delicate sweet-and-sour flavor.

SERVES 6

2 eggplants
extra virgin olive oil
salt
2 to 3 garlic cloves, crushed
1 pound tomatoes, skinned and chopped
2 teaspoons sugar
black pepper
1 1/2 tablespoons pomegranate molasses
one 14-ounce can chickpeas, drained
2 tablespoons chopped flat-leaf parsley

Cut the eggplants in half lengthwise and then into 1/2-inch slices. Brush them generously with oil, sprinkle lightly with salt, and cook them under the broiler for 15 minutes, or on an oiled griddle, turning them over once. They do not need to be cooked through as they will be stewed further in the sauce.

In a large saucepan, heat the garlic in 1 tablespoon olive oil for seconds only, stirring, until it just begins to color. Add the tomatoes and squash them gently in the pan. Add the sugar, salt, and black pepper and cook for 15 minutes. Add the pomegranate molasses, put in the eggplants and chickpeas, and simmer for 20 to 30 minutes, or until the eggplants are very soft.

Serve sprinkled with chopped parsley.

OKRA with BABY ONIONS and TOMATOES
Bamieh Bi Zeit

Cooked in this way, in olive oil, the dish is normally served cold as a salad, but I also like it hot with rice or as a side dish with meat or chicken.

SERVES 4 TO 6

1 pound medium okra

1/2 pound baby onions or shallots

6 whole garlic cloves, peeled

5 tablespoons extra virgin olive oil

1 pound tomatoes, peeled and chopped

salt and black pepper

1 teaspoon sugar

3 to 4 tablespoons chopped flat-leaf parsley or coriander

Wash the okra and, with a small sharp knife, carefully pare the conical stem ends without cutting through the pods. To peel the baby onions or shallots more easily, put them in boiling water and simmer for 5 minutes. Drain, and peel them when they are cool enough to handle.

In a large pan over low heat, gently fry the onions and garlic cloves in 3 tablespoons oil, shaking the pan to color them very lightly all over. Add the okra and sauté gently for about 5 minutes, turning the pods around in the pan.

Add the tomatoes, season with salt, pepper, and sugar, and simmer for 15 minutes, or until the okra are tender and the sauce is reduced. Taste and adjust the seasoning, stir in the chopped parsley or coriander, and cook a minute more. Stir in the remaining olive oil and serve at room temperature.

VARIATION

Add the juice of 1/2 lemon or 1 tablespoon pomegranate molasses toward the end of the cooking time. If adding molasses, omit the sugar.

ZUCCHINI with VINEGAR, MINT, and GARLIC
Koussa Bil Khal

These zucchini slices are usually fried but they are just as good grilled. They can be prepared hours before serving, even a day ahead.

SERVES 6

5 large zucchini (weighing about 2 pounds)
extra virgin olive oil
salt
2 tablespoons white wine vinegar
2 teaspoons dried, crushed mint
2 to 3 garlic cloves, crushed

Trim the ends of the zucchini and cut them lengthwise in slices about 1/3 inch thick. Arrange them side by side on a baking sheet lined with foil and brushed with oil. Brush the slices generously with olive oil and sprinkle lightly with salt.

Cook under a preheated broiler until lightly browned, then turn over and brush the other side with oil and return to the broiler until browned.

Mix the vinegar with the mint and garlic and brush a little onto each slice. Serve at room temperature.

VARIATIONS

❋ Instead of using raw garlic, heat it in 2 tablespoons oil in a small frying pan until the aroma rises, but do not let it color.

❋ Serve the grilled slices topped with strained Greek-style yogurt.

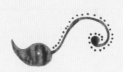

ROAST POTATOES with LEMON and CORIANDER
Batata Bel Lamoun Wal Cosbara

These potatoes are normally deep-fried or sautéed in olive oil but they are equally good roasted. They are served cold, although I admit I like them hot, too.

SERVES 6

2 pounds new potatoes, peeled
salt and black pepper
5 to 6 tablespoons extra virgin olive oil
4 garlic cloves, crushed
juice of 1 1/2 lemons
large handful of chopped coriander

Boil the potatoes in salted water for about 10 minutes, then drain and transfer to a wide baking dish. Cut them into 1/2-inch cubes and sprinkle over some salt and pepper, the olive oil, and the garlic. Mix and turn the pieces of potato so they are coated all over with the oil.

Roast the potato pieces in a very hot oven, preheated to 475°F, for 30 minutes, or until they are crisp and brown. Take them out, sprinkle evenly with the lemon juice and chopped coriander, and mix well, being careful not to break the potatoes.

CURLY ENDIVE *with*
CARAMELIZED ONIONS
Hindbeh

Wild chicory is used for this Lebanese mountain salad. The sweetness of the caramelized onion topping is a contrast to the slightly bitter leaves. You can sometimes find bunches of wild chicory, which has long, dark green leaves, in Middle Eastern stores, but ordinary curly endive—what the French call chicorée—will do very well. The salad can also be made with dandelion leaves.

SERVES 4 TO 6
about 2 pounds curly endive
2 large onions, sliced
6 tablespoons extra virgin olive oil
4 to 6 garlic cloves, crushed
salt and black pepper
2 lemons

Trim the stem ends of the endive and remove any discolored bits, then wash the leaves. Boil in salted water for a couple of minutes, or until it is soft, then drain and press out the excess water. Cut up the leaves into pieces 1 1/2 to 2 1/2 inches long.

Fry the onions in the oil in a large pan over medium heat until brown and caramelized, stirring often. Remove about three-quarters of the onions to use as the topping, draining them on paper towels. Add the garlic to the onions remaining in the pan, and as soon as the aroma rises, put in the endive. Add salt and pepper and the juice of 1/2 lemon, and cook, stirring, for a minute or so.

Serve cold on a flat serving dish with the caramelized onions sprinkled all over the top, accompanied by the remaining lemons, cut into quarters.

VARIATION

To the onions remaining in the pan, add one 14-ounce can chickpeas or haricot beans, well drained, at the same time as the endive.

SPINACH and BEANS with CARAMELIZED ONIONS
Sabanekh Bi Loubia

Use black-eyed peas or haricot beans for this dish. You can use frozen spinach (defrost it thoroughly). If using fresh, wash it well and remove the stems only if they are very thick.

SERVES 4 TO 6

1 large onion, sliced
6 tablespoons extra virgin olive oil
3 garlic cloves, chopped
1/2 pound fresh spinach
salt and black pepper
one 14-ounce can beans, drained
juice of 1/4 to 1/2 lemon

Fry the onion in 2 tablespoons oil, stirring often, until brown and caramelized.

In a large saucepan, heat the garlic in 2 tablespoons oil for moments only, until the aroma rises. Add the spinach, put on the lid, and cook until the spinach crumples to a soft mass. Add salt and pepper.

Stir the beans and the fried onions into the spinach; add lemon juice and cook through. Add the remaining oil and serve cold.

VARIATION
Chickpeas can be used in the same way instead of beans.

LENTILS with PASTA and CARAMELIZED ONIONS
Rishta Bi Addas

This can be eaten hot or at room temperature, like a pasta salad. The tagliatelle is usually cooked in the same water as the lentils, which gives the pasta a pleasant earthy color and flavor, but you can also boil them separately.

SERVES 4 TO 6
- 1 large onion, sliced
- 6 to 7 tablespoons extra virgin olive oil
- 1/2 cup large green or brown lentils
- 4 ounces dry tagliatelle nests
- salt and black pepper
- large handful of chopped flat-leaf parsley

Fry the onion in 2 tablespoons oil until brown and caramelized, stirring often. It is a good idea to start with the lid on; this allows them to soften more quickly.

Rinse the lentils and boil them in plenty of water until they are only just tender. Some brands take as little as 10 to 15 minutes, others take much longer. You should read the instructions on the package and watch the cooking carefully.

Break the tagliatelle into pieces by crushing the nests in your hands and drop the pieces into the pan with the lentils—there should be enough water to cover them. Add salt, stir, and boil vigorously until the pasta is cooked al dente.

Drain quickly and toss gently with the remaining olive oil, a little salt and pepper, the fried onions, and the chopped parsley.

CHICKPEAS with TOASTED BREAD and YOGURT
Fattet Hummus Bi Laban

A layer of chickpeas, spread over bread soaked in their cooking broth, smothered in yogurt with an elusive taste of tahini, and topped with pine nuts may sound heavy but it is surprisingly light and delicate in the eating, and the mix of textures, temperatures, and flavors is a joy. The bread must be the very thin flat bread known as khobz halabi, which is sold by Lebanese bakeries. You need either 1 large one measuring about 12 inches in diameter, or 2 smaller ones; or use 1 pita bread instead.

SERVES 6 TO 8 1 1/4 cups chickpeas, soaked for 2 hours or overnight

salt

2 garlic cloves, crushed

1 large or 2 small very thin Lebanese flat breads (see above)

2 1/2 tablespoons tahini

4 cups plain whole-milk yogurt, at room temperature

1/2 to 2/3 cup pine nuts

1 1/2 tablespoons extra virgin olive oil

Drain the chickpeas and put them in a pan with water to cover and simmer, covered, for 1 1/4 to 1 1/2 hours, until they are very soft. Add water, as needed, so that the level remains about 1/3 inch above the chickpeas throughout the cooking. Add salt when the chickpeas have begun to soften and the crushed garlic toward the end.

Toast the bread in an oven preheated to 400°F until it becomes crisp. Then place it at the bottom of an ovenproof dish and break it up into smallish pieces by pressing down on it with the palm of your hand. Pour the hot chickpeas and much of their cooking liquid over the pieces of bread so that they are well soaked. If you are not ready to serve, you can reheat this in the oven when you are.

Before serving, beat the tahini into the yogurt, and pour it over the chickpeas. Quickly fry the pine nuts in the oil, stirring, until lightly browned, and sprinkle over the dish.

VARIATIONS

✻ Fry the pine nuts in 3 tablespoons butter until lightly colored, and then add 2 tablespoons crushed dried mint and 1/2 tablespoon red or white wine vinegar.

✻ In a version called *tasseia*, the chickpeas are crushed and mixed with 2 to 3 tablespoons tahini, the juice of 1/2 lemon, and 1 crushed garlic clove. You can put these in a blender with a little of the cooking water. Squeeze a little lemon juice into the chickpea water before sprinkling it over the bread, spread the mashed chickpea purée over the top, and cover with yogurt, then garnish as above.

✻ Instead of toasting the bread, some people cut it into triangles and deep-fry them in hot oil. Drain the pieces on absorbent paper towels.

PRAWNS with GARLIC and CORIANDER
Kreidess Bi Cosbara

Use raw king prawns for this dish; they are gray and turn pink when they are cooked. Some supermarkets sell them ready-peeled.

SERVES 4

16 large, raw king prawns
3 tablespoons extra virgin olive oil
3 garlic cloves, finely chopped
handful of chopped coriander
1 lemon, cut in quarters

If the prawns need peeling, pull off the heads and legs, then peel off the shells, but leave the tails on. If you see a dark vein along the back, make a fine slit with a sharp knife and pull it out.

Heat the olive oil in a large frying pan, add the prawns, and cook for a minute. Turn them over, add the garlic and coriander, and cook for a minute more, until the prawns turn pink. They should not need any salt. Serve them hot with the lemon quarters.

CHEESE OMELETTE
Ijjit Al Jibne

This simple herby omelette can be served as a light main dish accompanied by a salad. It can be served hot or cold. To serve it as a mezze, cut it into small wedges, or make tiny pancakes (see Variation).

SERVES 4 TO 6   8 eggs, lightly beaten

6 ounces feta cheese, mashed with a fork

6 scallions, finely sliced

handful of chopped mint

large handful of chopped flat-leaf parsley

white pepper

3 tablespoons olive oil

In a bowl, lightly beat the eggs with the rest of the ingredients, except the oil.

Heat 2 tablespoons oil in a large, nonstick ovenproof frying pan. When it begins to sizzle, pour in the egg mixture. Cook over low heat for about 10 minutes, or until the bottom sets.

Drizzle the remaining oil over the top of the omelette, and cook under the broiler for a few minutes, until lightly browned. Serve it cut in wedges like a cake.

VARIATION

Drop small amounts of the egg mixture in batches—by the half ladle—in a nonstick frying pan filmed with oil and turn them over as soon as the bottoms become detached.

GRILLED CHICKEN WINGS with LEMON and GARLIC
Jawaneh

Chicken wings are a very popular mezze item. They should be quite lemony and garlicky. You eat them with your fingers.

SERVES 4

3 tablespoons extra virgin olive oil
juice of 1 lemon
salt and black pepper
2 to 4 garlic cloves, crushed
16 chicken wings
2 tablespoons chopped flat-leaf parsley

Mix the olive oil, lemon juice, salt, pepper, and garlic, and place the chicken wings in the marinade. Leave for 1 hour, covered with plastic wrap, in the refrigerator.

Remove the wings from the marinade and place them on a piece of foil on a baking tray and cook them under a preheated broiler for 7 minutes, turning them over once. Or barbecue them over glowing embers for the same amount of time. Serve them sprinkled with chopped parsley.

GRILLED QUAILS
Siman Meshwi

Quails are part of the mezze tradition. Use your hands to eat them.

SERVES 4

4 quails
2 tablespoons extra virgin olive oil
salt and pepper
1 tablespoon chopped flat-leaf parsley

Lay each quail breast side down. Cut along one side of the backbone, then along the other side and remove the bone. Open out the bird and turn it over. Cut the wing and leg joints just enough to pull them a little apart, then press down hard with the palm of your hand to flatten the bird.

Place the quails on a sheet of foil on an oven tray. Rub them with the olive oil and sprinkle with salt and pepper. Cook the birds under a preheated broiler for about 8 minutes, turning them over once.

Serve sprinkled with the chopped parsley.

LITTLE PUFF PASTRY CHEESE PIES
Sambousek Bi Jibne

These melt-in-the-mouth cheese pies make good party food. They can be eaten hot or warm. You can make them in advance and heat them through before serving. Use fresh or frozen and defrosted puff pastry.

MAKES
32 PIES

1 pound puff pastry
flour
2 to 3 tablespoons butter, melted

FOR THE FILLING
1/2 pound mozzarella cheese
1/2 pound feta cheese
2 eggs, lightly beaten

It is important to roll out the puff pastry as thinly as you possibly can. It is easier to do this if you cut it into four equal pieces and roll out each one separately. Dust the rolling surface and the rolling pin with flour. Roll out the first sheet of pastry, turning it over and dusting it with flour. Cut 6 rounds with a 4-inch pastry cutter. Make a ball out of the off-cuts, roll this out, and make 2 more rounds. Put the 8 rounds in a pile and wrap it in plastic wrap. Do the same with the remaining pastry.

For the filling, blend the mozzarella in the food processor. In a bowl, mash the feta cheese with a fork, add the mozzarella, and mix well together, then mix in the eggs.

Put a tablespoon of the filling on one half of each round of pastry. Dip your finger in water and slightly dampen the pastry edges (this will make them stick better), then fold the pastry over the filling to make a half-moon shape. Seal the pies by pinching the edges very firmly together. A traditional way is to finish the pies by twisting the edges, making a scalloped effect; another is to press down the edges with the prongs of a fork.

Arrange the pies on sheets of foil on baking trays. Brush the tops with melted butter and bake them in an oven preheated to 400°F for about 15 to 20 minutes, or until they are puffed up and lightly golden.

VARIATIONS

Instead of baking, deep-fry the pies in vegetable oil, turning them over once. Drain them on absorbent paper towels.

For a shiny golden color, instead of brushing with melted butter, brush the pies with an egg yolk mixed with a drop of water.

SPINACH PIES
Fatayer Bi Sabanikh

These little pies are a famous Lenten specialty; they are deliciously sharp and lemony. A good, commercial puff pastry will do very well for the dough. The pies are wonderful eaten hot and also good cold.

You may use frozen leaf spinach instead of fresh spinach. Defrost it and squeeze out the liquid.

MAKES ABOUT
24 PIES

1 pound fresh spinach leaves
1 large onion, chopped
4 tablespoons extra virgin olive oil
salt and pepper
1/2 teaspoon ground allspice
juice of 1 lemon or 1 tablespoon sumac (see page 7)
14 ounces puff pastry
flour

Wash the spinach and remove any thick stems (you can leave the thin stems of very young spinach). Put the leaves in a large saucepan with just the water that is clinging to the leaves and steam with the lid on for a minute or two, until the spinach crumples to a soft mass. Strain in a colander, then squeeze all the liquid out with your hands. Chop the spinach coarsely.

In a large frying pan, fry the onion in 3 tablespoons of the olive oil, stirring occasionally, until golden. Add the spinach, salt and pepper, allspice, and lemon juice or sumac and mix well, leaving the pan on the heat for a few moments so that any excess liquid can evaporate.

Cut the puff pastry in half to make rolling out more manageable. Lightly dust the rolling surface and the rolling pin with flour. Roll out each half into a thin sheet, turning the sheet over a few times and dusting it each time with a little flour. Cut it into rounds with a pastry cutter 4 inches in diameter. Off-cuts can be rolled into a ball and rolled out again, so you do not waste any part of the dough. Put the rounds in a pile and wrap it in plastic wrap. Do the same with the remaining pastry.

Take a round of pastry, lay it flat on one hand, and put a tablespoon of filling in the middle. To make the traditional Lebanese three-sided pie, lift up two sides and pinch the neighboring edges together, making a thin-ridged joint. Lift up the third side, join its two edges to the other two to make a small three-sided pyramid with a rounded base. Seal the openings by pinching the edges firmly all the way to the top. Repeat with the remaining pastry rounds and filling. Don't worry if the pies open a little at the top to reveal the filling when they are cooked.

Place the pies on sheets of foil on baking trays, brush the tops with the remaining olive oil, and bake in an oven preheated to 350°F for 25 to 30 minutes, or until golden.

VARIATION

Add 1/2 cup pine nuts to the fried onions, and stir until they begin to color, before adding the spinach.

LITTLE MEAT PIZZAS
Lahma Bi Ajeen

The dough given here is one of a variety used to make the famous Arab "pizzas" variously called lahma bi ajeen and sfiha. It contains yogurt and olive oil and is soft and moist. Small pizzas make good finger food; large ones make an excellent snack. They can be made in advance and reheated.

Do also try the different toppings given in the variations below.

MAKES
ABOUT 20
SMALL
PIZZAS

FOR THE DOUGH

about 1 cup warm yogurt

2 teaspoons dried yeast

pinch of sugar

1/4 cup warm water

3 1/3 cups strong white bread flour

1 teaspoon salt

1/4 cup extra virgin olive oil

FOR THE MEAT AND TOMATO TOPPING

1 large onion

1 1/4 pounds ground lamb

3 large garlic cloves, crushed

1/2 teaspoon ground allspice

salt and black pepper

2 tablespoons pomegranate molasses

1 pound tomatoes, unpeeled, finely chopped

1/4 cup pine nuts (optional)

To warm the yogurt, put the pot in a bowl or pan of hot, not boiling, water for about 1 hour. Dissolve the yeast with the sugar in the 1/4 cup of warm water and leave for about 10 minutes, until it froths. In a large bowl, mix the flour with the salt and oil, then add the yeast mixture and just enough of the yogurt to make the dough hold together in a ball. Begin by mixing with a fork, then work with your hands. Knead for about 10 minutes, or until the dough is smooth and elastic. Pour a drop of oil in the bowl and roll the dough around in it to grease it all over and prevent a dry skin from forming. Cover the bowl with plastic wrap and leave in a warm place for 1 1/2 hours, until it has doubled in bulk.

For the topping, finely chop the onion in the food processor and drain it of its juices. Put the meat, onion, garlic, allspice, salt, pepper, and pomegranate molasses in a bowl. Mix well and work into a soft paste with your hands. Then work in the tomato and the pine nuts, if using.

Punch down the risen dough and knead for 1 minute. Take lumps the size of a large walnut if making mini pizzas, or the size of an egg if making large ones, and roll out on a clean surface with a rolling pin. Do not flour these as the dough is very greasy and will not stick. Roll out thinly into rounds about 1/8 inch thick and place on oiled sheets of foil on baking trays.

Take lumps of the topping mixture and spread thickly over each round of dough— go right up to the edges as the topping tends to shrink while the dough expands as it cooks.

Bake one tray at a time in an oven preheated to 400°F for 15 minutes, placing each on the top shelf. Serve the pizzas hot.

VARIATIONS

✿ For a Meat and Yogurt Topping: Mix 1 1/4 pounds ground lamb, 1 large onion (finely chopped in the food processor and drained of its juices), 1/2 cup plain whole-milk yogurt, the juice of 1/2 lemon, salt and pepper, 1/2 teaspoon ground allspice, and 1/3 cup pine nuts.

✿ For Meat and Tomato with Chili: Work together to a paste 1 large onion (very finely chopped in the food processor and drained of its juices), 1/2 to 1 finely chopped chili pepper, 1 1/4 pounds ground lamb, 4 tablespoons concentrated tomato paste, 2 tablespoons pomegranate molasses, salt, and pepper.

RED LENTIL and RICE SOUP
Makhlouta

Serve this creamy soup with thin Lebanese flat bread cut into triangles, opened out, brushed with olive oil, and toasted in the oven until crisp.

SERVES 6 TO 8
2 large onions, sliced
3 tablespoons extra virgin olive oil
7 1/2 cups chicken stock (made with 2 bouillon cubes)
1 cup red lentils
1/2 cup short-grain or risotto rice
black pepper
2 teaspoons ground coriander
salt
1 teaspoon ground cumin
2 lemons

Fry the onions in the oil. Cover the pan and cook over low heat, stirring occasionally, until they soften. Then cook over high heat, stirring often, until they are very brown and caramelized. Drain on paper towels and keep them aside.

Bring the stock to the boil then put in the lentils and rice. Add the black pepper and the ground coriander, and simmer for about 35 to 45 minutes, until the lentils and rice fall apart and the soup has a creamy texture. Add a little salt toward the end of the cooking time, taking into account the saltiness of the bouillon cubes, and a little water, if necessary, to thin the soup to a light creamy consistency.

Serve, sprinkling each bowlful with a pinch of cumin and garnishing each with a topping of fried onions. Pass around lemon quarters.

GREEN VEGETABLE SOUP

This spring soup is green and aromatic. It becomes more substantial if served over rice. Other vegetables such as artichoke bottoms (frozen ones will do; see page 8) cut into pieces, peas, and broad beans can also be added.

SERVES 6 TO 8
1 cup long-grain or washed basmati rice
8 cups chicken or vegetable stock (made with 2 bouillon cubes)
2 leeks
1 small head of celery with leaves
salt and white pepper
3 to 4 garlic cloves, crushed
juice of 1 lemon
1 teaspoon sugar, or more to taste
7 ounces zucchini
2 tablespoons dried mint

To cook the rice, add it to plenty of boiling, salted water and simmer for 10 to 18 minutes (the time varies depending on the type of rice), or until tender, then drain quickly. Keep it aside until you are ready to serve.

Heat the stock in a large pan. Cut the leeks crosswise and the celery into slices about 1/3 inch thick and add them to the pan. Simmer for about 30 minutes, until they are tender. Add salt (taking into account the saltiness of the stock), white pepper, garlic, lemon juice, and sugar.

Trim the zucchini of their ends and cut in half lengthwise and then into 1/3-inch-thick slices. Add them to the pan and cook for 5 minutes, then add the mint and cook 5 minutes more. Taste and adjust the flavorings.

Serve in soup bowls over the rice.

Main Courses

Everyone in Lebanon appreciates the old traditional dishes that now make up the national cuisine. The repertoire is mainly represented by the refined, sophisticated dishes of the old Greek Orthodox and Sunni *grande bourgeoisie* of Beirut and those of the Maronite *grands seigneurs* of the mountains, combined with simple rural dishes and with the festive dishes associated with religious holidays. There are traditionalists, modernizers who may simply lighten the cooking and present the food in a novel way, and there are those who allow themselves to be creative.

SEA BREAM with SAFFRON RICE
Samak Wal Roz Bil Zafaran

Ask the fishmonger to clean and scale the fish, and remove the fins and gills, but ask him to leave the heads on. The rice, which is cooked with olive oil instead of the usual butter, is the traditional rice to accompany fish in Lebanon. Turmeric is sometimes used instead of saffron. Start cooking the rice first.

SERVES 4

FOR THE RICE

6 tablespoons extra virgin olive oil
1/2 teaspoon saffron powder or threads
1 1/2 cups long-grain rice
2 1/3 cups boiling water
salt and black pepper
2 medium onions, sliced
1/2 cup pine nuts

4 sea bream (weighing about 14 ounces each)
salt and black pepper
2 tablespoons extra virgin olive oil
To serve: 1 lemon

For the rice, heat 2 tablespoons oil in a pan. Stir in the saffron and add the rice. Stir well, until the rice acquires a transparent yellow glow. Add the boiling water, stir in the salt and pepper, and simmer over low heat, covered and undisturbed, for about 20 minutes, until the rice is tender and the water has been absorbed. Then stir in another 2 tablespoons oil.

Fry the onions in the remaining 2 tablespoons oil, stirring occasionally, until brown. Add the pine nuts, and stir until they are lightly colored.

Make 3 to 4 slashes about 1/3 inch deep in the thickest part of the fish so that they cook evenly. Put them side by side in a baking dish, sprinkle with salt and pepper, and rub them generously with olive oil. Bake in an oven preheated to 425°F for about 15 minutes.

Serve the fish with lemon quarters, and the rice separately, shaped in a mound and garnished with the pine nuts and onions.

PAN-FRIED RED MULLET with TAHINI SAUCE
Sultan Ibrahim Makli Bi Tehine

The most popular item on the menu in the fish restaurants along the long Lebanese coast are the deep-fried red mullet that come accompanied by a tahini sauce and very thin crisp deep-fried bread. They are fried whole, coated with flour, but at home I find it easier to pan-fry red mullet fillets.

SERVES 4

FOR THE TAHINI SAUCE
1/3 cup tahini
juice of 1 lemon
about 1/3 cup cold water
salt
1/2 to 1 clove garlic, crushed (optional)

8 red mullet fillets (weighing about 3 ounces each), skin on
salt and black pepper
2 to 3 tablespoons extra virgin olive oil
1 lemon, cut in wedges

First, make the sauce. Stir the tahini in the jar before using. With a fork, beat the tahini with the lemon juice. It will thicken to a stiff paste. Add the water, beating vigorously until you get the consistency of a pale, runny cream. Then add a little salt and the garlic, if using, and pour into a serving bowl.

Season the red mullet fillets with salt and pepper and fry in the oil over medium-high heat, preferably in a nonstick frying pan, for about 2 minutes on the skin side. Turn and cook the other side for half a minute more.

Serve the fish at once, with the lemon wedges, and let people pour the tahini sauce on the side.

VARIATION

Season 4 fish fillets (5 to 7 ounces each), such as cod or haddock, with salt and white pepper and 1/2 teaspoon ground cumin. Dip the fillets in flour to coat them all over, and shallow-fry in sizzling olive oil, turning over once. Drain on paper towels and serve with the tahini sauce.

FISH with PINE NUT SAUCE
Samak Bil Tarator Bi Senobar

This is a dish that is served cold and is especially good for a buffet party. It is beautiful and dramatic. Get a large white fish—sea bass would be great but is expensive; cod or haddock will do very well. (Although salmon is not a fish used in Lebanon, and not a fish of the Mediterranean regions, it is good to serve in this way.) Have the fish skinned and also filleted, if you like, and ask for the head and tail. Cooked in foil, the fish steams in its own juice and the flesh remains moist. The pine nut sauce, tarator bi senobar, has a very delicate flavor.

SERVES 8

2 tablespoons extra virgin olive oil

1 whole cod (weighing about 5 1/2 pounds)

salt

1 lemon, cut into thin slices

To garnish: 3 tablespoons pine nuts or 4 tablespoons chopped
     flat-leaf parsley, and 2 lemons, sliced

FOR THE PINE NUT SAUCE

2 slices good white bread, 1/2 inch thick

1 2/3 cups pine nuts

juice of 2 lemons

2 garlic cloves, crushed

salt

Brush a large sheet of foil with a little of the olive oil. Place the fish in the middle, sprinkle lightly with salt and rub with the remaining oil. Sprinkle the cavity of the fish with a little salt and put in the lemon slices. Wrap in a loose parcel, twisting the foil edges together to seal it. Wrap the head and tail separately in another piece of foil.

Bake the fish in an oven preheated to 400°F for 45 minutes, or until done. To test for doneness, cut into the thickest part and check that the flesh flakes and has turned white right through. The head and tail should come out of the oven after 20 minutes.

For the sauce, cut away the crusts from the bread (it should now weigh about 3 ounces) and soak the slices in water. Blend the pine nuts to a paste in the food processor. Then add the bread, squeezed dry, lemon juice, and garlic and blend well. Add a little salt and about 3 to 4 tablespoons of cold water—just enough to blend to the consistency of thick cream.

Serve the fish cold, covered with the sauce, and with the head and tail in place. Decorate with a pattern using pine nuts that have been fried gently in a drop of oil until slightly colored, or with parsley, and with lemon slices cut into half-moon shapes.

FISH with RICE and ONION SAUCE
Sayyadieh

The distinctive feature of this famous Arab fish and rice dish is the flavor of caramelized onions in the brown broth that suffuses the rice and colors it a pale brown. Use skinned fillets of white fish such as bream, turbot, haddock, or cod.

SERVES 4

About 1 1/4 pounds onions, sliced
4 to 5 tablespoons extra virgin olive oil
2 fish or chicken bouillon cubes
salt and black pepper
1/2 teaspoon ground cumin
1/2 teaspoon ground allspice
1 1/2 cups long-grain or washed basmati rice
4 fish fillets (each weighing 5 to 7 ounces)
1/2 to 1 lemon
2/3 cup pine nuts

In a large saucepan, fry the onions in 2 1/2 tablespoons oil over low heat, with the lid on until they are soft and transparent, stirring occasionally. Then take off the lid and let them get very dark brown and caramelized. Blend them to a cream in the food processor and return this to the pan.

Add about 4 1/2 cups boiling water and the crumbled bouillon cubes; season with salt, pepper, cumin, and allspice, and simmer for about 10 minutes.

Pour out the onion stock to measure the quantity you need for cooking the rice. Return 2 1/2 cups to the pan, and put the rest aside to use as the sauce. Add the rice and some salt, stir well, and cook, covered, over a low heat, for about 10 to 18 minutes, until the rice is tender. (Some brands that claim not to be parboiled or precooked now take as little as 8 to 10 minutes, so read the information on the package.) Set it aside until you are ready to serve.

Pan-fry the fish fillets, seasoned with salt and pepper, in the remaining oil, for 2 to 3 minutes on each side, until the flesh just begins to flake. Squeeze a little lemon juice over them. Fry the pine nuts in a drop of oil until lightly browned. Reheat the onion sauce, adding a little lemon juice to taste.

Serve the rice heaped in a mound with the sauce poured over. Arrange the pieces of fish on top or around the rice and sprinkle with the pine nuts.

✱ A way of preparing the dish in advance is to layer it in a deep baking dish—pine nuts first, then fish, then rice—and heat it through in the oven. Turn it out upside down just before serving, and serve the sauce separately.

✱ You can accompany the dish with the tahini sauce on page 290 as well as its brown sauce.

✱ For a "white" version of the same dish, the onions should be meltingly soft, but should not be allowed to brown.

CHICKEN PIE with ONIONS and SUMAC
Musakhan

This pie with a beguilingly flavorsome filling is a refined interpretation of musakhan, which is of Bedouin origin and is baked in thin Arab bread. It is delicious, and you must try it. It can be made in advance and reheated before serving. Use the large-size sheets of fillo (about 19 inches × 12 inches) that are sold frozen, and defrost for 2 to 3 hours; see page 9 for information about using fillo.

SERVES 6

1 1/4 pounds onions, sliced

2 1/2 tablespoons sunflower oil

6 boneless, skinless chicken thighs

1 1/2 tablespoons sumac (see page 7)

1 teaspoon ground cinnamon

1/2 teaspoon ground cardamom

juice of 1/2 to 1 lemon

salt and black pepper

7 sheets fillo pastry (about 7 ounces)

1/2 stick (4 tablespoons) butter, melted

For the filling, fry the onions in the oil until soft and beginning to color. Cook on low heat, with the lid on to start with, stirring occasionally, until they soften. Remove the lid and cook over medium-high heat. Cut the chicken into 3/4- to 1-inch pieces and add them to the onions. Cook, turning the pieces, until they are lightly colored all over. Add the sumac, cinnamon, cardamom, lemon juice, salt, and pepper and mix well.

Be ready to assemble the pie quickly so that the fillo does not dry out. Brush a large, round baking pan, about 11 inches in diameter, with melted butter. Place the first sheet of fillo in the pan so that it nestles in the bottom and the two ends hang over the side. Brush the sheet quickly with melted butter, pressing it into the corners with the brush. Repeat with four more of the sheets, so the sides of the pan are completely covered.

Spread the filling evenly in the pan over the sheets and fold the overhanging fillo back over the filling to enclose it, again brushing each bit with melted butter. Cover the surface with the remaining two sheets of fillo, brushing each with melted butter. Tuck them into the sides of the pan, trimming them with scissors to make this easier.

Bake the pie in an oven preheated to 350°F for 25 minutes, or until browned. Turn it out, upside down, on a large platter and serve hot. Use a finely serrated knife to cut it into wedges.

VARIATION

For a more homely snack, fill pita bread with the hot filling and heat through in the oven.

GRILLED POUSSINS with SUMAC
Farrouj Meshwi Bil Sumac

Poussins in this country tend to have a somewhat bland flavor, but with lemon, sumac, and olive oil they are a treat.

SERVES 2

2 poussins
juice of 1/2 lemon
2 tablespoons extra virgin olive oil
salt and black pepper
1 teaspoon sumac (see page 7)

Cut the poussins down both sides of the backbones with poultry shears or kitchen scissors and remove the bones. Cut the wing and leg joints just enough to pull them a little apart, then open the poussins out and flatten them by pressing down hard with the palm of your hand. Rub them with a mixture of lemon juice, olive oil, salt, and pepper. Leave in a cool place for 30 minutes to absorb the lemon juice.

Cook the poussins on a sheet of foil under a preheated broiler or on a barbecue, flesh side to the heat, for 10 minutes; then turn and cook the skin side for 5 to 10 minutes. Cut into a thigh with a pointed knife to check for doneness; they are ready when the juices no longer run pink but the meat is still juicy. Sprinkle with sumac and serve with pita or Lebanese bread.

OPTIONAL ACCOMPANIMENT

Slice 1 large red or white onion finely and sprinkle generously with salt. Leave for 30 minutes, until the juices run out and it loses its strong flavor. Rinse and drain the onion and mix it with 4 tablespoons chopped flat-leaf parsley.

CHICKEN and CHICKPEAS with YOGURT
Fattet Djaj

A number of dishes that go under the general name of fatta all have in common a bed of toasted bread, soaked in stock, and a topping of yogurt. The name denotes the manner of breaking up crisp, toasted bread with your hands. To me, they recall a special person, the late Josephine Salam.

Many years ago I received a letter from her from Beirut saying that she had a number of recipes she thought I would like. On our first meeting, at Claridge's tearoom in London, where a band played Noël Coward tunes, she offered to come to my house and show me how to make fatta with chicken. We made that and many more meals together. It was the time of the civil war in Lebanon, and as she came and went from the country, I received an ongoing account of everyday life in the ravaged city.

Her daughter, Rana, has become an artist and designer. For her thesis at the Royal College of Art in London, she asked me to give a lecture on the history of Middle Eastern food. She had ten portraits of me painted on cloth by a poster-painter in Egypt (he used photographs I gave Rana) and hung them around the college to publicize the event. She laid out foods and spices as in a souk, put on a tape of sounds and music recorded in an Egyptian street, and passed around Arab delicacies. When she visited me a few years later with her husband and new baby, I offered her the fatta with stuffed eggplants on page 300.

SERVES 8

4 cups plain whole-milk yogurt

3/4 cup strained Greek-style yogurt

2 garlic cloves, crushed

1 1/2 tablespoons crushed, dried mint

salt

1 large chicken

1 large onion, cut in half

1 large carrot, cut into pieces

2 bay leaves

1 cinnamon stick

6 to 8 cardamom pods

white pepper

3 very thin, Lebanese breads or 2 pita breads

3 to 4 tablespoons white wine vinegar

one 14-ounce can chickpeas, drained

2/3 cup pine nuts

2 tablespoons extra virgin olive oil

Mix the two types of yogurt in a bowl and beat in the garlic and mint with a little salt. Let it come to room temperature.

Put the chicken in a large saucepan and cover with water. Bring it to the boil and remove any scum. Add the onion, carrot, bay leaves, cinnamon stick, cardamom pods, and salt and pepper. Simmer, covered, for 1 to 1 1/2 hours, until the chicken is very tender and almost falls off the bone. Lift out the chicken and cut it into pieces, removing the skin and bones. Strain the stock.

Open out the Lebanese or pita breads. Toast them in the oven, or under the broiler, until they are crisp and only lightly browned. Then break them up into pieces in your hands and spread them at the bottom of a wide baking dish. Mix the wine vinegar in about 1 1/4 cups of the strained chicken stock, and pour over the bread, adding more if necessary, so that the bread is thoroughly soaked and soggy. Sprinkle the chickpeas over it.

Spread the chicken over the soaked bread and chickpeas and cover the dish with foil. Heat it through in a medium oven 20 minutes before you are ready to serve—it should be very hot.

Just before serving, pour the yogurt evenly all over the dish. Briefly fry the pine nuts in the olive oil until lightly golden and sprinkle over the top.

VARIATION
Instead of adding mint to the yogurt, beat in 3 tablespoons tahini.

STUFFED EGGPLANTS, TOASTED BREAD, TOMATO SAUCE, and YOGURT
Fattet Batinjan

This dish is complex and requires time, but it has dramatic appeal and it is quite delicious with layers of different textures and flavors. I like to add two ingredients that are optional: pomegranate molasses (see page 7), which gives a brown color and sweet-and-sour flavor to the tomato sauce, and tahini (see page 7), which gives a nutty flavor to the yogurt. Look for small eggplants, 4 to 4 1/4 inches long, which can usually be found in Middle Eastern and Asian stores.

SERVES 6

2 to 3 tablespoons vegetable oil

3/4 pound lean ground beef or lamb

salt and black pepper

1 teaspoon ground cinnamon

1/2 teaspoon ground allspice

1/2 cup pine nuts

6 small eggplants (weighing about 1 3/4 pounds)

2 pounds tomatoes, peeled and chopped

2 teaspoons sugar

1 1/2 tablespoons pomegranate molasses (optional)

2 pita breads

2 cups plain whole-milk yogurt, at room temperature

2 tablespoons tahini (optional)

2 garlic cloves (optional)

For the eggplant stuffing, heat 2 tablespoons oil in a frying pan. Put in the meat and add the salt, pepper, cinnamon, and allspice. Cook over medium-high heat, crushing the meat with a fork and turning it over, for about 5 to 8 minutes, until it has changed color and the liquid has evaporated.

In another small frying pan, fry the pine nuts in a drop of oil, shaking the pan to brown them slightly all over. Stir half the pine nuts into the meat.

Wash the eggplants, cut a slice off at the stem end, and, using an apple corer, hollow out the flesh. Insert the corer, digging it in while gently turning it, then give a sharp, quick twist as you reach near the end, and pull out the flesh. Repeat this action with the corer, or scrape the sides with a sharp knife to leave a shell with walls about 1/4 inch thick, being careful not to pierce the skin. Fill the cavities with the meat and pine nut mixture.

Put the tomatoes in a wide pan with the sugar, a little salt and pepper, and, if you like, the pomegranate molasses. Stir well and simmer for 5 minutes. Put in the eggplants and simmer over low heat for 45 minutes, or until the eggplants are very soft, turning them over once.

Open out the pita breads by cutting around them with scissors or a serrated knife, and toast them under the broiler until they are crisp and lightly browned. Mix the yogurt with the tahini and garlic, if using.

Just before serving, assemble the different components in a wide and deep serving dish. Break the toasted pita breads into small pieces with your hands into the bottom of the dish. Take the eggplants out of the tomato sauce and pour the sauce over the toast, which will become soft and swollen. Pour the yogurt all over the sauce, and arrange the stuffed eggplants on top. Finally, sprinkle with the remaining pine nuts.

NOTE

You can use up the extracted eggplant flesh for a salad or an omelette. So that it does not discolor, put it in a bowl of water with salt and a squeeze of lemon juice. Then drain and sauté in olive oil before dressing with lemon juice or mixing with eggs to make an omelette.

STUFFED ZUCCHINI in TOMATO SAUCE
Koussa Mahshi Bi Banadoura

This makes a satisfying homely meal and is especially good when served with Vermicelli Rice (see page 304).

SERVES 4 TO 6 — 2 pounds small zucchini (4 to 4 3/4 inches long)

FOR THE FILLING
5 ounces lean ground lamb
1/4 cup short-grain or risotto rice
salt and pepper
1/2 teaspoon ground cinnamon
1/2 teaspoon ground allspice

1 large onion, chopped
2 tablespoons sunflower oil
3 garlic cloves, crushed
2 pounds tomatoes, peeled and chopped
salt and black pepper
1 tablespoon tomato paste
1 to 2 teaspoons sugar
1 to 1 1/2 lemons
1 teaspoon crushed, dried mint

Wash the zucchini, slice off the stem ends, and shave off the brown skin on the other ends. With a long apple corer, make a hole at the stem end of each vegetable and scoop out the flesh, being careful not to break the skin, or to break through the other end, which must remain closed. This is done by digging in while gently turning the corer, then giving a sharp, quick twist as it reaches near the end, before pulling out the flesh. It is a skill that is acquired with a little practice. With the corer or a small, sharp knife, cut out a little more of the flesh, if necessary, but the shell must be left intact.

Put the filling ingredients together in a bowl and knead well by hand until thoroughly blended. Fill each zucchini, packing in the filling to within 1/2 inch of the end to allow for the expansion of the rice.

For the sauce, fry the onion in the sunflower oil until golden. Use a pan that will hold the zucchini in one or two whole layers. Add the garlic and stir until the aroma rises, then add the tomatoes. Season with salt and pepper and stir in the tomato paste, sugar, and juice of half a lemon.

Place the stuffed zucchini side by side in one or two layers in the sauce. Add water, if necessary, to cover them and simmer very gently, with the lid on, over low heat, for about 45 minutes, or until the zucchini are soft.

Carefully lift the zucchini out of the pan and place them on a serving dish. Stir the mint and the juice of the remaining lemon into the sauce, and continue cooking for a moment or two, then pour over the zucchini.

NOTE

Use the extracted zucchini flesh for a salad: Simmer it in a little water for a minute or two, drain, and dress it with olive oil, lemon juice, salt, and pepper.

STUFFED ZUCCHINI in YOGURT SAUCE
Koussa Mahshi Bi Laban

Prepare the stuffed zucchini as in the recipe above and arrange them in a wide pan. Only just cover with lamb or chicken stock (use 1 1/2 bouillon cubes), and simmer gently, covered, for about 25 minutes, until the water is absorbed and the zucchini are nearly done.

In another saucepan, beat 4 cups of plain whole-milk yogurt with a little salt until it is liquid. Mix 1 tablespoon cornstarch with 2 to 3 tablespoons water to make a creamy paste, add it to the yogurt, and beat well. This will stabilize the yogurt and prevent it from curdling when it is cooked. Bring to the boil slowly over low heat, stirring constantly with a wooden spoon *in one direction only* (this is important). Reduce the heat as low as possible and let the yogurt barely simmer, *uncovered* (this, too, is supposed to be important), for about 10 minutes, until it has thickened.

Pour the yogurt over the zucchini and simmer for about 20 minutes. Before serving, crush 3 garlic cloves with a little salt, add 2 teaspoons dried, crushed mint, and mix well. Fry this mixture in 1 tablespoon butter for moments only and stir into the yogurt.

VERMICELLI RICE
Roz Bil Shaghrieh

Roz bil shaghrieh is the everyday rice that accompanies stews, stuffed vegetables, and grills in Lebanon. People also eat it by itself with yogurt poured over. The short-grain rice from Egypt is the traditional rice used, but today basmati is preferred. Middle Eastern stores sell Italian "cut" vermicelli called filini and similar Turkish Şehriye, but otherwise you can buy vermicelli nests and break them in your hands into small 3/4-inch pieces.

SERVES 4

1 1/4 cups basmati rice
2/3 cup filini or broken vermicelli nests
2 tablespoons butter
about 2 cups boiling water
salt

Wash the rice briefly in cold water, pour into a strainer and then rinse under cold running water, and drain. Toast the *filini*, or broken vermicelli, in a dry frying pan over medium heat or in a tray under the broiler until they are lightly browned, stirring so that they brown evenly. Watch them, as they brown very quickly.

Heat the butter in a saucepan over medium heat, add the rice, and stir until the grains are coated. Pour in the boiling water, add the browned vermicelli and some salt, and stir well. Simmer, covered, over low heat until the rice is tender and the water absorbed. Some brands of basmati now cook in only 10 minutes while others can take up to 20 minutes, so be sure to read the instructions on the package and be ready to turn off the heat after 10 minutes.

STUFFED ARTICHOKE BOTTOMS
with MEAT and PINE NUTS
Ardishawki Mahshi

Look for the frozen artichoke bottoms—a flat cup variety from Egypt—in Middle Eastern stores. There are about 9 in a 14-ounce package. Serve the dish hot with Vermicelli Rice (page 304).

SERVES 4

1 large onion, chopped

3 tablespoons sunflower oil

11 ounces ground lamb or beef

salt and black pepper

1/2 teaspoon ground allspice

1/4 cup pine nuts

14 ounces frozen artichoke bottoms, defrosted

1 tablespoon flour

juice of 1/2 lemon

Fry the onion in 2 tablespoons oil until golden. Add the meat, salt, pepper, and allspice and stir, turning the meat over and crushing it with a fork until it changes color. In a small pan, fry the pine nuts in the remaining oil, stirring, until lightly colored, and add them to the meat.

Place the artichoke bottoms side by side in a shallow baking dish and fill them with the meat mixture. Mix the flour with lemon juice and blend well, then gradually stir in about 3/4 cup water, and pour into the dish. Cover with foil and bake in an oven preheated to 350°F for 25 minutes, or until the artichokes are tender.

"NEW-STYLE" SHISH BARAK

Traditional shish barak are tiny tortellini-like pies with a meat filling that are first baked and then cooked in a yogurt sauce. This "new-style" version of large, individual, coiled pies is inspired by Kamal Mouzawak (for his vegetarian alternative, see the variation). It is an exciting mix of flavors, textures, and temperatures and makes a beautiful presentation. The pastry used in Lebanon, rakakat, is different from fillo—it is softer and more pliable, like a paper-thin pancake—but fillo will do very well. Use the large sheets measuring about 19 × 12 inches that are normally sold frozen; see page 9 for hints on using fillo.

SERVES 12 AS
A FIRST
COURSE,
6 AS A MAIN
DISH

FOR THE FILLING

2 large onions, chopped

3 tablespoons sunflower oil

1 pound lean ground lamb

salt and black pepper

2 teaspoons ground cinnamon

1/2 teaspoon ground allspice

1/2 teaspoon ground nutmeg

1 to 2 tablespoons pomegranate molasses

1/2 cup pine nuts

FOR THE PASTRY

6 sheets of fillo (about 6 ounces)

3/4 stick (6 tablespoons) butter, melted

FOR THE SAUCE AND GARNISH

4 cups plain whole-milk yogurt, at room temperature

salt

2 to 3 cloves garlic, crushed (optional)

4 tablespoons extra virgin olive oil

1 tablespoon crushed, dried mint

For the filling, fry the onions in the oil until golden, stirring occasionally. Add the ground meat, salt and pepper, cinnamon, allspice, and nutmeg. The filling needs to be well seasoned and strongly flavored as it is balanced with the fillo pastry and yogurt, which are bland. Stir, turning over the meat and crushing it to break up any lumps, until it changes color and the juices have been absorbed. Then stir in the pomegranate molasses and cook 1 to 2 minutes more. In a small pan, fry the pine nuts in a drop of oil, stirring, for moments only, until they just begin to color. Stir them into the meat and let it cool.

Cut the sheets of fillo in half, into 2 rectangles that measure about 12 inches × 9 inches, and pile them on top of each other with the long sides nearest to you. Brush the top sheet with melted butter. Put a line of filling (about 3 to 4 tablespoons) along the long edge, to reach to about 3/4 inch from either end, and roll up into a long thin roll. Then shape the roll into a tight coil, creasing it a little as you do, so that the pastry does not tear, and place it on a piece of foil (you do not need to grease it) on a baking sheet. Repeat with the remaining sheets of fillo and the filling, placing the coils next to each other so that they are held tight. Brush the tops with melted butter.

About 30 minutes before you are ready to serve, bake the pies in an oven preheated to 400°F for about 25 minutes, until golden.

For the sauce, beat the yogurt with a little salt and the garlic, if using. For the garnish, mix the olive oil and the dried mint.

Serve the pies as they come out of the oven. Pour about 3 tablespoons yogurt over each, and drizzle a little of the minty olive oil (about a teaspoon) over the top.

VARIATION

For Kamal's vegetarian filling, fry 4 large sliced onions in 4 tablespoons oil until brown. Add 1 cup pine nuts, salt, pepper, 3 teaspoons of ground mixed spices (cinnamon, allspice, nutmeg, ginger, cloves, cumin), and 1 1/2 tablespoons pomegranate molasses.

GROUND MEAT KEBAB
Kafta Meshwiyeh

The ground meat for this kebab—I usually buy shoulder of lamb—should have a good amount of fat so that it remains moist and juicy. Most of it will melt away in the heat of the grill. You will need skewers with a thick, wide blade to hold the meat and prevent it from rolling around. Alternatively, it is easier and equally good to shape the meat into burgers. Serve them with Arab flat breads or the very thin, Lebanese markouk (see page 245), and accompany them with a salad and a choice of mezze.

SERVES 4

2 medium onions
1/2 to 2/3 cup chopped flat-leaf parsley
1 1/2 pounds lamb, taken from the shoulder with some fat
salt and black pepper

Grate or finely chop the onion in the food processor, drain, and turn it into a bowl. Add the chopped parsley to the onion. Cut the meat into chunks, then blend it in the food processor to a soft paste, adding salt and pepper. Mix the meat paste with the parsley and onion, and knead with your hand until well blended.

Divide the meat into 8 balls and wrap each one around a skewer, pressing it firmly so that it holds together in a long, flat, sausage shape. Alternatively, flatten the balls into burgers. Place the skewers, or burgers, on the oiled grill of a barbecue, over the embers of a charcoal fire or on a rack under the broiler, and cook for 5 to 8 minutes, turning them over once, until browned outside but still pink inside.

Kafta Yogurtliya

Using the recipe above, roll the meat into little balls the size of a large walnut. Sauté in batches in a little oil in a large frying pan, turning them until they are browned all over but still a little pink inside. You can do this in advance, if you wish, and heat them through, covered with foil, in the oven when you are ready to serve.

Open out a pita, toast it under the broiler, and break it into small pieces at the bottom of a serving dish. Just before serving, pour 4 cups plain whole-milk yogurt, which should be at room temperature, over the toast and drop the meatballs on top. Fry 3 tablespoons pine nuts very briefly in 1/4 stick (2 tablespoons) butter and sprinkle them over the dish with their butter.

MEATBALLS with PINE NUTS in TOMATO SAUCE
Daoud Basha

The dish takes its name from the governor who administered Mount Lebanon between 1861 and 1868 in Ottoman times. Serve it with plain or Vermicelli Rice (page 304).

SERVES 6

2 medium onions
1 1/2 pounds lean ground lamb
salt and pepper
1 1/2 teaspoons ground cinnamon
1/2 teaspoon ground allspice
2/3 cup pine nuts
vegetable oil
2 pounds tomatoes, peeled or not
2 teaspoons sugar
3 garlic cloves, crushed (optional)

Grate or finely chop the onions in the food processor, drain, and turn them into a bowl. Add the ground lamb with salt, pepper, cinnamon, and allspice, and work into a paste with your hands. Roll the paste into small walnut-size balls. Make a hole in each ball with your finger, stuff the cavity with a few pine nuts, and close the hole. Alternatively, and more easily, work the pine nuts into the meat paste, then roll it into balls.

Put a little oil in a soup plate and roll the meatballs in it. Put them in a baking dish and bake in an oven preheated to 400°F for 15 to 20 minutes, until their color changes.

For the sauce, cut up the tomatoes and liquefy them in the food processor or blender. Add a little salt and pepper, the sugar, and garlic, if using, and pour over the meatballs. Bake them for another 35 minutes, turning the meatballs over once.

VARIATION
Add the juice of 1 lemon and a good pinch of chili flakes to the sauce.

BAKED KIBBEH with ONION and PINE NUT TOPPING
Kibbeh Saniyeh

Kibbeh forms a major part of the national dishes of Lebanon. There are countless versions, from a raw meat paste to little, oval shells stuffed with a ground meat filling and deep-fried or cooked in yogurt or bitter orange juice, as well as vegetarian kibbeh with pumpkin or potato, and one with fish—each version having a number of regional variations. One thing they all have in common is bulgur (burghul in Lebanon). Since most are labor-intensive and require skill and application, they are not the kind of thing you undertake if you are not part of the culture.

So I was very happy to discover a traditional kibbeh that was truly delightful and relatively easy, with only one layer of kibbeh and a flavorsome onion and pine nut topping. I found it in a little restaurant in Beirut called Kibbet Zaman (Yesterday's Kibbeh). It can be served hot or cold (I prefer it hot) as a main dish or cut up small as a mezze. It is really worth doing—I guarantee you will surprise your guests. Accompany it with baba ghanouj (page 248), hummus (page 249), and a salad.

SERVES 6

FOR THE KIBBEH BASE
2/3 cup fine-ground bulgur
1 medium onion, cut in quarters
1 pound lean, boneless leg of lamb
1/2 teaspoon salt
black pepper
1 teaspoon cinnamon
2 tablespoons vegetable oil

FOR THE TOPPING
1 pound onions, sliced
3 tablespoons extra virgin olive oil
1/4 to 1/3 cup pine nuts
salt and black pepper
1/2 teaspoon ground cinnamon
pinch of ground allspice
1/2 to 1 tablespoon pomegranate molasses (optional)

For the kibbeh base, rinse the bulgur in a fine sieve under cold running water and drain well. Purée the onion in the food processor. Add the meat, salt, pepper, and cinnamon and blend to a paste. Add the bulgur and blend to a smooth, soft paste.

With your hand, press the paste into the bottom of an oiled, round, shallow baking dish or tart dish, about 11 inches in diameter. Flatten and smooth the top and rub with 2 tablespoons oil. With a pointed knife, cut the contents into 6 wedges through the center, and run the knife round the edges of the dish. Bake in an oven preheated to 375°F for about 30 minutes, until browned.

While the *kibbeh* base is baking, prepare the topping. Fry the sliced onions in the olive oil until they are golden brown, stirring often. Add the pine nuts and stir until lightly colored. Add a little salt and pepper, the cinnamon, and allspice and, if you like a slightly sweet-and-sour flavor (I do), the pomegranate molasses. Cook, stirring for a minute or so.

Serve the *kibbeh* with the topping spread over the top.

VARIATIONS

✱ Instead of pine nuts, use 2/3 cup shelled walnuts, broken into pieces and, if you like, 2 tablespoons raisins soaked in water for 15 minutes and drained. (If you are using raisins, omit the pomegranate molasses.)

✱ Add 1 tablespoon sumac (see page 7) to the onion topping and omit the pomegranate molasses.

LAMB STEW with VINEGAR and EGGPLANTS
Lahma Bi Khal

This dish does not look very nice—it is a muddy brown—but the flavors are deliciously rich and strong, and the meat is meltingly tender. Serve it with plain or Vermicelli Rice (page 304).

SERVES 6 TO 8

1 pound baby onions or shallots

2 pounds boned shoulder of lamb

sunflower oil

8 whole garlic cloves

salt and pepper

1 teaspoon ground cinnamon

1/2 teaspoon ground allspice

1 teaspoon sugar

3 medium eggplants

4 tablespoons red or white wine vinegar

1 tablespoon crushed, dried mint

To peel the baby onions or shallots, drop them in boiling water and poach for 5 minutes to loosen the skins. Drain and peel them while still warm.

Cut the meat into 8 large pieces and trim off only some of the fat. Heat 2 tablespoons oil in a large pan, put in the meat, and turn to brown it all over, then lift it out. It will have released quite a bit of fat. Fry the baby onions or shallots and the whole cloves of garlic in the fat, stirring until golden. Lift them out and set aside.

Pour off the fat, and return the meat to the pan. Cover with water bring to the boil, and remove the scum. Add the garlic, salt, pepper, cinnamon, allspice, and sugar. Simmer, covered, for about 1 1/2 hours, until the meat is very tender, adding water, as necessary, to keep it covered.

Cut the eggplants into 1/2-inch-thick rounds. Brush them with oil and cook them under the preheated broiler or in a grill pan, turning them over once, until browned; they do not need to be cooked through.

Put the onions in with the meat, add the vinegar and mint, and simmer, covered, for 10 minutes. Add the eggplants and cook for a further 20 minutes.

LAMB SHANKS COOKED
in YOGURT
Laban Ummo

The name of this dish, which means "his mother's milk," implies that the meat of a young animal is cooked in its own mother's milk. It can be made with small lamb shanks or with knuckle of veal (osso buco) or slightly fatty, cubed meat. I have used lamb shanks. Serve it with plain or Vermicelli Rice (page 304). The yogurt makes a wonderful, soupy sauce—so provide spoons, too.

SERVES 6

6 lamb shanks (each weighing 11 to 14 ounces)
salt and white pepper
1 pound shallots or baby onions
8 cups plain whole-milk yogurt
2 tablespoons cornstarch
3 garlic cloves, crushed (optional)
To serve: crushed, dried mint

Put the lamb shanks in a large pan and cover them with water. Bring to the boil, remove any scum, and add salt and pepper. Cook them with the lid on for 2 hours, adding water to keep them covered. Peel the shallots or baby onions: drop them in boiling water and blanch them for 5 minutes to loosen the skins, then drain and peel them while still warm. Add them to the meat and cook for 30 minutes more, until they are soft and the meat is so tender that it falls off the bone.

You need to prepare or stabilize the yogurt to prevent it from curdling during cooking. Pour it into a large saucepan and beat well until it is liquid. Mix the cornstarch to a light paste with 3 to 4 tablespoons water and add this to the yogurt, beating vigorously until well mixed. Now bring the yogurt to the boil slowly, stirring constantly *in one direction only*, and then reduce the heat to as low as possible and let it barely simmer, uncovered, for about 10 minutes. Do not cover the pan with a lid: they say that a drop of steam falling back into the yogurt could ruin it. I am not sure that is true.

Drain the cooked shanks—you can remove the bones or not, as you wish—and the onions and add them to the yogurt. Stir in a little salt and the garlic, if using, and simmer gently, uncovered, for 10 to 15 minutes.

When serving, pass around a little bowl of dried mint so people can stir a teaspoonful or so into their sauce, if they wish.

ROAST LAMB with RICE, GROUND MEAT, and NUTS
Ouzi

A central part of every grand Arab feast is lamb—shoulder or leg—cooked à la cuillère (to such tenderness that you can eat it "with a spoon"), accompanied by rice with ground meat and nuts.

 This recipe comes from the caterer Nazira Bitar, who is the queen of wedding cakes all over the Arab world. She prepared a banquet in Stockholm that was hosted by the King of Jordan for King Carl Gustav and Queen Silvia.

SERVES 6 TO 8

1 leg of lamb (weighing about 5 pounds) or 2 shoulders

1 teaspoon ground cinnamon

1/2 teaspoon ground allspice

1/2 teaspoon ground cumin

1/2 teaspoon ground cardamom

salt and black pepper

2 tablespoons sunflower oil

1 onion, cut in quarters

1 head of garlic, cut in half

FOR THE RICE

2 1/2 cups basmati or long-grain rice

1 large onion, chopped

3 tablespoons sunflower oil

1/2 pound ground beef

salt and black pepper

1 teaspoon ground cinnamon

1/2 teaspoon ground allspice

1/2 teaspoon ground nutmeg

1/2 teaspoon ground cloves

4 1/4 cups lamb or chicken stock (use 2 bouillon cubes)

1/3 cup sliced almonds

1/3 cup pistachios

1/3 cup pine nuts

Rub the leg of lamb all over with the spices, salt, pepper, and oil. Place it in a large roasting pan and put it into an oven preheated to 425°F. After 20 minutes, take the pan out of the oven, pour in 4 1/4 cups water, and add the onion and garlic. Cover the meat with a large sheet of foil and put it back in the oven. Lower the heat to 300°F, and cook for 3 hours.

While the meat is cooking, prepare the rice. If using basmati, wash the rice in cold water, rinse in a strainer under cold running water, and drain. In a large pan, fry the onion in 2 tablespoons oil until it is soft and beginning to color. Add the ground beef and cook, stirring, turning it over and crushing it with a fork to break up any lumps, until it has changed color. Add salt and pepper and all the spices: cinnamon, allspice, nutmeg, and cloves. Stir well and add the rice, then stir again.

Pour in the boiling stock, mix well, and simmer, covered, for about 10 to 20 minutes until the rice is tender. (Some brands that claim not to be parboiled or precooked now take as little as 8 to 10 minutes, so read the information on the package.) Add a little stock or water if it becomes too dry. Drain and keep it on the side until you are ready to serve.

Fry the almonds, pistachios, and pine nuts separately in the remaining oil until they just begin to color. When the leg of lamb is ready, place it on a serving dish with the rice. You can cut the meat off the bone into slices, if you wish. Sprinkle the fried nuts all over the rice. Serve the flavorsome meat broth produced at the bottom of the roasting pan as a sauce. Heat it through and serve it in a jug, first pouring off as much of the fat from the top as you can.

Desserts

In Beirut and other cities in Lebanon, people do not make any of their pastries at home—they buy them—apart from those attached to religious festivals, and even then, they make them only during those festivals. Pastry making is one of the legendary trades of the country and the great pastry capital of Lebanon is the city of Tripoli. I was allowed into the kitchens of one of the celebrated pastry-makers there, Abdul Rahman Hallab and Sons, where I saw dozens of different types of pastries being made. I was also taken by a local man, Abdel Karim al Chaar (a friend of the friends who took me to Tripoli) around the *souks* of the old city to taste yet more pastries made by small artisans. Abdel Karim is a famous singer, who sings verses from the Koran in mosques and holds concerts of the classic Arab-Andalusian mode called *tarab*. He came with his daughter Ranine, who was, at that moment, a finalist in the inter-Arab singing competition *Superstar* on Future TV. Abdel Karim was greeted by all the old men in the *souk* while young girls with headscarves clustered around Ranine and assured her that they would be voting for her. And we got special treatment in the pastry shops.

In the center of the *khan* that specialized in perfumed soaps we saw rose water, *mai ward*, and orange blossom water, *mai zahr*, being made in a row of primitive alembics (see pages 6 and 7). The waters lend a delicate perfume to many Lebanese puddings and pastries. Here, even out in the open, the perfume was intoxicating.

In Beirut, I went to see a pastry-maker called Nazira Bitar whose wedding cakes are famous all over the Arab world. She showed me photograph albums of her fantastically elaborate cakes with edible flowers, birds, butterflies, fruits, shells, and jewels. Her latest are chandeliers that reach from the ceiling to the floor.

MILK PUDDING
Muhallabiya

*Muhallabiya is the most popular Lebanese dessert. In restaurants it is usually made with corn-
starch. At home, ground rice or a mixture of both is used. It is a special refinement to pour a little
honey syrup over the top and to garnish it with a large amount of chopped nuts. It is very easy to
make, but it needs attention and patience during the long stirring.*

SERVES 6

2 tablespoons cornstarch

1/4 cup ground rice

4 1/2 cups milk

1/2 cup sugar, or more to taste

1 tablespoon orange blossom water (see page 6)

1 1/2 tablespoons rose water (see page 7)

3 tablespoons clear honey

1/3 cup blanched almonds, coarsely chopped

1/3 cup pistachio nuts, coarsely chopped

Mix the cornstarch and ground rice with about 1/2 cup cold milk and beat well, making
sure that you break up any small lumps. Bring the rest of the milk to the boil in a large,
preferably nonstick, pan. Add the cornstarch and ground rice mixture, stirring vigorously with a wooden spoon.

Keep over low heat, and stir constantly, until you feel a slight resistance. Continue
to cook gently over low heat for 15 to 20 minutes, or until the cream thickens further,
stirring occasionally. Be very careful not to scrape the bottom of the pan; the cream
burns slightly at the bottom, and if it is scraped it will give a burnt taste to the pudding.
Add the sugar toward the end.

Stir in the orange blossom water and 1 tablespoon rose water, and cook a few
moments more. Let the cream cool a little before pouring into a glass serving bowl. Let
it cool, then chill in the refrigerator, covered with plastic wrap.

When the pudding is cold, prepare a honey syrup in a small pan by bringing to the
boil the honey with about 1/2 cup water. Stir well and add the remaining 1/2 tablespoon
of rose water. Let it cool and pour over the cold, firmed cream; it will seep in a little.

Serve sprinkled with a pattern of chopped almonds and pistachios.

VARIATION

Instead of garnishing with chopped nuts, serve topped with rose petal jam, which is
available from Middle Eastern stores.

MILK ICE CREAM with
GUM MASTIC and ROSE WATER
Bouza Bi Halib

A brilliant white milk ice cream with a chewy texture made with sahlab (called salep in Turkey), the ground-up root tuber of a member of the orchid family, is very difficult to make successfully at home, so here is a modern version that I also love. It is without sahlab, so not chewy, but the traditional flavorings of mastic and rose water give it a special appeal.

You should pound, then grind the tiny lumps of gum mastic (see page 6) with a teaspoon of sugar to a fine powder with a pestle and mortar (or use a spice grinder). Use very little as otherwise the taste can be quite unpleasant.

SERVES 4 TO 6 4 egg yolks
1/2 cup sugar
1 1/4 cups light cream
1 to 2 tablespoons rose water, to taste
1/4 teaspoon pulverized gum mastic
1 1/4 cups heavy cream

Beat the egg yolks with the sugar to a thick, pale cream in a bowl. Bring the light cream to the boil and gradually pour over the yolk mixture, beating all the time.

Put the bowl in a pan of boiling water or in the top part of a double boiler, and stir constantly until the mixture thickens into a custard. Add the rose water, take it off the heat, and sprinkle the gum mastic over the whole surface (if it falls in one place it sticks together in a lump) and stir it in vigorously. Let cool.

Beat the heavy cream until firm and fold this into the cooled custard.

Pour the mixture into a mold lined with plastic wrap and cover with more plastic wrap. Freeze overnight. Take out of the freezer 5 to 10 minutes before serving, remove the plastic wrap, and turn the ice cream out of its mold.

RICE PUDDING with APRICOT COMPOTE
Roz Bi Halib Wal Mish Mish

Rice pudding is a homely pudding. Topped by a fruit compote such as stewed apricots, it becomes elegant, dinner-party fare. It is also good served with rose petal jam, which you can buy in Middle Eastern stores. Gum mastic (see recipe on page 321) gives the pudding an intriguing, and to me, very delicious flavor, but it is optional. Serve the pudding cold.

SERVES 6

1 cup short-grain or risotto rice

1 1/2 cups water

4 1/2 cups milk

3/4 cup sugar, or to taste

2 tablespoons orange blossom or rose water (see pages 6 and 7)

1/2 teaspoon pulverized gum mastic (optional) (see page 6)

APRICOT COMPOTE

2 pounds apricots

1 3/4 cups water

3/4 cup sugar

1 lemon

Boil the rice in the water for 8 minutes, or until the water is absorbed. Add the milk and simmer over very low heat for about 30 minutes, stirring occasionally to make sure that the bottom does not stick and burn.

When the rice is very soft and the milk not entirely absorbed, add the sugar and stir until dissolved. If it is a bit dry, add a little more milk. Add the orange blossom or rose water, or a mix of the two, and cook for a minute longer. Turn off the heat, sprinkle on the mastic, if using, and stir very well before pouring into a serving bowl. There should still be quite a bit of liquid. It will be absorbed as the pudding cools; the result should be creamy. Pour the pudding into a wide serving dish and chill in the refrigerator, covered with plastic wrap.

For the apricot compote, wash the apricots, cut them in half, and remove the pits. Put them in a large heavy-bottomed pan with the water, sugar, and lemon juice. Cook, covered, over low heat for 10 minutes, or until the apricots fall apart. Let the fruit cool, then chill it in the refrigerator before spreading it over the rice pudding.

KATAIFI with CREAM FILLING
Osmaliyah Bil Ashta

Osmaliyah has been known for generations in my family in Egypt as konafa and I have featured it before. I include it here again because, of all the Lebanese pastries that are good to make at home and to serve at a dinner party, this is one of the best; it is my mother's recipe. It is meant to be served hot but it is also good cold.

You can buy the soft white vermicelli-like dough frozen in Lebanese, Turkish, and Greek stores. In Lebanon, it is called knafe but in America it is sold by its Greek name, kataifi, usually in 1-pound packages; it should be defrosted for 2 to 3 hours. The quantities below will make one large pastry to serve 10, but you can also make two half the size—one to serve fewer people and one to put in the freezer to bake at a later date. It freezes well uncooked.

SERVES 10

FOR THE SYRUP

2 1/2 cups sugar

1 1/4 cups water

1 tablespoon lemon juice

2 tablespoons orange blossom water (see page 6)

FOR THE CREAM FILLING

1/2 cup rice flour

4 cups milk

1/2 cup heavy cream

4 tablespoons sugar

FOR THE PASTRY

1 pound kataifi (knafe) pastry, defrosted

2 sticks or 1/2 pound unsalted butter, melted

To garnish: 2/3 cup pistachios, chopped finely

Make the syrup first. Boil the sugar with the water and lemon juice over low heat for 5 to 8 minutes, until it is just thick enough to coat the back of a spoon. Another way to test it is to pour a drop onto a cold plate, and if it does not spread out like water, it is ready. Stir in the orange blossom water and cook a moment more. Let it cool and then chill in the refrigerator. (If you have overcooked the syrup and it becomes too thick to pour when it is cold, you can rescue it by adding a little water and bringing it to the boil again.)

For the filling, mix the rice flour with enough of the cold milk to make a smooth, creamy paste. Bring the rest of the milk with the cream to the boil, preferably in a non-stick pan (this stops the cream sticking at the bottom and burning). Add the rice flour

paste, stirring vigorously with a wooden spoon. Leave it on very low heat and continue to stir constantly for 15 to 20 minutes, until the mixture is quite thick, being careful not to scrape any burnt bits from the bottom of the pan. Then add the cream and sugar and stir well.

Put the *kataifi* pastry in a large bowl. With your fingers, pull out and separate the strands as much as possible. Melt the butter and when it has cooled slightly, pour it over the pastry and work it in very thoroughly with your fingers, pulling out and separating the strands and turning them over so that they do not stick together and are entirely coated with butter.

Spread half the pastry on the bottom of a large round pie pan, measuring 11 to 12 inches in diameter. Spread the cream filling over it evenly and cover with the rest of the pastry. Press down firmly and flatten it with the palm of your hand. Bake in an oven preheated to 350°F for about 45 minutes. Some like to brown the bottom, which comes out on top when the pastry is turned out, by running it over heat on the stove top for a brief moment only. Others prefer the pastry to remain pale.

Just before serving, run a sharp knife around the edges of the *osmaliyah* to loosen the sides, and turn it out onto a large serving dish. Pour the cold syrup all over the hot pastry and sprinkle the top lavishly with the chopped pistachios.

Alternatively, you can pour only half the syrup over the pastry and pass the rest around in a jug for everyone to help themselves to more, if they wish.

OSMALIYAH with CHEESE FILLING
Osmaliyah Bil Jibne

This is another wonderful dessert, which I strongly recommend. It is quicker and easier to make than the previous one with cream. Make the pastry as in the recipe on page 324, but instead of the cream filling, use 1 pound mozzarella cheese blended in the food processor with 1/2 pound ricotta, 2 tablespoons sugar, and 2 tablespoons orange blossom water. Bake as above and pour the cold syrup over the hot pastry as it comes out of the oven, just before serving. Serve hot, or at least warm, while the cheese is soft.

Bellawrieh

This is made with *kataifi* pastry in the same way as the recipe for *Kataifi* with a Cream Filling (see page 324). Instead of the cream filling, use 1 pound or 3 1/2 cups whole pistachios or chopped walnuts mixed with a few tablespoons of the sugar syrup to bind them together. Serve this pastry cold.

PANCAKES STUFFED with WALNUTS
Atayef Bil Jawz

To make these spongy pancakes stuffed with walnuts and dipped in syrup takes time (and I should warn you that they are fattening) but they are heavenly and when you have made them more than once, you will find them not too difficult. The amount of syrup is more than you need, but it is good to serve separately as well, in case anyone would like to pour a little more on their pastry.

MAKES
ABOUT 20
PANCAKES

FOR THE BATTER
1 teaspoon active dry yeast
1 teaspoon sugar
1 1/2 cups lukewarm water
1 1/3 cups plain flour
sunflower or vegetable oil, for frying

FOR THE SYRUP
2 1/2 cups sugar
2 cups water

1 tablespoon lemon juice
1 to 2 tablespoons orange blossom or rose water (see pages 6 and 7)

1 3/4 cups walnuts, chopped finely
1/2 cup sugar
1 1/2 teaspoons rose water

For the batter, dissolve the yeast with the sugar in about 1/2 cup of the warm water. Let it stand for 10 minutes, or until it froths. Put the flour into a large bowl. Add the yeast mixture and the remaining water gradually, beating vigorously, to make a creamy, lump-free batter. Cover the bowl with plastic wrap and leave in a warm place for about 2 hours, until the batter rises and becomes bubbly and elastic.

To make the syrup, bring the sugar and water to the boil in a pan with the lemon juice and simmer for 5 to 8 minutes, until it is thick enough to coat the back of a spoon.

Then stir in the orange blossom or rose water and simmer for a few seconds more. Allow to cool; then chill in the refrigerator.

For the filling, mix together the walnuts, sugar, and rose water.

When the batter is ready, beat it again vigorously. Using a piece of paper towel, rub a nonstick frying pan with oil, ensuring it is thoroughly greased with a very thin film of oil. Heat the frying pan until it is very hot, then reduce the heat and keep it at medium.

In batches of 3, pour one-third of a ladle (about 2 tablespoons) of batter into the pan. Spread the batter a little with the back of a fork (it does not spread by itself) so that it becomes a round, 3 1/2 to 4 inches in diameter, or an oval. Cook one side of the pancake only. The other side must remain uncooked and moist so that its edges will stick together. When the pancakes lose their whiteness and tiny holes appear, and as they become detached from the pan, lift them out and pile them up on a plate. Continue with the rest of the batter and filling.

Put a tablespoon of filling in the middle of each pancake, on the uncooked side. Fold the pancake in half over the filling to make a half-moon shape, and close the pastries by pinching the edges very firmly together to seal them.

Working in batches, deep-fry the pancakes *very briefly* in sizzling but not too hot oil, turning them over once, until they just begin to color. (They become hard if they are fried too long.) Then lift them out with a slotted spoon and drain on paper towels. Dip them, while still hot, on both sides in the syrup so they absorb some, and transfer to a serving plate.

Serve them warm or cold. Pour any remaining syrup into a bowl and offer extra to those who have a sweet tooth.

VARIATION

Instead of deep-frying the pancakes, you can bake them. Arrange them on an oiled baking dish, brush them with oil or melted butter, and bake them in an oven preheated to 400°F for 15 to 20 minutes.

PANCAKES STUFFED *with* CHEESE
Atayef Bil Jibne

Follow the above recipe, and instead of walnuts use the following filling: blend in the food processor 13 ounces mozzarella cheese with 4 tablespoons sugar and 2 teaspoons rose water.

TINY OPEN PANCAKES *with* CREAM *and* ROSE PETAL JAM
Atayef Bil Ashta

These are easy and a treat. Make the pancakes as in Pancakes Stuffed with Walnuts (page 326), but use just 1 tablespoon batter for each pancake, and turn them to cook the other side. The quantity of batter will make about 30 little pancakes. Dip the little pancakes into the syrup and arrange on a flat serving plate. Spread each with a heaped teaspoon of crème fraîche (you will need about 1 cup) and top with a teaspoon of rose petal jam. Alternatively, instead of the rose petal jam, sprinkle finely chopped pistachios over the cream (you will need about 1 cup whole pistachios).

ALMOND PUFF PASTRY PIES
Sambousek Bi Loz

These little pies, which are filled with nuts—almonds, pine nuts, pistachios, or walnuts—can be served with tea or coffee, either dusted with confectioners' sugar or dipped in syrup. Use commercial fresh or frozen and defrosted puff pastry.

MAKES 24 PIES

1 pound puff pastry
flour, for dusting
1/3 stick (2 1/2 tablespoons) unsalted butter, melted
confectioners' sugar

FOR THE ALMOND FILLING
2 1/2 cups ground almonds
1 1/4 cups superfine sugar
3 tablespoons orange blossom water (see page 6)

It is important to roll out the puff pastry as thinly as you possibly can. It is easier to do so if you cut the block into four equal pieces and roll out each one separately. Dust the surface and the rolling pin with flour, and roll out the sheet of pastry, turning it over and dusting it with flour, until you can cut out 6 rounds with a 4-inch pastry cutter. Put the rounds in a pile and wrap the pile in plastic wrap. Do the same with the remaining pastry.

Mix the filling ingredients to a paste. Put a tablespoon of the filling in the center of each round and bring the edges up together over the filling to make a half-moon shape. Seal the edges by pinching them very firmly together. A traditional way is to twist the edges making a scalloped effect; another is to press down the edges with the prongs of a fork. Moistening the edges with a finger dipped in water helps to make the pastry stick.

Arrange the pies on sheets of foil on baking trays. Brush the tops with melted butter and bake in an oven preheated to 400°F for about 15 minutes, or until they are puffed up and lightly golden. Let them cool before dusting with confectioners' sugar.

VARIATIONS

❈ For a pine nut filling, blend 3 cups pine nuts in the food processor with 1 cup superfine sugar and 4 tablespoons orange blossom water.

❈ For a pistachio filling, blend 3 cups pistachios in the food processor with 1 cup superfine sugar and 4 tablespoons rose water (see page 7).

❀ For a walnut filling, blend 3 cups walnuts in the food processor with 1 cup sugar, the grated rind of 1 orange, and 4 tablespoons fresh orange juice.

❀ For the pastries in syrup, bring to the boil 1 1/4 cups water and 2 3/4 cups sugar with 1 tablespoon lemon juice. Lower the heat and simmer for 3 to 5 minutes, or until the sugar is completely dissolved. Let it cool and then chill it in the refrigerator. Make the pastries as in the above recipe, or with any of the fillings in the listed variations. Do not dust them with confectioners' sugar but dip them in the cold syrup immediately after they come out of the oven.

PISTACHIO PASTE STUFFED with CREAM
Bohsalino

I had never come across this pastry before. I tasted it in Beirut, where a few patisseries claim to have invented it. One called Bohsali gave it the name Bohsalino; another calls it Taj el Malek. It involves a little skill—akin to pottery making—that improves with practice. In Lebanon they are filled with the thick cream that rises to the top when rich buffaloes' milk is boiled. They do not keep more than a few days because of the cream and must be kept in the refrigerator.

> 1 1/2 cups shelled pistachios
> 1/2 cup superfine sugar
> 2 tablespoons rose water (see page 7)
> about 1/4 cup thick clotted cream or crème fraîche
> Confectioners' sugar to sprinkle on

Grind the pistachios in the food processor, then add the sugar and rose water (don't be tempted to put in any more rose water) and blend until it forms a soft, malleable, slightly oily paste. The mix will appear like wet sand at first, but the oil released by the pistachios will bind it into a workable paste.

Rub your hands with oil so that the paste does not stick. Take little lumps the size of a small egg, roll each into a ball, then make a hole in it with your finger and enlarge it by pinching the sides and pulling them up to make a little dome-shaped pot.

Fill the hole with about 1 tablespoon clotted cream. Put the pot down on a plate rubbed with oil and make a lid for it: take a lump of paste the size of a large olive, flatten it between the palms of your hands, and lay it over the cream. Stick the edges well together and place the pastry flat-side down in a pastry case.

Alternatively, you can line tiny cake molds with plastic wrap and press the paste around the sides, fill the hollow with the cream, and cover with a lid.

Keep the pastries in the refrigerator—the cream needs to be refrigerated and the paste will firm—until you are ready to serve them, sprinkled with confectioners' sugar.

VARIATION

Do the same with almonds and use 2 tablespoons of orange blossom water instead of rose water.

Acknowledgments

Over the decades that I have been involved with the foods of the Middle East and North Africa, very many people have given recipes, advice, bits of information, stories, and memories that have found their way into this book. I will not thank them all here, but they should know that their contributions were much valued and that I always think of them fondly.

Of those who have helped me most when I was preparing *Arabesque*, I am especially grateful to Nevin Halici, who has been a fantastic guide in Turkey. The late Turkish gastronome Tuğrul Şavkai was extremely helpful, and I miss him deeply. Kamal Mouzawak was my all-important, entertaining, and gracious guide in Lebanon. I cannot thank him enough, and I also thank his mother, Fariba, for her hospitality and valuable information. Others who have made me love Lebanon (and love them too) and have helped me with my research are my friends Mai Ghoussoub, her husband, Hazim Saghie, and their families: Hazim's mother, Khalida Saghie; Mai's mother, Maggie; her sister, Hoda, brother-in-law, Kamal, nephew, Maher, and Natasha, his new bride. I am also indebted to the caterer Nazira Hadad Bitar. I owe much to Fatema Hal, who is a Moroccan restaurateur (her Mansouria is, for me, the best in Paris), anthropologist, and food writer. I met her in Morocco, Sicily, Paris, and Barcelona.

I thank my editor, Camilla Stoddart, for her vision and her enthusiastic support; Jenny Dereham for her intelligent and painstaking editing; Jason Lowe for the beautiful photographs; my agent, Jacqueline Korn, for her unceasing encouragement. I have very special thanks for Judith Jones. She took an interest in the project from the start and, as always, offered much valuable advice and encouragement throughout.

Index

lamb
  couscous with lamb, onions and raisins,
    117–18
  ground meat kebab, 99, 309
  little meat pizzas, 282–3
  meatballs with pine nuts in tomato sauce,
    310
  "new style" shish barak, 305–8
  roast shoulder with caramelized baby
    onions and honey, 102
  roast shoulder with couscous and date
    stuffing, 100–1
  roast with rice, ground meat and nuts,
    316–17
  shanks cooked in yogurt, 208, 315
  shanks with egg and lemon sauce, 209–12
  stew with eggplant sauce, 205–6
  stew with shallots and chestnuts, 207
  stew with vinegar and eggplants, 314
  stuffed zucchinis, 302–3
  tagines with caramelized baby onions, 106–8
  tagine with apricots, 108–9
  tagine with chestnuts, 112
  tagine with dates and almonds, 109–10
  tagine with potatoes and peas, 105
  tagine with prunes and almonds, 111
  see also meat
Lebanon, 234–45
  recipes, 248–332
leeks with egg and lemon sauce, 160
lemons
  egg and lemon sauces, 160–1, 209–12
  seared tuna with lemon dressing, 191
lemons, preserved, 7, 35–7
  artichoke and fava bean salad with, 55–6
  skate with preserved lemon and green
    olives, 82
  spinach salad with preserved lemon and
    olives, 56
  tagine of chicken with artichoke bottoms,
    preserved lemon, and olives, 95
  tagine of chicken with preserved lemon and
    olives, 93–4
lentils
  chickpea and lentil soup, 70–1
  with pasta and caramelized onions, 271
  red lentil and rice soup, 284

mackerel with walnut sauce, smoked, 188
mahya, 33
main courses, 75–121, 187–215, 287–317
meat, 187
  cigars, 64–5
  ground meat kebab, 99
  kofte kebab with tomato sauce and yogurt,
    203–5
  Lebanon, 282–3, 295, 302–3, 305–17
  Morocco, 64–5, 95–6, 99–112, 117–18
  "new style" shish barak, 305–8
  puff pastry pies with raisins and pine nuts,
    201
  stuffed artichoke bottoms with meat and
    pine nuts, 305
  stuffed eggplants, 212–13
  stuffed quinces, 215
  Turkey, 201–13, 215
  see also chicken; lamb; poussins; veal
meze, Turkish, 146, 153–85
mezze, Lebanese, 240–2, 247–85
milk
  and almond pudding, 225
  ice cream with gum mastic and rose water,
    321
  pudding, 320
mint
  mint tea, 33
  and parsley salad with rice, 255
  tea, 137
Morocco, 14–35
  recipes, 36–137
mozzarella cheese
  little puff pastry cheese pies, 278
  pancakes stuffed with cheese, 328
mune, 237

nuts
  roast lamb with rice, ground meat and,
    316–17
  see also individual types of nut

okra with baby onions and tomatoes, 264
olive oil, 6
olives, 35
  little pies with fresh goat cheese and, 63–4
  orange, olive and onion salad, 48

A NOTE ABOUT THE AUTHOR

Claudia Roden was born and raised in Cairo. She completed her formal
education in Paris and then moved to London to study art. She travels
extensively as a food writer. Her previous books include the James Beard
Award–winning *The Book of Jewish Food*, as well as *The New Book of Middle
Eastern Food*, *Coffee: A Connoisseur's Companion*, *The Good Food of Italy—Region
by Region*, *Everything Tastes Better Outdoors*, and *Mediterranean Cookery*, which
was published in conjunction with her BBC television series on the
Mediterranean. In 1989 she won the two most prestigious food prizes in
Italy, the Premio Orio Vergani and the Premio Maria Luigia, Duchessa di
Parma for her London *Sunday Times Magazine* series "The Taste of Italy."
She has won six Glenfiddich prizes, including 1992 Food Writer of the
Year for articles in the *Daily Telegraph* and *The Observer* magazine, and the
Glenfiddich Trophy awarded "in celebration of a unique contribution to
the food that we eat in Britain today." In 1999, she won a Versailles Award
in France, and Prince Claus of the Netherlands presented her with the
Prince Claus Award "in recognition of exceptional initiatives and
achievements in the field of culture." She lives in London.

A NOTE ON THE TYPE

The text of this book was set in Quadraat. The Dutch typographer Fred
Smeijers began designing this digital font in 1992, and it was released
by FontShop. Quadraat is a very legible face that looks back to the
sixteenth century from a contemporary point of view. Its eighteen styles,
including serif and sans serif versions, make it useful for both text and
display. Smeijers specializes in typographic research and development
for product manufacturers and is also known for the design of the
typefaces Renard and Fresco.

Composed by North Market Street Graphics, Lancaster, Pennsylvania
Printed and bound by SNP Lee Fung Printers Ltd. China